DEFEATING DICTATORS

FIGHTING TYRANNY IN AFRICA AND AROUND THE WORLD

GEORGE B. N. AYITTEY

palgrave
macmillan

ALSO BY GEORGE B. N. AYITTEY
AND AVAILABLE FROM PALGRAVE MACMILLAN

Africa Betrayed
Africa in Chaos
Africa Unchained

DEFEATING DICTATORS
Copyright ©, George B. N. Ayittey, 2011.
All rights reserved.

First published in 2011 by PALGRAVE MACMILLAN® in the United
States—a division of St. Martin's Press LLC, 175 Fifth Avenue, New York,
NY 10010.

Where this book is distribut[ed in the rest of the] world, this is by Palgrave M[acmillan, a division of Macmillan Publishers] Limited, registered in Engla[nd, company number 785998, of Houndmills,] Basingstoke, Hampshire R[G21 6XS.]

Palgrave Macmillan is the gl[obal academic imprint of the above companies] and has companies and repr[esentatives throughout the world.]

Palgrave® and Macmillan® a[re registered trademarks in the United States,] the United Kingdom, Europ[e and other countries.]

ISBN: 978-0-230-10859-2

Library of Congress Cataloging-in-Publication Data
Ayittey, George B. N., 1945–
    Defeating dictators : fighting tyranny in Africa and around the world /
George B.N. Ayittey.
        p. cm.
    Includes bibliographical references and index.
    ISBN 978-0-230-10859-2 (hardback)
    1. Democratization—Africa. 2. Regime change—
Africa. 3. Dictatorship—Africa. 4. Africa—Politics and
government—1960– 5. Democratization. 6. Regime
change. 7. Dictatorship. I. Title.
JQ1879.A15A98 2011
320.96—dc23

A catalogue record of the book is available from the British Library.

Design by Letra Libre Inc.

First edition: November 2011

10 9 8 7 6 5 4 3 2 1

Printed in the United States of America.

Dedicated to the freedom activists who have died in the last few years fighting tyrannical regimes

Abdelbaki Djabali, Ahmed Benchemsi, Lounes Matoub (Algeria)

Oleg Bebenin (Belarus)

Wang Bingzhang, Hu Jia, Gao Zhisheng, Liu Xiaobo, Yu Jie (China)

Delphie Namuto, Caddy Adzuba, and Bruno Koko Chirambiza (Congo DR)

Khaled Mohamed Saeed, Salaheddin Mohsen, Saad Eddin Ibrahim (Egypt)

Matewos Habteab, Amanuel Asrat, Medhanie Haile, Yusuf Mohamed Ali, Saïd Abdelkader, Fessehaye Yohannes, Yusuf Mohamed Ali, Saïd Abdelkader, and Medhanie Haile (Eritrea)

ShiBire Desalegn, Tensae Zegeye, Habtamu Tola, Binyam Degefa, Behailu Tesfaye, Kasim Ali Rashid, Teodros Giday Hailu, Adissu Belachew, Milion Kebede Robi, Desta Umma Birru, Tiruwork G. Tsadik, Elfnesh Tekle, Abebeth Huletu, Regassa Feyessa, Teshome Addis Kidane, and Birtukan Midekssa (Ethiopia)

Deyda Hydara, Sarata Jabbi, Pa Modou Faal, Pap Saine, Ebrima Sawaneh, Sam Sarr, and Abubacarr (The Gambia)

Sanah Jaleh, Mohamad Mokhtari, Neda Agha-Soltan, Klan Tajbakhsh, Muhammad-Reza Ali-Zamani (Iran)

Idrees Boufayed, Daif Al Ghazal, Abd al-Raziq al-Mansuri, Fathi Eljahmi, and the rebels (Libya)

Kamsulum Kazeem, Tunde Oladepo, and Tunde Salau (Nigeria)

Hwang Jang Yop and other pro-democracy activists (North Korea)

Anna Politkovskaya, Anastasia Baburova, Natalya Estemirova, Stanislav Markelov, Mikhail Beketov, Oleg Kashin, Anatoly Adamchuk, and others (Russia)

Jean-Leonard Rugambage, Andre Kagwa Rwiserek, and Victoire Ingabire (Rwanda)

Yousif Kuwa Mekki (Sudan)

Tal al-Mallohi (Syria)

Mohammed Bouazizi, Lahseen Naji, Ramzi Al-Abboudi, Mohamed Ammari, Chawki Belhoussine El Hadri (Tunisia)

Jimmy Higenyi, Dr. James Rwanyare (Uganda)

Godknows Dzoro Mtshakazi, Gift Tandere, Shepherd Ndungu (Zimbabwe)

CONTENTS

ACKNOWLEDGMENTS

IN MY STRUGGLES, VARIOUS PEOPLE, both Americans and Africans, as well as foundations, institutes, and agencies have provided me with support and encouragement. I owe each one of them a huge debt of gratitude.

The Earhart Foundation in Ann Arbor, Michigan was helpful with funding to enable me to complete this book. The J. M. Kaplan Fund in New York was extremely helpful, as was the Cato Institute in Washington, DC.

The Board of Directors of The Free Africa Foundation, its staff, scholars, and associates must also be mentioned. Keith Colburn of North Brook, Phil Harvey of DKT International, Mary Kaplan of New York, and Ed Claflin, my literary agent, among others, have been extremely supportive.

There are many others (Americans, Canadians, South Africans, and other nationalities) to whom I still owe a debt of gratitude: Lynne Criner, John Fund (*The Wall Street Journal*), Georgie Ann Geyer (nationally syndicated columnist), Ashleigh Emmerson, Elizabeth Dickinson of *Foreign Policy*, Sandy and Margaret Matheson, Maggie Beddow, Luba Ostashevsky, Alan Bradshaw, and others were particularly helpful.

Last but not least have been the numerous Ghanaians and other Africans who have shown unflappable support for my work and writings. Worthy of mention are Dr. Shaka Ssali of *"Straight Talk Africa,"* Mohamed Idris, Karanta Kalley, Dr. Charles Mensa, Ablorh Odjijah, Rev. G. B. K. Owusu, Vivian Boafo, and many, many others.

A special gratitude is owed to Emmanuel Odamtten, an administrative assistant at The Free Africa Foundation, for his diligence, steadfast support, and research.

In the final analysis, however, the views expressed in this book are my own, and any errors or misstatements are my sole responsibility.

George B. N. Ayittey, Ph.D.
Washington, D.C.
USA
July 2011

INTRODUCTION

ADVANCING THE CAUSE OF LIBERTY

DEMOCRACY HAS SUFFERED A STEADY DECLINE five consecutive years in a row. In its 2011 annual report, Freedom House describes this as a continuing "freedom recession." It suggests that conventional ways of fighting dictators are not working and that a re-evaluation is imperative. Despots are gaining the upper hand; they have learned new tricks and honed their skills to beat back the democratic challenge.

The purpose of this book is not to present a catalog of grotesque atrocities and scandalous human rights violations that despots around the world perpetrate against their own people. The singular purpose is to advance the cause of liberty. There are millions of people—in Africa, Asia, Central Asia, the Middle East, and South America—who still labor under the yoke of tyranny and who yearn to be free. This book seeks to help liberate them. It may seem like a formidable and impossible task that is strewn with obstacles. But it depends upon the way the problem—dictatorship—is viewed and tackled.

In the past, and even conventionally, much effort, money, and time have been spent to reason with, persuade, cajole, or bribe dictators, or even threaten them with sanctions. Western governments have spent billions in this effort to no or little avail. A new way of thinking or a different approach is imperative. Leave the dictators alone for now. They are stone-deaf and impervious to reason. Railing daily about their abuses of human rights, acts of brutality, and violence will not alone bring about change. It is time to think about the other side, the opposition, the pro-democracy activists and reformers. That is the focus of this book.

Dictators have proliferated, especially in postcolonial Africa, not so much because of their ingenuity but because of the nature and character of the opposition forces—both domestic and international—arrayed against them. To be sure, dictators are crafty, evil geniuses with awesome firepower at their disposal. They are also brutally efficient at intimidation, terrorism, and mass slaughter.

However, a force is able to dominate because the counterforce is either nonexistent or weak. Despots have prevailed for decades because the opposition forces are weak or crumbling. The purpose of this book, based in part upon my own personal experience and on lessons garnered from several developing countries, is to strengthen the opposition forces.

Too many in the West have become complacent or tolerant of despots, especially in African nations. The standard arguments are, "They have no democratic tradition"; "Despotism is part of the political culture"; "Dictatorship is acceptable to them"; and, as French president Jacques Chirac once said, "Africa is not yet mature enough for Western-style democracy." Such misconceptions, resulting from mythology and false assumptions, have informed many Western policies and foreign aid programs that have failed miserably after costing hundreds of billions of dollars. The intentions of the policies and programs might have been laudable, but it is absurd to seek to help a people one doesn't understand.

Despotism is not a new political phenomenon to the people of the developing world. They have encountered it in their traditional societies and devised various measures to check and deal with it. Chapter 2 takes a look at these traditional societies, many of which still exist—their social structures, political organizations, and governments—in which kinship is the articulating principle. The chief, king, or ruler is not chosen by voting but is appointed with the approval of a council; governance is based upon consultation with councils, and decisions are reached by consensus. This appears to be the near-universal style of governance among the natives of the developing world. Despotism is incompatible with such systems and is fundamentally alien to most of the natives of developing countries. Yet the fact that the natives were very much aware of the threat of despotism suggests that the proliferation of despots in modern times is the result of the near-total absence of the curbs and checks and balances that exist in traditional systems. Chapter 3 looks at these curbs.

This way of looking at despotism is different from the conventional and has two advantages. First, it dispels the offensive notion held by some in the West that "despotism is acceptable to these people." It has *never* been acceptable! Second, it frames the arguments against despotism in *cultural terms,* not the standard Western narrative. This approach invokes a sense of *cultural betrayal* by the despots and inoculates the case for freedom against the charge of being "Western sponsored." Casting the cause for freedom in a Western or religious framework polarizes the debate and detracts from the basic issue of *liberty.* The West should not tolerate despotism in the developing countries; nor should despots use their traditional systems to justify their tyrannical rule.

On the battlefield one must know the enemy—his strengths, weaknesses, and tactics. Chapter 4 discusses the modus operandi of despotic regimes. Like a table, a despotic regime has "legs"—props or supports. For despotic regimes, these supports are both external and internal. One does not fight a regime by climbing on top of the table to fight it where it is strongest. Instead, one identifies its props and systematically severs them. The law of gravity then takes care of the rest.

Despotic regimes' external props come in the form of foreign aid, foreign loans, diplomatic recognition, and so on. The internal support comes from security forces, civil servants, intellectuals, and students, among others. Support is often bought with patronage, government appointments, and perks.

A despotic regime does not last forever. It violates the natural order of things and eventually collapses under the weight of its own internal contradictions. Paranoia and insecurity often plague despotic regimes, and palace intrigues often lead the despot to suspect plots by everyone, even his own military. He may create layers upon layers of security, just in case one layer fails. In the end, however, he may be hoisted by his own petard—overthrown or killed by members of his own security apparatus. The demise of a despotic regime is the subject of chapter 5.

Freedom lovers and democracy activists, however, cannot wait for a despotic regime to self-destruct. It may take decades—witness the military regimes of Than Shwe of Myanmar (Burma) and Colonel Muammar Qaddafi of Libya. And even if a regime self-destructs sooner, another dictator may take the place of the one who has been overthrown. Therefore, a *proactive* stance or strategy must be forged to hasten his demise and ensure a peaceful transition. Toward this end, chapter 6 examines successful prodemocracy revolutions in the Philippines (February 1986),

Estonia, Latvia, and Lithuania (1987–1990), the Czech Republic (November 1989), Ghana (December 2000), Georgia (November 2003), Ukraine (November 2004), and Tunisia and Egypt (2011). Why were they successful and what lessons can be learned?

This author was one of the architects of the nonviolent democratic change in Ghana in 2000 and takes pride in the fact that Ghana was the first sub-Saharan African country visited by President Barack Obama in July 2009. He chose Ghana because it is a "model of good governance and democracy."[1] The author's role in bringing about change in Ghana is briefly described in chapter 6, which also looks at unsuccessful revolutions in Iran (June 2009), Zimbabwe (March 2008), Kenya (January 2008), Myanmar or Burma (September 2007), Venezuela (November 2007), Ethiopia (November 2005), and China (April 1989). What were the reasons for these failures?

With lessons learned and mistakes to be avoided, in chapter 7 we seek to lay out a smart and effective opposition strategy. It takes an intelligent or a smart opposition to make democracy work—not the rah-rah noisy type that simply chants "Mugabe Must Go!" A smart opposition must know the weaknesses of the enemy and exploit them, which is the first rule of combat. One does not fight an enemy on the turf on which he is strongest; one exploits his weaknesses.

Toppling a dictator, however, is only the first step; it does not necessarily establish freedom and prosperity. Many countries have experienced "revolution reversals." A dictator is toppled, only to be replaced by another tyrant. As Africans are fond of saying: "We struggle very hard to remove one cockroach from power and the next rat comes to do the same thing or worse. Haba! [Darn!]"

Africa is not unique in this regard, however. The "color" or "flower" revolutions in post-communist republics in Central Asia have faded or wilted in Georgia (Rose), Kyrgyzstan (Tulip), and Ukraine (Orange). In East and Southeast Asia, some Filipinos yearn for a return of Ferdinand and Imelda Marcos, and some Indonesians are contemplating making Suharto a national hero. Chapter 8 offers a sobering assessment of the reversals of revolutions and the reasons for them.

Chapter 9 examines what role—if any—the international community or the West can play to assist pro-democracy movements. The picture is not pretty. Like their domestic counterparts, international opposition or resistance to despots is generally weak, impotent, and crumbling. The international effort is led by a cacophonous gallery of Western donors, multilateral financial institutions, development experts, human rights advocacy groups, Hollywood stars, rock stars, pro-democracy activists, and a whole bunch of others. There is no coordination among them, no road map. Some even work at cross-purposes with one another. Massive confusion prevails.

Dictators have been responsible for many of Africa's humanitarian catastrophes. Providing relief aid to the victims of repressive rule and leaving the dictators in place makes little sense. It is a Band-Aid solution. The Darfur crisis in Sudan, in which the international community simply cleans up after the dictator, Omar al-Bashir, is the most obscene. To be sure, he has been indicted by the International Crimes Commission (ICC) for crimes against humanity, and there is an international warrant for his arrest. Yet he travels freely in Africa and the Middle East, thumbing his nose at the world.

A dictatorship is a closed society that needs reform in many areas: intellectual, political, constitutional, institutional, and economic. Oftentimes, the international community pushes one type of reform out of sequence and compounds the problem. For example, pushing economic liberalization before political reform amounts to putting the cart before the horse. Economic liberalization will engender economic prosperity, but without political reform that prosperity will not be evenly distributed. It will enrich the ruling vampire elites, leaving the mass of people in poverty (crony capitalism). The elite's ostentatious lifestyles, the public perception of corruption, and the growing social inequality will eventually provoke civil unrest if food prices are raised sharply or if there are no jobs for the youth. That is when the political day of reckoning will arrive. If the political space is not opened up, the country may implode, dissipating all the economic gains: Indonesia, Ivory Coast, and Yugoslavia are examples of this. China currently faces this dilemma. Thus, political reform must precede economic liberalization. In the same vein, intellectual freedom must precede political reform because the people need the intellectual freedom to determine the type of political system they want.

Real reform begins with intellectual freedom; continues with political, constitutional, and institutional reform; and concludes with economic liberalization. Call it "Ayittey's Law." The West underestimates the reformist potency of freedom of expression and its corollary, the free media. Free media in Liberia, Rwanda, Sierra Leone, and Somalia, for example, would have saved those countries from implosion. And it is free media, not sanctions, that will halt Iran's nuclear ambition. Free media in North Korea would spank that incorrigible tyke into good behavior. And free media would clip China's "chopsticks mercantilism" down to size. The free media are the most effective weapon against *all* dictatorships. So why is the West trying to reason with or appease dictators?

Chapter 10 provides an epilogue and lessons learned—most poignantly, from the author's perspective.

Finally, a few cautionary notes. First, the term "opposition group or leader" is applied throughout this book to *pro-democracy* groups and leaders, although, in practice, there may be groups and leaders whose democracy credentials are dubious. Second, it is acknowledged from the outset that this book has a slant toward Africa—in the sense that many examples and illustrations are taken from that continent—although every effort has been made to include evidence from other continents. There are numerous despots in Africa and only a smattering on other continents. Of the 54 African countries, only 15 can be said to be democratic. Thus, by dint of logic or reason, Africa presents a trove of information about despotism that can be mined. However, regardless of their nationality, race, religion, or ideology, despots use the same modus operandi. Third, though the terms "freedom" and "democracy" are used interchangeably throughout this book, the two are not necessarily identical. Democracy can result in an "elected tyranny," or tyranny of the majority.

Fourth, this author foresaw the upheavals in North Africa that spread to the Middle East. Back in 2005, I wrote *Africa Unchained*, which warned of the "cheetah generation"—a new generation of angry Africans. They are young, educated, and tech savvy. They brook no nonsense about corruption or dictatorship. They understand democracy, accountability, and the rule of law. They won't sit there and wait for dysfunctional governments to come and do things for them. They are taking back Africa—one village at a time: Tunisia and Egypt have been re-claimed. More countries soon will be as well.

Fifth, mention must be made of a noteworthy contribution by Gene Sharp in *From Dictatorship to Democracy*. He covers the same terrain with astonishing brevity, but his approach tends to be somewhat theoretical and lacks a cultural perspective. Furthermore, this author, having been part of the struggle for democracy in Ghana, speaks from experience.

CHAPTER 1

DESPOTIC REGIMES TODAY

"A political system based on force, oppression, changing people's votes, killing, closure, arresting and using Stalinist and medieval torture, creating repression, censorship of newspapers, interruption of the means of mass communications, jailing the enlightened and the elite of society for false reasons, and forcing them to make false confessions in jail, is condemned and illegitimate."

—Grand Ayatollah Hossein Ali Montazeri[1]

THE TERMS "DESPOT," "AUTOCRAT," "TYRANT," AND "DICTATOR" are used interchangeably throughout this book to refer to a ruler with absolute or unlimited power, but there are subtle differences. A *despot* may be more reminiscent of medieval monarchs who were convinced that they were endowed with the divine right to rule over their people. In other words, despotism is often infused with a dose of narcissism. An *autocrat* may have no such grand delusions about himself, but he still wields enormous power. A *tyrant* is a ruler who exercises power oppressively and harshly. The word *dictator* may be more applicable to a ruler with a military background who barks orders, issues diktats or edicts, and expects full compliance and obedience. It is possible to make other distinctions, such as "benign" or "benevolent" dictatorship, but this book does not do so.

Modern dictators come in different shades, races, skin colors, and religions, and they profess various ideologies. However, in general, they share common characteristics and idiosyncrasies. They are rulers who are neither chosen by their people nor represent their people.

The political watchdog Freedom House found in 2011 that 60 of the world's 194 countries are "partly free" and 47 are considered "not free." That means that the populations of roughly 55 percent of the world's nations are oppressed.

The continent of Africa has the dubious distinction of harboring more dictators per capita than any other region in the world. Teeming with tyrants, it is the most *un-free continent in the world*. The usual suspects received the lowest possible ratings for both political rights and civil liberties: Myanmar (Burma), Equatorial Guinea, Eritrea, Libya, North Korea, Somalia, Sudan, Tibet, Turkmenistan, and Uzbekistan.[2] But China, Egypt, Iran, Russia, and Venezuela are cited for having stepped up repressive measures with greater brazenness.

Despots are constantly refining their tactics and learning new tricks from each other in their efforts to control pro-democracy forces. To maintain their iron grip on power, despots invent new "enemies." This enables them to mobilize their security forces, keep their countries on a war footing, and suspend civil liberties. These enemies are often foreign, but they might also come from within, in which case they are labeled "neo-colonial stooges," "imperialist lackeys," or "CIA agents."

In some countries, despots justify their repressive rule by rallying the people around some nationalistic cause or some farcical "revolution." In Sudan, for example, Lieutenant-General Omar al-Bashir proclaimed an "Islamic Revolution" that will deliver the Sudanese from abject poverty and squalor by tapping the country's oil and mineral riches to create a model economy.

The despots have grown bolder as the resistance against them appears to be collapsing. The weakness of domestic opposition and inadequate support from democratic countries for that opposition, as well as fatigue, appear to be contributing factors. Unless the resistance—both domestic and international—is strengthened and democratic countries join forces, the despots will continue to gain momentum and win.

THE GALAXY OF DESPOTS: THE WORLD'S MOST ODIOUS AND DESPICABLE DICTATORS

On April 8, 2010, a coalition of opposition groups ousted Kyrgystan's dictator, President Kurmanbek Bakiyev, from power in Bishkek. A continent away, Africans like myself cheered: "One coconut down, 54 more to harvest!" Then, on January 14, 2011, came a loud *thud!* Another coconut down, this one in Tunisia, inspiring others to shake coconut trees vigorously. Then another in Egypt on February 11, 2011, with more to follow.

The West was caught completely off guard by the upheavals in North Africa. In fact, the West—or the international community—had lost the will to fight dictators, preferring "dialogue," "partnership," or "rapprochement" with such hideous tyrants as Muammar Qaddafi in Libya. Pundits intoned that "these people preferred strong men." But this author foresaw these upheavals. Despotism has never been acceptable to "these people," despite the veneer of "stability" despotism projects. There is one insidious and odious aspect of despotism that is particularly infuriating and galling—the political and cultural betrayal. As in Kyrgyzstan, many despots began their careers as erstwhile "freedom fighters," who were supposed to have liberated their people from repressive rule. Back in March 2005, Bakiyev rode the crest of the Tulip Revolution to oust another dictator, President Askar Akayev. So familiar are Africans with this phenomenon that, it may be recalled, we have this saying: "We struggle very hard to remove one cockroach from power and the next rat comes to do the same thing. Haba! [Darn!]."

In an article published in *Foreign Policy*, I denounced these revolutionary-turned-tyrant "crocodile liberators" who were joining the ranks of other fine specimens: the Swiss bank socialists, who socialize economic losses and stash personal gains abroad; the quack revolutionaries, who betray the ideals that brought them to power; and the briefcase bandits, who simply pillage and steal. I drew up a list of the "Worst of the Worst" dictators and warned of their imminent demise. Here is my list,[3] based on these insidious, ignoble qualities of perfidy, cultural betrayal, and economic devastation. These criteria are decidedly *non-Western*.

THE LIST: THE MOST ODIOUS AND DESPICABLE

1. **Omar al-Bashir of Sudan:** A megalomaniac zealot who has quashed all opposition, Bashir is responsible for the deaths of more than 4 million Sudanese and has been indicted by the International Criminal Court for war crimes. His Arab militia, the Janjaweed, may have halted its massacres in Darfur but it continues to traffic black Sudanese as slaves. Bashir himself

has been accused of having several Dinka and Nuer slaves, one of whom escaped in 1995.[4]
Years in power: 21

2. **Kim Jong Il of North Korea:** A personality-cult-cultivating isolationist with a taste for fine French cognac, Kim has pauperized his people, allowed famine to run rampant, and sent hundreds of thousands to prison camps (where as many as 200,000 languish today)—all while spending his country's precious few resources on creating a nuclear program. As he succeeded his father, Kim Il Sung, Kim Jong Il is being succeeded by his son, Kim Jong Eun. The country is a "family business and property."[5]
Years in power: 16

3. **Robert Mugabe of Zimbabwe:** A liberation "hero" in the struggle for independence who has since transformed himself into a murderous despot, Mugabe has arrested and tortured the opposition, squeezed his economy into astounding negative growth and billion-percent inflation, and funneled off a juicy cut for himself using currency manipulation and offshore accounts.
Years in power: 29

4. **Than Shwe of Myanmar (Burma):** A heartless military coconut-head whose sole consuming preoccupation is power, Than Shwe has decimated the opposition with arrests and detentions, denied humanitarian aid to his people after the devastating Cyclone Nargis in 2008, and thrived off a threatened black-market economy of natural gas exports. This vainglorious general, bubbling with swagger, sports a uniform festooned with self-awarded medals, but he is too cowardly to face an untampered-with ballot box.
Years in power: 18

5. **Mahmoud Ahmadinejad of Iran:** Inflammatory, obstinate, and a traitor to the liberation philosophy of the Islamic Revolution, Ahmadinejad has pursued a nuclear program in defiance of international law and the West. Responsible for countless injustices during his five years in power, the president's latest egregious offense was leading his paramilitary

goons, the Basij, toward the violent repression of protests after the June 2009 disputed presidential election, which many believe he lost.
Years in power: 5

6. **Meles Zenawi of Ethiopia:** A "rat" worse than the "cockroach" (former Marxist dictator Mengistu Haile Mariam) he ousted, Zenawi has clamped down on the opposition, stifled all dissent, and rigged elections. After he stole the May 2005 election, his security thugs opened fire on peaceful demonstrators, killing more than 200 of them, and jailed more than 1,000 opposition leaders and supporters. Like a true Marxist revolutionary, Zenawi has stashed millions in foreign banks and acquired mansions in Maryland and London in his wife's name, according to the opposition—even as his barbaric regime collects a whopping US$1 billion in foreign aid each year. He won 99.6 per cent of the vote in the May 2010 election—just shy of the 100 percent Saddam Hussein won in a 2002 referendum for another seven-year term.[6]
Years in power: 19

7. **Isaiah Afwerki of Eritrea:** Another crocodile liberator, Afwerki has turned his country into a national prison in which independent media are shut down, elections are categorically rejected, military service is mandatory, and the government would rather support Somali militants than its own people.
Years in power: 17

8. **Hu Jintao of China:** A chameleon despot who beguiles foreign investors with a smile and a bow but ruthlessly crushes any political dissent with brutal abandon, Hu has an iron grip on Tibet and is now seeking what can only be described as new colonies in Africa from which to extract the natural resources his growing economy craves and in which to resettle surplus Chinese population.
Years in power: 7

9. **Muammar al-Qaddafi of Libya:** An eccentric megalomaniac infamous for his indecipherably flamboyant speeches and equally erratic politics, Qaddafi today runs a police state based on his version of Mao's Red Book—the Green Book—which

includes a solution to "the problem of democracy." Under siege by rebels, he vowed to crush "the rats and traitors." After they seized his compound on August 24, the rebels vowed to smoke out the rat from the labyrinth of tunnels beneath the compound. So who's the real rat?
Years in power: 42

10. **Hugo Chávez of Venezuela:** The quack leader of the Bolivarian Revolution, Chávez promotes a doctrine of participatory democracy in which he is the sole participant, having jailed opposition leaders, extended term limits indefinitely, and closed independent media outlets. He has vowed to rule till 2021.
Years in power: 10

11. **Gurbanguly Berdymukhammedov of Turkmenistan:** Succeeding the eccentric tyrant Saparmurat Niyazov (who even renamed the months of the year after himself and his family), this obscure dentist has continued his late predecessor's repressive policies, explaining that, after all, he has an "uncanny resemblance to Niyazov."
Years in power: 4

12. **Idris Deby of Chad:** Having led a rebel insurgency against former dictator Hissene Habre, today Deby faces a rebel insurgency led by his own brother. Deby has drained social spending accounts to equip the military, co-opted opposition leaders, and is now building a moat around the capital, N'Djamena, to repel would-be insurgents.
Years in power: 20

13. **Teodoro Obiang Nguema Mbasogo of Equatorial Guinea:** Obiang and his family literally own the economy in one of the world's most unequal countries; the masses are left in desperate poverty in a country where oil wealth yields a GDP per capita that should be on a par with many European states. (How much oil revenue the country earns is a "state secret.") Obiang is a vicious despot who tolerates no dissent and has amassed a fortune exceeding US$600 million. When he accused his government of corruption, incompetence, and poor leadership, the entire government resigned in protest in

2006. He became the chairman of the African Union in 2011. Imagine.

Years in power: 31

14. **Yahya Jammeh of Gambia:** An eccentric military buffoon who has vowed to rule for 40 years and claims to have discovered the cure for HIV/AIDS, Jammeh insists on being addressed as "His Excellency President Professor Dr. Al-Haji Yahya Abdul-Azziz Jemus Junkung Jammeh." He claims he has mystical powers and will turn Gambia into an oil-producing nation; no luck yet. He has threatened to behead gays. He is terrified of witches and evil sorcerers, who, he claims, are harming his country. To root out witches, villagers at Jambur were rounded up and forced to drink a foul-smelling potion in 2009. Six people later died.

Years in power: 16

15. **Blaise Compaoré of Burkina Faso:** A tin-pot despot with no vision and no agenda save perpetuating himself in power by liquidating all political opponents and stifling dissent, Compaoré rose to power after murdering his predecessor, Thomas Sankara, in a 1987 coup. He dishonors the name of his own country, Burkina Faso, which in the Dioula language means "men of integrity."

Years in power: 23

16. **Bashar al-Assad of Syria:** A pretentious despot trying to fit into his father's shoes, which are too big for him, Assad has squandered billions on foreign misadventures in such places as Lebanon and Iraq. After neglecting the needs of his people, they rose up against him in May 2011. But he used tanks and his extensive security apparatus to crush them and maintain his tight grip on power.

Years in power: 10

17. **Islam Karimov of Uzbekistan:** A ruthless thug since Soviet times, Karimov has banned opposition parties, tossed as many as 6,500 political prisoners into jail, and labels anyone who challenges his iron grip on power as an "Islamic terrorist." What does he do with "terrorists" once they are in his hands? Torture them: Karimov's regime earned notoriety for boiling

two people alive and torturing many others. Outside the prisons, the president's troops are equally indiscriminate, massacring hundreds of peaceful demonstrators in 2005 after a minor uprising in the city of Andijan.
Years in power: 20

18. **Yoweri Museveni of Uganda:** After leading a rebel insurgency that took power in 1986, Museveni declared, "No African head of state should be in power for more than 10 years." He is still in power, winning one coconut election after another. Political parties can be formed legally, but a political rally of more than seven people is illegal.
Years in power: 26

19. **Paul Kagame of Rwanda:** A true liberator who saved the Tutsis from complete extermination in 1994, Kagame now practices the same ethnic apartheid he sought to end. His Rwanda Patriotic Front dominates all levers of power: the security forces, the civil service, the judiciary, banks, universities, and state-owned corporations. Those who challenge him are accused of being "hatemongers" or "divisionists" and are arrested. Such was the case with opposition leaders who were jailed days before the August 2003 election. A similar campaign of vilification was waged against the opposition in the run-up to the August 2010 election.
Years in power: 16

20. **Raul Castro of Cuba:** Afflicted with intellectual astigmatism, Castro is pitifully unaware of the fact that the revolution he leads is obsolete, an abysmal failure, and totally irrelevant to the aspirations of the Cuban people. He blames the failure of the "revolution" on "foreign conspiracies," which he then uses to justify even more brutal clampdowns that lead to more failures. He operates from the offensive notion that the entire Cuban economy belongs to the Castro family alone.
Years in power: 2

21. **Alexander Lukashenko of Belarus:** An autocrat and former collective farm chairman, Lukashenko maintains an iron grip on his country, monitoring opposition movements with a secret police distastefully called the KGB. His brutal style of

governance has earned him the title "Europe's last dictator"; he even gave safe haven to Kyrgyzstan's toppled leader during the uprising in that country in the spring of 2010.
Years in power: 16

22. **Paul Biya of Cameroon:** A suave bandit who has reportedly amassed a personal fortune of more than US$200 million and the mansions to go with it, Biya has beaten the opposition into complete submission. Not that he's worried about elections—he has rigged the term-limit laws twice to make sure the party doesn't end any time soon.
Years in power: 28

The list, of course, is not exhaustive or static; it keeps evolving.

DESPOTIC REGIMES AROUND THE WORLD

An analysis or a discussion of despotic regimes around the world would involve a tedious repetition of brutal acts of repression, injustices, indignities, and grotesque human rights violations. Moreover, despite regime differences, the modus operandi of one despot is strikingly similar to that of all the others. Most despotic regimes are characterized by the following:

- Unyielding grip on power: Elections, if any, are farcical and are *always* won by the despot.
- Political repression: Opposition parties are banned or afforded little political space to operate; key opposition leaders are arrested, intimidated, hounded, or even killed.
- Intellectual repression: Censorship may be imposed; journalists, editors, and writers are harassed, intimidated, jailed, or killed; newspapers and radio and television stations that are critical of government policies are shut down.
- Brutal tactics: Street protests are disrupted with batons, water cannons, tear gas, and even gunfire.
- Flagrant violations of human rights: Opponents of the regime are detained without trial; disappearances and murder are common; freedom of expression, movement, and assembly are nonexistent.

Rather than discuss these traits for each despotic regime, I will just list the countries where such practices are most prevalent:

- **Africa:** Algeria, Eritrea, Ethiopia, Sudan, Uganda, and Zimbabwe
- **Asia:** Myanmar (Burma), Cambodia, and Vietnam
- **Central Asia:** Kazakhstan, Tajikistan, Turkmenistan, and Uzbekistan
- **Eastern Europe:** Belarus
- **Latin America:** Venezuela
- **Middle East:** Iran, Jordan, Saudi Arabia, Syria, and Yemen

Across Eurasia (comprising 12 states), governments are characterized by strong executives and weak legislatures. The primary focus of politics is on elections and on the constant tussle between presidents and parliaments over their respective authority. Presidents routinely rig elections and rule by decree, bypassing parliaments. Opposition political parties are not well organized and offer few viable alternatives. As such, "there are few intermediaries between high politics and the people, and the press that might play that role relies on the patronage of the state or powerful business cliques with their own agendas."[7]

The picture is much the same in Latin America. The *caudillos* (military strongmen) may be back in the barracks but despots now emerge from the ballot box.[8] Once elected, they succeed in neutering and debauching the state institutions. As reported in the *Economist:*

> Mr Chávez has turned Venezuela's courts into a tool of the executive and used them to jail, harass or disqualify a growing number of his opponents. Nicaragua's president, Daniel Ortega, has abused his power to rig both municipal elections and the supreme court. Less blatantly, Ecuador's Mr Correa has tried to muzzle the media, and the Kirchners in Argentina have used the presidency to bully opponents in business and the press. Yet the leaders of the region's main powers have stayed silent about these abuses.[9]

Even in countries where the separation of powers exists, weak institutions are unable to uphold the rule of law, provide effective government, and advance the rights and freedoms of the people. In Peru, neither the incumbent, Alan García, nor his predecessor, Alejandro Toledo, have commanded much clout or popularity. Political parties in

Peru, the *Economist* went on to say, are just personal vehicles for self-aggrandizement: "For local elections in Oct 2009, no fewer than 60,000 candidates registered in 14,000 municipalities for just 2,000 slates. There is no civil service. There are constant demonstrations, some violent. In a recent poll 22% of respondents outside Lima approved of blocking roads as a form of protest."

The Middle East is the region most bereft of democracy. Until the recent upheavals, only 3 of the 22 countries in the Arab League—Iraq, Lebanon, and the Palestinian territories—could be said to be democratic, even with some caveats. With access to the media restricted, chaotic general elections produce predictable results: the autocrats and vampire elites retain power; the opposition is demoralized, even radicalized; and the word "democracy" is bastardized. As the *Economist* notes:

> Every Arab country now has a form of representative legislature, even if most have little power and some, like Saudi Arabia's, are appointed by a king. Some of these autocracies allow more pluralism than others. Morocco, for instance, has widened its space for debate. Others, such as Kuwait, allow a directly elected parliament, but the ruling royal family, still ultimately in charge, has often rued the legislative near-paralysis that followed.[10]

Whether they are monarchies or republics, the Arab states tend to act much the same. Says Larry Diamond, a senior fellow of the Hoover Institution and board member of the Free Africa Foundation: "The Arab League has become, in effect, an autocrats' club."[11] Elections are for show, a window-dressing to let off steam. Technically, they are meaningless. But now the youth have started to change things. Angry street protesters sent Tunisian dictator Zine el-Abidine Ben Ali fleeing into exile on January 14, 2011, and brought down Hosni Mubarak of Egypt on February 11, 2011. In Burkina Faso, Libya, Syria, Uganda, and others, dictators put up a fierce resistance. In the end, however, the forces of liberty will triumph.

THE DEVASTATING TOLL

The act of repression not only assails our human conscience and dignity but also exacts a toll in terms of human lives and economic activity. Despotism wreaks economic, social, and human devastation.

Consider the impact on economic activity: An error made by a despot who does not have the necessary experts advising him could result in commodity shortages, overproduction, or a breakdown in the productive process. Since a despot is not likely to admit this, the problems can fester until they erupt into a full-blown crisis. This was the cause of the demise of the former Soviet Union. To be sure, impressive rates of economic growth are possible under authoritarian or despotic regimes. China and the Asian Tigers (Hong Kong, Singapore, South Korea, and Taiwan) are often cited as examples, but there is a caveat. Exceptions do not make the rule. A final day of reckoning eventually arrives. In an interview, South Korea's former president, the late Kim Dae-jung, asserted in an interview that placing economic development ahead of democracy was "the fundamental cause of the Asian financial crisis in 1998" because "the authoritarian style of government permitted corruption and collusive intimacy between business and government to flourish."[12]

Economic Underperformance and Collapse

In a dictatorship, the normal order of things and even common sense have been turned completely upside down. There is no freedom of speech, no rule of law, and state institutions are packed with sycophants and praise-singers. Professionalism disappears from the security forces and the civil service. Fealty to the despot counts more than competence or efficiency. Promotions and job security depend upon who can shout the loudest praise of the despot.

Infrastructure such as roads, bridges, schools, telecommunications, and ports begins to crumble because contracts are awarded by the despot to family members, cronies, and loyal supporters. To sustain the heavy patronage doled out to supporters, the despot may impose heavy taxation and tariffs. Prices—especially food and fuel prices—start to shoot up. The public might vent its outrage in street protests. The despot may clamp down brutally on these street protests and take drastic measures to prevent future price hikes. The hikes are blamed on foreign saboteurs. Property rights are scoffed at. Commercial properties of businessmen alleged to be "anti-government" may be confiscated or seized for distribution to the poor masses in the name of social justice. Such was the case for more than a decade (2000–2010) in Zimbabwe, where the despotic regime of Robert Mugabe organized ruthless thugs to violently seize white commercial farmlands. Similarly, in Venezuela, Hugo Chávez "seized rural estates and factories the government deemed to be unproductive, including some assets of Lorenzo Mendoza, Venezuela's second-wealthiest man, and of H. J. Heinz Co., the world's largest ketchup maker."[13] Chávez also seized control of or nationalized oil refineries in 2008. Such contempt for property rights scares off investors, who fear that their commercial properties may be the next to be seized without due process. They flee the country and, without investment, the economy contracts.

The crisis in Zimbabwe, for example, has cost Africa dearly. Foreign investors have fled the region, and the South African rand has lost 25 percent of its value since 2000. Zimbabwe's economic collapse caused US$37 billion worth of damage to South Africa and other neighboring countries.[14] Although South Africa has been most affected, Botswana, Malawi, Mozambique, and Zambia have also suffered severely.

Foreign investors fled Venezuela, too. According to *Bloomberg News,* such investors "sold $778 million more in Venezuelan assets than they bought in the first nine months of 2006, according to the central bank; a decade ago, in the same period, they added $5.9 billion more than they disposed of."[15]

This is also true of other Latin American countries where private property rights are not well protected because the rule of law is weakly enforced. As a result, despite Latin American economic growth rates that averaged more than 5 percent in 2004 and 2005, capital flows were negative, meaning more money left the region than entered it. The basic reason was an ongoing lack of confidence among long-term investors. Latin America expert Andres Oppenheimer was cited as saying that "only 1 percent of the world's investment in research and development currently goes to Latin America."[16]

Rash diktats and reckless mismanagement inevitably produce economic crises. To deal with these crises, despots may take desperate and drastic measures, such as imposing strict economic/price controls, printing currency, and/or revaluing the old currency. However, as we shall see in chapter 5, none of these measures solves the economic crisis. Instead, they exacerbate it, creating black markets, greater scarcities, and even higher prices, resulting in a vicious downward spiral to economic collapse and a failed state (as has occurred in North Korea and Zimbabwe) unless the despot has access to substantial revenues from a mineral resource, such as oil, as has been the case with Saddam

Hussein of Iraq, Mahmoud Ahmadinejad of Iran, and Muammar Qaddafi of Libya.

The Human Toll

The cost of despotism in human terms is impossible to estimate. A handful of despots around the world inflict misery, despair, hopelessness—and even death—on millions of people who have protested against tyrannical rule. Hundreds of thousands have been jailed. Millions have been killed and millions more have fled their countries to become refugees elsewhere. Among the most infamous despots was Pol Pot of Cambodia, who ruthlessly eliminated anyone who posed a threat to him. Out of a population of 8 million in 1975, 2 million were executed. Another was Idi Amin of Uganda, who butchered as many as 200,000 Ugandans in the 1970s. It should be no surprise that about 70 percent of the world's refugee population is in Africa and the Middle East—the two regions that harbor the most despots.

Particularly treacherous have been massacres condoned or orchestrated by despotic regimes against particular groups for ethnic, religious, political, or other reasons. Pogroms are violent acts by mobs that are characterized by killings and the destruction of homes, businesses, property, and religious centers. The past four decades have seen attacks on the Copts in Egypt in the 1980s, on the Tamils in Sri Lanka in the 1980s, and on ethnic Armenians in Azerbaijan in the 1990s.[17] The human toll of despotism can be seen even more dramatically in the pogroms against the Igbo that led to the 1967–1970 Biafran War in Nigeria, the 1994 Rwandan genocide against the Tutsis, and the ongoing genocide against blacks in the Darfur region of Sudan. Postcolonial African leaders—mostly autocrats—have caused the deaths of more than 19 million Africans since 1960:

- 1 million Nigerians died in the Biafran War (1967–1970).
- 200,000 Ugandans were slaughtered by Idi Amin in the 1970s.
- 100,000 were butchered by President Macias Nguema in Equatorial Guinea in the 1970s.
- Over 400,000 Ethiopians perished under Mengistu Haile Mariam.

- Over 500,000 Somalis perished under Mohammed Siad Barre.
- Man-made famines claimed over 2 million lives between 1980 and 2000 in Chad, Ethiopia, Niger, Somalia, and Sudan.
- Over 2 million have died in the wars of Liberia (1993–1999), Sierra Leone (1994–1999), and Ivory Coast (2000–2005).
- Over 1 million died in Mozambique's civil war in the 1970s.
- 1.5 million died in Angola's civil war, which began in 1975 and continued intermittently until 2002.
- 800,000 perished in Rwanda's genocide in 1994.
- 300,000 died in Burundi in 1993–1994.
- 4 million perished in Sudan's civil wars from 1960 to 2006.
- 6 million died as a result of Congo's wars from 1996 to 2006.

The rough total of 19.8 million does not include conflict-related deaths in Chad, Western Sahara, and Algeria and those who perished at refugee camps. Historians estimate that the total number of black Africans shipped as slaves to the Americas in the sixteenth, seventeenth, and eighteenth centuries was about 10 million. Africa lost another 10 million people through the trans-Saharan and East African slave trade run by Arabs. This means that, in a space of just 50 years after independence in the 1960s, postcolonial African leaders have slaughtered about the same number of Africans as were lost to both the West and East African slave trades over several centuries. Think about it.

Failed States

Every year, the social and economic toll of despotism is driven home by the publication of two indices. The first is the Index of Failed States, drawn up by *Foreign Policy* magazine in collaboration with the Fund for Peace, an independent research organization. Using 12 indicators of state cohesion and performance, compiled through a close examination of more than 30,000 publicly available sources, the Index ranks 177 states in order from most to least at risk of failure.[18] In the 2010 Index, most of the 20 failed states at the bottom are ruled by despotic regimes. Afghanistan, Iraq, and Pakistan may be regarded as exceptions because of ongoing wars in 2009. The majority of the failed states—12 out of 20—are in sub-Saharan Africa, and 11 out of those 12 African countries are ruled by despots.

INDEX OF FAILED STATES, 2010[19]

Somalia
Chad
Sudan
Zimbabwe
Democratic Republic of the
    Congo
Afghanistan
Iraq
Central African Republic
Guinea
Pakistan

Haiti
Ivory Coast
Kenya
Nigeria
Yemen
Myanmar (Burma)
Ethiopia
East Timor
North Korea
Niger

Even more telling is the United Nations Human Development Index. Of the 24 at the bottom, a staggering 22 are in sub-Saharan Africa.[20]

HUMAN DEVELOPMENT INDEX, 2010[21]

Togo
Malawi
Benin
Timor-Leste
Ivory Coast
Zambia
Eritrea
Senegal
Rwanda
Gambia
Liberia
Guinea
Ethiopia

Mozambique
Guinea-Bissau
Burundi
Chad
Democratic Republic of the
    Congo
Burkina Faso
Mali
Central African Republic
Sierra Leone
Afghanistan
Niger

Despite its immense wealth of mineral resources, Africa remains mired in abject poverty, misery, deprivation, and chaos. The World Bank adjusted its yardstick for extreme poverty from US$1.00 to US$1.25 a day, which means that 389 million of the 875 million people in sub-Saharan Africa lived in poverty in 2005.[22]

Millions of lives have been lost, economies have collapsed, and whole states have failed under brutal repression. The toll of despotism has been especially devastating for Africa. Africa is poor because she is not free. However, a failed state evolves through various stages. It begins as a vampire state, metastasizes into a coconut republic, and then finally implodes, becoming a failed or collapsed state.

Vampire States

"Anyone who gets to the presidency ends up with way more than he had before, while the poor and working class are the ones always left behind."
—Roberto Pedroza, a newspaper vendor in Mexico City[23]

The most remarkable aspect of despotism is the rapid deterioration of the institution of government. "Government," as it is known in the West, does not exist in countries ruled by despots. Leaving aside the democratic requirement that a government must be "of the people, by the people, and for the people," one expects a government, at a minimum, to care for and be responsive to the needs of the people, or at least to perform some basic services for its people. But even these minimal requirements are often lacking in a dictatorship, where government as an entity is totally divorced from the people and perceived by those running it as a vehicle not to serve but to fleece the people. Dishonesty, thievery, and embezzlement pervade the public sector. Public servants embezzle state funds, and high-ranking ministers are on the take. Government then becomes irrelevant to the people.

What then exists is a vampire state—a government hijacked by a phalanx of bandits, gangsters, crooks, and scoundrels who use the machinery of the state to enrich themselves, their cronies, supporters, and members of their own ethnic, racial, or religious group and to exclude everyone else. It is an apartheid-like system based on the politics of exclusion. One is poor if one does not belong to that charmed circle. The richest people in Africa and many Third World countries are the ruling vampire elites and government ministers. And quite often, the chief bandit is the head of state himself.

Examples of vampire states abound. In fact, one can characterize all communist states as such. They suck the economic vitality out of their people for the enrichment of the ruling communist apparatchiks. Even in post-communist Russia corruption has become a nearly insurmountable obstacle to the country's economic development. Berlin-based NGO Transparency International rates Russia 146th out of 180 nations in its Corruption Perception Index, saying "bribe-taking is worth about $300 billion a year."[24]

The PRI party, which ruled Mexico for more than 70 years, though not communist, is another example (its replacement was scarcely better). Said Lino Korrodi, finance manager for Vicente Fox's 2000 presidential campaign: "It is evident that he (Vicente Fox) got rich during his six years in office, in a very shameless and cynical way."[25] Mexican presidents are limited to one six-year term. Their last year in office is cynically derided by Mexicans as *"el año del dinero"* (year of the money). That is when Mexican presidents bare their fangs and suck as much as they can in a frenzy. Carlos Salinas de Gortari, who served from 1988 to 1994, was probably the most bloodthirsty. His name became synonymous with fraud, corruption, and economic devastation, and he fled in disgrace into a self-imposed exile in Ireland. The *New York Times* reported that "In 2002, Swiss banking authorities found more than US$100 million sitting in a Swiss bank account once controlled by his brother Raúl Salinas and froze it." The loot "was held in the name of a Cayman Islands shell corporation, Trocca Ltd., secretly controlled by Mr. Salinas."[26]

The regimes of several other Latin American countries ruled by oligarchies and *caudillo*s in the 1980s and 1990s can also be characterized as vampire states. Their rule deepened social and economic inequalities, provoking social discontent and sparking revolutionary movements in such countries as Colombia and Nicaragua. Widespread government dysfunction, corruption, and economic despair forced many Latin Americans to migrate and settle in the United States, often illegally. Known as the "undocumented," their number now exceeds 10 million.

In the Middle East, the classic example of a vampire state is Saudi Arabia. Others include regimes in Tunisia (under the ousted dictator Ben Ali), Egypt (under Hosni Mubarak), Iraq (under the late Saddam Hussein), Iran, Syria, and Yemen. More examples can be found in Africa, where the state has been reduced to a mafia-like bazaar in which anyone with an official designation can pillage at will. Dictators seize and monopolize both political and economic power to advance their own selfish and criminal interests, not to develop their economies, and they don't care about the poor. Their overarching obsession is to amass personal wealth, gaudily displayed in flashy automobiles, fabulous mansions, and bevies of fawning women. Helping the poor, promoting economic growth, or improving the standard of living of their people is anathema to the ruling elites. "Food for the people!" "People's power!" "Houses for the masses!" are simply empty slogans that are designed to fool the people and the international community.

Nigeria is the mother of all vampire states. Between 1970 and 2004, more than US$450 billion in oil revenue flowed into Nigerian government coffers, but much of it was looted by Nigeria's reckless military bandits. Mallam Nuhu Ribadu, the chairman of the Economic and Financial Crimes Commission set up in 2003, confirmed the theft of $412 billion over the period from 1960 to 1999. "We cannot be accurate down to the last figure but that is our projection," said Osita Nwajah, a commission spokesman.[27]

For 18 months (from February 1999 to August 2000), Nigeria's vampire state was paralyzed by legislators' wrangling over perks. Its 109 senators and 360 representatives passed just five pieces of legislation, including a budget that was held up for five months. Immediately upon taking office, the legislators voted themselves hefty allowances, including a 5 billion *naira* (US$50 million) furniture allowance for their official residences and offices. The now-impeached ex-chairman of the Senate from President Olusegun Obasanjo's own People's Democratic Party (PDP), Chuba Okadigbo, was the most greedy, according to *New African:*

> As Senate President, he controlled 24 official vehicles but ordered 8 more at a cost of $290,000. He was also found to have spent $225,000 on garden furniture for his government house, $340,000 on furniture for the house itself ($120,000 over the authorized budget); bought without authority a massive electricity generator whose price he had inflated to $135,000; and accepted a secret payment of $208,000 from public funds, whose purpose included the purchase of "Christmas gifts."[28]

And it gets better: President Obasanjo went after the loot that former president Sani Abacha and his family had stashed abroad. There was much public fanfare regarding the sum of about US$709 million and another £144 million recovered from the Abachas and the former president's henchmen. But then, this recovered loot itself was quickly *re-looted!* The Senate Public Accounts Committee found only US$6.8 million and £2.8 million of the recovered booty in the Central Bank of Nigeria (CBN).[29]

In case after case, government officials in the developing countries get rich by misusing their positions. Faithful only to their foreign bank accounts, these official buccaneers have no sense of morality, justice, or even patriotism. They kill and maim their own people and destroy their own countries to acquire and protect their booty because, functionally illiterate, they are incapable of using the skills and knowledge they acquired from education to get rich on their own in the private sector. Needless to say, they are "derided by some experts as 'the extractors,' people who squandered wealth without building for the future."[30]

The inviolate ethic of the vampire elites is self-aggrandizement and self-perpetuation in power. To achieve these objectives, they take over and subvert every key institution of government: the civil service, judiciary, military, media, and banking. As a result, state institutions and commissions become paralyzed. Laxity, ineptitude, and unprofessionalism thus flourish in the public sector. Of course, the country may have a police force and judiciary system to catch and prosecute the thieves. But the police are themselves highway robbers who are under orders to protect the looters in power, and many of the judges are themselves crooks.

Obviously, there are no checks against brigandage. The worst offender is the military—the most trenchantly perverted institution, especially in Latin America and Africa. In any normal civilized society, the function of the military is to defend the territorial integrity of the nation and its people against external aggression. But under despotic regimes, the military is instead locked in combat with the very people it is supposed to defend. Witness the barbaric brutalities meted out against street protesters by Iran's Basij militiamen in June 2009. Or those of North Korean security guards against market traders in December 2009. And think of Muammar Qaddafi sending jet fighters to bomb street demonstrators in February 2011. In *We Wish to Inform You that Tomorrow We Will Be Killed with Our Families*, Philip Gourevitch writes that, "Across much of Africa, a soldier's uniform and gun had long been regarded—and are still seen—as little more than a license to engage in banditry."[31] Wole Soyinka handed the postcolonial soldiers a blistering rebuke:

> The military dictatorships of the African continent, parasitic, unproductive, totally devoid of social commitment or vision, are an expression of this exclusionist mentality of a handful; so are those immediately post-

colonial monopolies that parade themselves as single-party states. To exclude the sentient plurality of any society from the right of decision in the structuring of their own lives is an attempt to anesthetize, turn comatose, indeed idiotize society, which of course is a supreme irony, since the proven idiots of our postcolonial experience have been, indeed still are, largely to be found among the military dictators.[32]

A simple rule of thumb on development has emerged: the index of economic well-being of a developing country is inversely related to the length of time the military holds political power. The longer it stays in power, the greater the economic devastation. Again, a few exceptions may be noted, as in the case of Augusto Pinochet of Chile, but exceptions do not make the rule.

Meanwhile, the vampire state wobbles as it lurches from one crisis to another. Its legitimacy is openly questioned. Some sections of the population are in open revolt and others may even mount roadblocks to keep out state officials, as occurred in many Latin American countries in the 1990s. Such was also the case in Libya in February 2011. The despot barks orders but is routinely ignored. His ruling vampire elites, clueless about how to resolve the economic crisis, resort to desperate measures to keep things under control, but they fail to arrest the deterioration. They readily give up and flex their muscle, daring anyone to hold them accountable or take power away from them. Steadily, the vampire state, infused with the arrogance of power, hardens into a coconut republic and provokes a rebellion: Tunisia, Egypt, Libya, and elsewhere in North Africa and the Arab world.

Coconut Republics

This invites a distinction. In a banana republic, one might slip on a banana peel but things *do* work for the people now and then, albeit inefficiently and unreliably. Electric supply is spasmodic and the water tap has a mind of its own. Occasionally, it might spit some water and then change its mind. Buses operate according to their own internal clock. By the grace of God or Allah, a bus might arrive, belching thick black smoke. Food and gasoline are generally available but expensive, if one is willing to contend with occasional long lines. The police are helpful when they are bribed and will then protect the people by catching real crooks. There is petty corruption. Now and then, a million dollars here and a million there might be embezzled. Such a banana republic often slips into suspended animation or arrested development.

A coconut republic, on the other hand, is ruthlessly inefficient, lethal, and eventually implodes. Instead of a banana peel, one might step on a live grenade. Here, common sense has been butchered and arrogant tomfoolery rampages with impunity. The entire notion of "governance" has been turned completely on its head by the ruling vampire elites, who wield absolute power, commit crimes, and plunder with supercilious arrogance.[33] They are not answerable or accountable to anybody and one dares not ask. Impunity reigns supreme. It is here where one finds tyrants chanting "People's Revolution" and "Freedom!" while standing on the necks of their people. A "revolution" is a major cataclysmic event that brings about an overthrow of the ancien régime. It makes a clean break with the existing way of doing things and establishes a *new* way or order. In politics, for example, a "revolution" occurs when the subjugated and exploited class rises up to overthrow the oppressors—as occurred with the American and French Revolutions. But in a coconut republic, it is the other way around. It is the dictators who are chanting revolution! Have you ever noticed that those Third World leaders who vociferously claim they are fighting against terrorism in order to receive Western aid are themselves sponsors of state terrorism against their own people?

In a coconut republic, the rule of law is a farce; bandits are in charge, their victims in jail. The police and security forces protect the ruling vampire elites, not the people. The chief bandit is the head of state himself. He and his family and his henchmen have a constant supply of electricity and their water taps run *all the time;* the people can collect rain water. There are inexhaustible supplies of food and gasoline for *them,* but not for the people. And there are no buses for the people, period. Those shiny buses that ply the road are for vampire elites. The people can walk. The republic sits atop vast reserves of oil and exports oil, but there is no gasoline for the people since the country's oil refineries have broken down. Funds earmarked for repairs have been stolen, and refined petroleum products must be imported. The country may also be rich in mineral deposits such as diamonds, gold, and coltan, yet the mineral wealth has produced misery—or a curse.[34]

Here are some examples of life in a coconut republic:

1. Hugo Chávez of Venezuela forces everyone to listen to his hours-long tirades but dozes off when he listens to them himself.

2. Saparmurat Niyazov, the late president-for-life of Turkmenistan, erected statues and portraits of himself everywhere and named cities, airports, and even a meteorite after himself. The months and days of the week were named after him and his family, and a family feast was celebrated every day.

3. When a presidential election was held in Uzbekistan in 2007, President Islam A. Karimov's three opponents each publicly endorsed him. In the 2009 parliamentary election, all four parties in the race staunchly supported Karimov. Asked if there was any real political opposition and competition in his country, Karimov replied that the 2009 race for the parliament's lower chamber "had injected genuine competition into the process, largely because the four parties have vocally criticized one another."[35]

4. Uganda's agriculture minister, Kibirige Ssebunya, declared that: "All the poor should be arrested because they hinder us from performing our development duties. It is hard to lead the poor, and the poor cannot lead the rich. They should be eliminated."[36] He advised local leaders to arrest poor people in their areas of jurisdiction. He died four years later.

5. A former minister of finance was found hiding—where else?—in a coconut tree: "[Zambia's] former finance minister, Katele Kalumba, was arrested and charged with theft after the police found him hiding in a tree near his rural home. Mr. Kalumba, who had been on the run for four months, is being charged in connection with some US$33 million that vanished while he was in office."[37]

6. The late president of Liberia, General Samuel Doe, summoned his finance minister, "only to be reminded by aides that he had already executed him."[38]

7. Tanzania's anti-corruption czar, Dr. Edward Hosea, was himself implicated in a corruption scandal involving the award of a US$172.5 million contract to supply 100 megawatts of emergency power to a Texas-based company that did not exist.[39]

Coconut Security Forces   In a coconut republic, the police are scarcely professional. Tell a police officer that you saw a minister stealing the people's money and it is *you* he will arrest! After the brutal murder of politician Robert Ouko in 1990, the *Washington Post* reported that, according to Kenyan police, "Foreign Minister Robert Ouko was presumed to have broken his own leg, shot himself in the head and set himself afire. Two years earlier, Kenyan officials suggested that a British tourist, Julie Ward, lopped off her own head and one of her legs before setting herself aflame."[40]

The ever-ready security forces can unleash the full force of their fury on unarmed civilians with batons, tear gas, water cannons, and rubber bullets. But how brave are the security forces really? Ambushed by a bunch of ragtag cattle rustlers, Kenya's elite presidential guards quickly surrendered. Johann Wandetto, a reporter for the *People Daily*, a newspaper in Kitale, Rift Valley province, published a story in the March 6, 1999, edition with the title: "Militia Men Rout 8 Crack Unit Officers: Shock as Moi's Men Surrender Meekly." Wandetto was arrested and sentenced to 18 months in prison on what the court described as an "alarmist report."[41]

And the mother of all security forces? When the African Union (AU) peacekeepers' base on the edge of Haskanita, a small town in southern Darfur, came under sustained rebel assault on September 29, 2007, the AU soldiers fled. According to the *Economist*, "Ten were killed; at least 40 fled into the bush. The attackers looted the compound before Sudanese troops arrived to rescue the surviving peacekeepers."[42]

Coconut Elections   Coconut elections are, essentially, farcical elections in which the incumbent writes the rules and then serves as a player, the referee, and the goalkeeper. The deck is hideously stacked against the opposition candidates, who are starved of funds, denied access to the state-controlled media, and brutalized by government-hired thugs as the police watch. Opposition parties may be banned too.

By contrast, the incumbent enjoys access to enormous state resources: state media, vehicles, the police, the military, and civil servants are all commandeered to ensure his re-election. Further, the entire electoral process itself is rigged: voter rolls are padded with ruling-party supporters and phantom voters while opposition supporters are purged. The electoral commissioner is in the pocket of the ruling party, as are the judges who might settle any election disputes. During the election campaign, posters of the incumbent are everywhere while pro-government thugs terrorize the populace and anyone perceived to be a supporter of the opposition parties. Innocent civilians are force-marched to attend the incumbent party's rallies, while opposition rallies are violently disrupted and opposition supporters are brutalized and even killed as the police look on.

On election day, the ruling party resorts to various tricks to steal the election. Ballot papers do not arrive on time, inducing frustrated opposition supporters to leave polling stations. Ballot boxes may eventually arrive but are already stuffed with votes for the incumbent. (Mayoral elections were held in Kampala, Uganda, on February 18, 2011. When the polls opened at 7:00 A.M., ballot boxes were already full of pre-ticked ballots for the ruling National Resistance Movement candidate, Peter Samatimba. This led to the cancellation of the results. Queried, Samatimba denied any involvement. "This could have been done by my opponents to discredit me," he said.[43]) And if during the vote count the opposition appears to be winning, the process can be halted and the ballot boxes transported to a secret location where the votes are counted in camera. Most often, posted election results do not reflect actual voting. This was the case in Ghana's 1996 elections, where Major Emmanuel Erskine, a challenger to the brutal regime of Fte./Lte. Jerry Rawlings, did not even get one single vote in his own constituency. That is, the results indicated that he did not vote for himself and his wife and four children did not vote for him. After he complained bitterly about the rigging, the electoral commission tossed six votes his way.

Here is a short list of instances that indicate coconut elections:

- The electoral equipment for coconut elections, the results of which are stolen anyway, was itself stolen (Nigeria, December 9, 2010).[44]
- Both candidates—Laurent Gbagbo and Alassane Ouattara— claimed victory and installed themselves as presidents after Ivory Coast's November 2010 elections.
- For the November 7, 2010, elections in Myanmar (Burma), military rulers bestowed upon their country a new flag, a new seal, and a new anthem. The old flags were to be lowered by people born on a Tuesday and the new flags were to be raised by people born on a Wednesday. Then all the old flags were to be burned. Many parties were blocked from participating by fees set so high that in many districts only government-backed

candidates could register, by stipulations that the military could allot close to one-quarter of all seats after the election took place, and by the harassment and threatening of opposition candidates who tried, against all odds, to compete. No international observers were permitted, and no foreign journalists were allowed in.[45] The military junta declared victory even before voting started.

• At the time of the August 25, 2003, elections in Rwanda, opposition leader Faustin Twagiramungu found his campaign stymied at every turn by government security forces. His rallies were canceled, his workers arrested, and his brochures seized. On the eve of the voting, "police arrested 12 of Twagiramungu's provincial organizers, saying they were preparing election day violence."[46] Additionally, "In Mr. Twagiramungu's home town, soldiers reportedly looked at ballot papers and ordered those who voted the wrong way to try again."[47] For the August 2010 elections, preparations for the September victory celebration by the incumbent despot, Paul Kagame, began before the voting did.

The year 2010 reaped a harvest of coconut elections in Belarus, Burkina Faso, Myanmar (Burma), Egypt, Ethiopia, Ivory Coast, and Rwanda. No incumbent lost an election.

Belarus, a country of 10 million, held its presidential elections on December 19, 2010. Long-term dictator Alexander Lukashenko, who had been in power for 16 years, won handily. His government controls the media, and opposition candidates were denied airtime. An agency called the KGB watched over the people. Intimidation was the order of the day. The government machine that pressured people into early voting was in place, and those who failed to vote early were threatened with the loss of their jobs in the state sector.

Lukashenko won nearly 80 percent of the vote and his closest rival 1.8 percent. Opposition activists and critical journalists denounced the vote as fraudulent, and over 10,000 demonstrators poured into the streets in a protest march toward Independence Square in the heart of Minsk. But heavily armed security and police forces unleashed their full fury on the demonstrators, who were savagely beaten. Seven of the nine opposition candidates were arrested, and over 600 protesters were taken into custody.[48]

The opposition candidate Vladimir Neklyayev, who received 1.8 percent of the vote, was beaten unconscious and rushed to the hospital. While he was being treated for head wounds, he was abducted by several men in civilian clothes. Also severely beaten and rushed to a hospital was another presidential candidate, Andrei Sannikov. And what was the reaction of the head of the Central Elections Commission, Lidiya Ermoshina—who was appointed by Lukashenko? According to an article in *Der Spiegel,* she "said that her office was aware of only very few complaints about the elections."[49] Naturally.

Coconut Reform   It is clear that the vampire state or the coconut republic must be reformed and replaced with a well-functioning state. To establish one, reform is needed in many areas—in the political system, the economic system, the judicial system, the educational system, and the electoral system. But reform is anathema to the ruling vampire elites and coconut heads, for it would threaten their lucrative businesses and their hold on power.

- Ask them to privatize inefficient state enterprises and they will sell the companies to themselves and their cronies at fire-sale prices: examples are Uganda under Yoweri Museveni and Egypt under Hosni Mubarak. Said Muhammad Al Ghanam, the former director of legal research in Egypt's Ministry of Interior: "The Mubarak era will be known in the history of Egypt as the era of thievery."[50]
- Ask them to develop their economies and they will develop their pockets. Ask them to seek foreign investment and they will seek a foreign country in which to invest their loot.
- Ask them to enforce the rule of law and they will force the law to respect their whims. Said *The Economist*: "In Zimbabwe, the thieves are in charge and their victims face prosecution."[51]
- Ask them to trim their bloated bureaucracies and cut government spending and they will establish a "Ministry of Less Government Spending." Ask them to establish a market-based economy and place more emphasis on the private sector and they will create a "Ministry of Private Enterprise," as Ghana did in 2002.
- Ask them to reform their abominable political and economic systems and they will perform the "coconut boogie"—one swing forward, three swings back, a jerk to the right, and a tumble

to land hard on a frozen Swiss bank account. Swiss authorities froze the bank accounts of Laurent Gbagbo of Ivory Coast, Zine el-Abidine Ben Ali of Tunisia, Hosni Mubarak of Egypt, and Muammar Qaddafi of Libya in 2011.

- Ask them to establish democratic pluralism and they will create surrogate parties, appoint their own electoral commissioners, empanel a gang of lackeys to write the constitution, inflate the voters' register, manipulate the electoral rules, and hold coconut elections to return themselves to power. Even African children could see through this chicanery and fraud. Said Adam Maiga from Mali: "We must put an end to this demagoguery. You have parliaments, but they are used as democratic decoration."[52]

Reform becomes a charade. The reform process has stalled through vexatious chicanery, willful deception, and vaunted acrobatics. The ruling vampire elites and the coconut heads are just not interested in reform, period. They benefit from the rotten status quo. But without reform, their countries could implode or collapse in a Tunisian-type revolution. In fact, the adamant refusal of despots to reform their odious and dysfunctional political systems has ignited revolutions:

- **Nicaragua:** In 1979, a revolutionary movement called the Sandinistas, led by Daniel Ortega, ousted from power Anastasio Somoza, whose family had ruled the country since 1936.
- **Indonesia:** In 1998, Suharto, who had held power for 32 years, was forced to resign following the Asian financial crisis. In May 1999, *Time Asia* estimated Suharto's family fortune at US$15 billion in cash, shares, corporate assets, real estate, jewelry, and fine art. Of this, US$9 billion was reported to have been deposited in an Austrian bank. Suharto was placed highest on Transparency International's list of corrupt leaders with an alleged misappropriation of between US$15 and 35 billion during his 32-year presidency.[53] His ouster led to the breakaway attempts by East Timor and Aceh.

However, Africa abounds with examples of despots who refused to heed the call to reform and, as a result, saw their countries implode in a violent vortex of chaos, carnage, and destruction, ending with their own deaths: Somalia (1991), Rwanda (1994), Liberia (1991), and Zaire (1996), among others. The cost of rebuilding each country devastated by war is in the billions. Rebuilding Liberia alone would cost at least US$15 billion.

The Coconut Cure   Alas, there is a cure for coconut heads. In Dar es Salaam, Tanzania, there is a place called "the magic corner," where all and sundry, including politicians, come to be relieved or cured of their problems. "Even those top leaders of the government come to that tree," said Shabuni Haruni, a private security guard. "Yes, during the election."[54]

Upon the payment of a small fee, a traditional healer will take a patient to a huge baobab tree, reputed to be the abode of ancestral spirits. Patients remove their shoes and kneel in front of the tree with their eyes closed. At one session described by the *Washington Post* correspondent Karl Vick,

> Rykia Selengia, a traditional healer, passed a coconut around and around the head of her kneeling client. The coconut went around the man's left arm, then the right, then each leg. When she handed the coconut to the client, Mussa Norris, he hurled it onto a stone.
>
> It shattered, releasing his problems to the winds.[55]

CHAPTER 2

TRADITIONAL SOCIETIES

MYTHOLOGY ABOUT TRADITIONAL SOCIETIES

THERE ARE MANY MYTHS ABOUT THE INSTITUTIONS and cultures of the peoples of the developing world that need to be dispelled. During the colonial era, these people were denigrated as "primitive barbarians" or "noble savages" who had no history or important institutions. Colonialism, therefore, was believed to be good for them because it civilized them and liberated them from their terrible and despotic rulers. In fact, there is a long history of such deprecation in the West, an example of which can be found in the writing of John Stuart Mill, an early advocate for individual rights.

Mill's classic essay *On Liberty* asserted forcefully, "Over himself, over his own body and mind, the individual is sovereign."[1] But Mill was unapologetic about the need for a double standard on individual rights:

> We may leave out of consideration those backward states of society in which the race itself may be considered as in its nonage [childhood]. Despotism is a legitimate mode of government in dealing with barbarians, provided the end be their improvement . . . Liberty, as a principle, has no application to any [such] state of things.[2]

Despotism is neither a legitimate nor an acceptable form of government for the people of the developing world. The source of much of this mythology was the failure to distinguish between the *existence* of an institution and *different forms* of the same institution. The absence of a *particular form* of an institution does not mean a total absence of that institution. The focus of our study here is the institution of democracy.

Democratic decisions can be taken in two ways: by majority vote and by consensus. Each method has both advantages and disadvantages. Decision-making by vote is fast and transparent. This is the Western way, but its downside is that it ignores minority positions and can result in "mob rule" or "tyranny of the majority."

Taking decisions by consensus has the advantage of taking *all* minority positions into account. Once such a decision has been reached, it is certain that *all* will go along with it because their viewpoints have already been considered. The downside, however, is that it takes an awfully long time to reach a consensus with a large number of participants. Thus, consensus is feasible in small gatherings: the Nobel Committee, the World Trade Organization (WTO), and many tribal councils or conclaves in the developing world make decisions by consensus. Again, the absence of ballot boxes—*a particular form of democracy*—does not imply the absence of democracy. When the Nobel Committee meets, formal votes are rarely taken within the committee, according to Geir Lundestad, director of the Nobel Institute. Rather, "they discuss it until they reach a consensus . . . They are always unanimous to the outside world."[3]

The Western-style majority vote, "winner-takes-all-and-eats-all," should not be taken as the gold standard as it lies at the source of many of the political problems in the developing world. It is a "zero-sum game" (I win, you lose), and in multiethnic societies in the developing world, minority groups will always be losers, which gives rise to ethnic tensions and strife. As we shall see later, it is another reason why despots have proliferated in modern times: they *never* lose Western-style elections.

Similarly, other institutions—money, the market, free enterprise, free trade, law, and justice, among others—existed in *other* forms. In fact, it can be stated categorically that the European colonialists introduced no new institutions into the Third World—only different and more efficient forms of already existing institutions; for example, paper currency versus commodity money.

Contrary to Western misconceptions, the natives have had their own functional institutions that have served them well for centuries. In fact, when a developing country implodes, the two institutions left standing are the religious ones (churches and mosques) and the traditional political structures. When the coastal town of Al-Bayda in Libya fell to anti-Qaddafi protesters on February 23, 2011, the town elders met to begin rebuilding. Angry pro-democracy fighters had captured hundreds of pro-Qaddafi soldiers and wanted to execute them. But when the tribal elders ordered restraint, the youth obeyed. "When the tribe says stop, the youth stop," said Abdullah Mortady, a prominent architect in the town.[4] The elders later asked the detainees' families and tribal leaders to come and pick them up. "We are not killers," said one elder. "Qaddafi made us killers," he added.[5]

The typical Westerner may find this story bizarre, and it is precisely the principal reason why the West got it so wrong and was caught by surprise by the upheavals in North Africa and the Middle East. Apparently, the West was trying to help people it didn't understand. Its foreign policies were predicated upon mythology or false premises.

In what follows, we shall discuss the main features of peasant societies—their social systems and, in particular, their institutions. This may sound like a formidable task due to the immense cultural and ethnic diversity, but the focus is on the striking similarities that characterize these institutions. Of particular importance to this study are democracy, markets, money, and capitalism.

The object of all this is two-fold. The first is to dispel certain Western myths and enable better policies to be formulated for people in developing countries. Contrary to Western misconceptions, strongmen are not acceptable to people in traditional societies. In fact, despotism and statism (centrally controlled or directed economic activity) are fundamentally *alien* to most such societies. The second goal is to help build democratic models that are more suitable and in consonance with these people's traditional political heritage. The modern systems, often foisted upon them by their leaders with Western acquiescence, are at variance with their traditional systems; hence, the constant upheavals and political turmoil. For example, Mobutu Sese Seko, the late president-for-life of Zaire (now the Democratic Republic of the Congo), once justified his autocratic rule with the statement that in traditional Africa, there was one chief and he ruled for life. He neglected to add that the chief was appointed—he did not appoint himself—and he could be removed at any time. The House of Saud is another example: it claims to rule in consultation with tribal leaders who receive petitions from citizens. However, in the traditional system, there is freedom of expression and there are sanctions against rulers who ignore citizens' petitions. The

West should not tolerate despotism in developing countries; nor should despots use traditional systems to justify their tyrannical rule.

In this discussion, the nouns—tribe, ethnic society, nation, groups, peasants, clans, indigenes, aborigines, and natives—as well as the adjectives—indigenous, traditional, aboriginal, autochthonous, and native—are used interchangeably without emotive content or pejorative intent. Native American Indians refer to their societies as "nations," while African indigenes use "tribes."

Social Structure

In the West, the individual is the basic economic and social unit—the reference point of social organization, attitudinal behavior, accountability, motivation, and achievement. In traditional societies in the developing world, kinship—descent from common ancestry—is the articulating principle of social organization as a whole and the basis of social integration. The lowest social unit within the lineage system is the nuclear family, which normally consists of a man, his wife (or wives), and children. A number of nuclear families tracing their descent from a single ancestral line make up a family group. A collection of family groups then becomes the clan, lineage, kinship, or the extended family. Another term for this might be the phratry, or tribal subdivision, for Native Americans.

Each social unit has a head, who is usually a male. In the nuclear family, the father or the oldest male is the head—politically, socially, economically, and religiously. Family and clan heads are generally referred to as sachems or chiefs in the case of American Indians or as elders in Africa. They oversee the welfare of the family or the community, serving as intermediaries between the family's ancestors and living members, helping educate children, resolving disputes, settling cases against family members, caring for the less fortunate members, and ensuring prosperity. Because they are imbued with wisdom, respect for elders is a near universal cultural command.

The clan provides vital services and protection to its individual members. It also affords economic security by providing insurance to individual householders undertaking risky ventures, as well as against liabilities its members might incur under customary law. The clan is answerable, in most cases, to a court of law with respect to the actions of its individual members. This is akin to the statutes governing the activities of a modern corporation. When an employee causes damage to a third party, the corporation may be sued or held liable. Similarly, the clan serves as a "corporate body" that is held liable for any damage caused by its members.

A group of extended families cohabitating a place but in different huts forms the village or a pueblo (among some Native Americans). The next unit up is the town, a collection of related villages. The hierarchical structure of a traditional society might then extend to the tribe, the province (or sultanate), and ultimately to the kingdom (or caliphate) in the case of monarchies or an empire.

Individual Rights and Responsibilities

In peasant societies, the community is paramount. The perspective is from the community to the individuals making up the community, not from the individual to the community as in the West. Tribal survival and prosperity are always the paramount prerogatives of clan leaders and chiefs. To achieve these objectives, group effort or cooperation is vital since individuals cannot survive on their own. This imperative also defines other social values: conformity, compassion, respect, human dignity, humanistic orientation, and collective unity. Parallel to the strong sense of community is the almost universal set of beliefs and practices centering upon ancestors, the original founders of the community and settlement. The peasant believes he owes his existence to his ancestors and therefore owes them a duty to carry out their commands and uphold their name and dignity. Although they are dead physically, they are spiritually ever present, influencing the course of daily life and mediating between the earthly and the supernatural. Whereas in the West religion supplies the moral code, in most peasant non-Muslim societies this code is provided by the ancestors.

Within the clan or tribe, however, the individual is free and independent, but his rights and freedoms are subordinate to those of the community. As the Ga of Ghana say, "Individuals don't live to be a hundred years old; the tribe does." And there is an Igbo saying: "*Ofu onye ada akali oho*" (No one individual can be greater or bigger than the community or country).

The individual has rights and freedoms, but they must be expressed within certain boundaries. These are prescribed by bio-evolutionary necessity, cultural norms, and religion. These norms are, in turn, influenced by custom, tradition, and the behavioral rules required by ancestors as well as by supernatural forces. In other words, philosophical beliefs, social mores, obligations, and value systems merely set the parameters within which the individual can operate freely. These boundaries are, in general, not imposed by the chief or king, which would constitute the hallmark of dictatorship. Furthermore, the boundaries vary from one ethnic group to another, and the degree of individualism or independence also varies across ethnic groups. There are some ethnic groups that place a cultural premium on individualism and show a strong attachment to egalitarianism. Others place greater emphasis on group identity, solidarity, and effort. Regardless, the preeminence of societal interests prevails in all tribal systems.

However, group effort—necessary for the survival of the tribe—does not preclude individual responsibility. No group will survive if it is made up of lazy men. Laziness is frowned upon in many tribal societies. Able-bodied peasants are expected to have an occupation (hunting, fishing, farming, craftsmanship, etc.) to support their families. "You reap what you sow," "Life is as you make it," and "He who does not cultivate his field will die of hunger" are some common proverbs in peasant societies. The African proverb "It takes a village to raise a child" does not absolve anyone of parental irresponsibility.

The individual can also own wealth and property that can be accumulated in social or physical forms: cattle, tradable goods, buildings, canoes, hunting gear, clothes, guns, trinkets, and so on. Prestige, status, honor, and influence are all attached to wealth in indigenous systems. The wealthy are "important people" with influence in social and governmental affairs. Inequities in wealth distribution are recognized since not all members of the lineage are engaged in the same occupation. Since each occupation offers different fortunes and opportunities, differences in wealth are bound to occur. Clans generally have a "family fund" or "family pot" from which a peasant can borrow initial start-up capital for business. The loans are expected to be paid back. More importantly, the extended family system can also serve as a launching pad for a peasant who wishes to undertake highly risky economic ventures, such as manufacturing and long-distance trading. It serves as insurance or a social security net. If a peasant fails in his endeavors, the extended family system will always be there to catch his fall. If he succeeds and becomes wealthy, he brings pride not just to himself but to his clan as well. The wealth he accumulates is private property, not communal property to be expropriated by the chief and divided equally among all tribal members. The rich are expected to help their less-fortunate brethren or kinsmen. By how much is left to their discretion. Further, the pursuit of wealth—just like individual freedom—must be conducted within certain boundaries that are set either by social norms or by religion (as in Islam). It is wrong for an individual to pursue wealth at the expense of his kinsmen or in a way that results in injury to his kinsmen. Islam forbids stealing and the charging of interest. If only modern-day Islamic kleptocrats would be true to their faith!

Peasants pool their resources together, cooperate, and help one another. This may be referred to as communalism or communitarianism, but it is not the same as socialism or communism. One can be communalistic or socialistic without being a socialist. Being social implies a desire to interact with others—as in "man is a social animal." Socialism, however, is an economic ideology that entails, among other things, state direction of economic activity (dirigisme). Peasants go about their economic activities on their own free will, not at the behest of their tribal government. Communism involves state ownership of the means of production and, hence, all goods and services produced. But in peasant societies the means of production are owned by the clan, the lineage, which, as noted earlier, acts as a corporate body or unit. However, the clan is not the same as the tribal government; it is a private entity and, therefore, the means of production are privately owned. Communal ownership is a myth.

The source of this myth is as follows: in the West the basic economic and social unit is the individual, whereas in peasant societies it is the collective—the clan or the extended family. When the first European settlers arrived in Africa or North America and asked a native, "Whom does this land belong to?" they were expecting to be told, "This land belongs to Mr. Smith"—an individual. Instead, they were told, "This land belongs to us." By "us," the native meant his clan or lineage, but the Europeans mistook that to mean the entire tribe. Hence, the myth of communal ownership. The original owners of land in peasant societies were the ancestors. They secured ownership by right of first occupation. When they passed away, their land fell into the possession of their descendants and, ultimately, the lineage. Thus, land in peasant societies is generally lineage-owned or -controlled. In addition, there may be tribal lands, which are acquired through conquest or by right of first possession.

A chief may send warring parties to stake out and claim an unoccupied piece of land. If he puts outposts there to guard against en-
croachment, young men from the village are required to defend such
lands. Such tribal lands do not belong to the chief, and he cannot sell
them without the full concurrence of the council of elders. He acts as
a caretaker of the lands for the tribe, and he may grant access to these
tribal lands to any tribesmen—or even to strangers—upon the offer of
a "customary gift." This gift varies from tribe to tribe. It may consist of
beads, two white goats, or a bottle of schnapps.

Those granted access to the land become tenants, not owners. They
exercise only usufructuary rights. Only what they produce on the land,
not the land itself, belongs to them. In some tribal systems, such tenants
are required to give a certain proportion of the harvest to the chief; others ask for an annual token donation. Tenants are free to use the land as
long as they want, but if they abuse it, they can be evicted.

Unfortunately, early European colonists did not understand this
scheme of things and mistook the presentation of a "gift" to mean
"purchase" of the land. Although several such misinterpretations took
place in Africa and North America, the most celebrated was that of
the purchase of Manhattan. In 1626, to gain access to Manhattan, the
Dutch colonists presented a token gift of beads and mirrors worth
about 60 guilders to a Native American chief. The Dutch thought they
had "bought" Manhattan whereas the Native Americans regarded the
transaction as granting access only.

POLITICAL ORGANIZATION

In most traditional societies, four main sociopolitical groupings can be
distinguished. The first is the "founder group," that is, all those members of the ethnic group who are related by blood to and descended
from the original forefather who is reputed to be the origin and founder
of the settlement. The terms "royal" and "governing" are also used to
refer to this lineage, to which is usually reserved the privilege of providing the "ruler" for the settlement.

The second group is the "commoners," the "common" members of
the ethnic group who are not genealogically related to the governing
group and who usually form the majority of tribal members. The third
are the "strangers" who have come to reside in the territory of the ethnic
group after having requested and been granted permission. They may

live as individuals, single families, family groups, or tribal subgroups that might be breakaways from other ethnic groups or remnants of other tribes. The fourth group is the "servants" or the servile class. In many West African ethnic societies, this class would include "slaves" attached to dignitaries or other prominent members of the ethnic group. However, "slaves" have a different social standing in traditional Africa; they can own property and can even become kings.[6]

In general, there are two main types of political organization. Of course, variations have occurred in different tribal societies, but the structures and foundations are essentially the same. In the first general type, Group A, ethnic groups exist as separate political entities and govern themselves independently. In the second, Group B, some ethnic societies come under the hegemony or rule by others either through conquest or through voluntary submission. Within each grouping, there is further differentiation in political organization.

In Group A are societies with centralized authority (sachems, sheikhs, chiefs), administrative machinery, and judicial institutions—chiefdoms, sultanates, or states.[7] There is, however, one fascinating alteration, namely, tribal societies that dispense with centralized authority altogether. These societies believe that any centralized authority is necessarily tyrannous, and their fear of oppression led them to do away with any centralized authority in whose hands power is concentrated. They are called acephalous or stateless societies—"tribes without rulers." Among them are the Igbo and the Fulani of Nigeria, the Kru of Liberia, the Tallensi of Ghana, the Konkomba of Togoland, the Somali, the Jie of Uganda, and the Mbeere of Kenya. Africa is unique in having the largest collection of stateless societies, but a few can be found among the aborigines of Australia, the Hmong of Southeast Asia, and the Kurds of the Middle East.

In this discussion, the term "king" will be used to denote the head of a kingdom, and the heads of constituent village governments will be called "chiefs." The term "kingdom" will be used for a political entity composed of a homogenous stock although the size may vary. "Empire" will be used to denote a political configuration in which different ethnic groups are ruled under a single monarch or emperor.

The existence of Group B, in which ethnic groups come under the suzerainty of others, underscores the fact that imperialism was not invented by the West. In this group, there are also two discernible political cultures: One is an imperial rule under which extensive domestic independence and autonomy are granted to the vassal states. The other type is predicated upon assimilation of the "superior foreign culture" by the subjugated.

Tribal Governments

In most traditional societies, political organization began at the village level. When migrating families formed a village, the original founder became the "owner of the village." His clan would then constitute the "royal family," to which was reserved the right to provide a "chief" for the village, though there may be different names for the holder of this position. Structurally, a chiefdom is composed of four basic units of government:

1. The chief, who is the central authority.
2. The inner or privy council, which advises the chief.
3. The council of chiefs or elders. If there are ten lineages in the village, for example, their heads would form the council of ten elders.
4. The village assembly of commoners, or the meeting.

The chief, often a male, is chosen by the queen or clan mother of the royal family after consultation with the elders and dignitaries of the royal family. In the Arab world, the chief is a sheikh or *naib* and is chosen by a council of elders. In some tribes, where royal lineage does not exist, different lineages offer candidates for the position. A group of elders then chooses the chief from a number of contestants or rotates the chieftaincy among the lineages. If none of these proves satisfactory, a stranger—even a white man—may be selected as a chief. Such was the case when an Englishman, Jimmy Maxen, was chosen *odikro* (village chief) in 1968 and named Nana Onyaisi of Aburi in Ghana.[8]

Note that no one makes himself a chief; he is selected not by voting but by consultation and consensus among the queen mother and the elders. Once selected, the chief is secluded for a couple of days and instructed on the rules of behavior and injunctions pertaining to chiefship. He is forbidden to go after women, to become a drunkard, to gamble, and to abuse his people, among other taboos. Then he must swear an oath to serve his people, seek their advice, follow customs and tradition, and rule with their consent. If he breaks any of the taboos or his own oath of office, he can be "recalled" by the queen/clan mother—"dehorned," as among some Native Americans, or "destooled," as in Africa. The possibility of removal or threat of impeachment as a penalty for breaking the oath serves as an effective deterrent against autocracy.

Once installed, the new chief may select his own inner or privy council of advisers from respectable notables or prominent men of distinction in the village. These inner councilors are the first group the chief may bounce ideas off or solicit advice from. In general, the chief is not obliged to take their advice, but he would, of course, be wise not to ignore them. If he does, they could withdraw their support and abandon him. This inner council constitutes the first line of defense against despotism.

The next powerful unit of government is the council of elders, or council of chiefs among many Native Americans, which is a near-universal unit of government among peasant societies from Asia through the Middle East and Africa to North and South America. The council of elders generally has two functions. The first is to advise and assist the chief in the administration of the ethnic group, and the second is to act as a brake on the chief, voicing dissatisfactions and preventing the abuse of power. The council of elders also advises him on the policies he pursues in both the internal and external affairs of the chiefdom. In executing those policies and in administering his office, the chief constantly has to consult the elders. He may be forbidden to do anything that affects the interest of the chiefdom without the knowledge, approval, and concurrence of the council, except in an emergency. Without the authority of the council, no new law can be promulgated. In some tribal systems, the chief cannot even receive foreigners unless a member of the council is present. Without the council, the chief is powerless and cannot initiate any law. All decisions initiated by the chief must be approved by the councilors. The council is an autonomous body and cannot be corrupted or suborned by the chief. It is made up of the heads of the extended families in the village, who are chosen by the extended families themselves. As such, the chief cannot remove or appoint a councilor and therefore cannot turn the council of elders into a rubber-stamp parliament.

Council meetings are open to the public. Among the Iroquois, warriors could appear before the council of chiefs and express their views upon public issues; women could do the same, but only through orators they selected.[9] In the Arab world, a council meeting is called a *majlis* (or *majalis*). "The Ruler of Fujairah, for example, holds an open *majlis* at least once a week, attended by both citizens and expatriates. To these *majlises* come traditionally minded tribesmen who may have waited months for the opportunity to discuss with their ruler directly, rather than pursuing their requests or complaints through a modern governmental structure."[10] During the *majlis* the leader hears grievances and mediates disputes; anyone under the leader's rule must be granted access to the *majlis*.[11]

The repository of the greatest political power or influence in all peasant societies, however, is the village assembly of commoners. In Africa, village assemblies are variously called *asetena kese* among the Ashanti of Ghana, *ama-ala* among the Igbo of Nigeria, *guurti* among the Somali, *kgotla* among the Tswana of Botswana, *dare* among the Shona of Zimbabwe, *pitso* among the Xhosa, and *ndaba* among the Zulu of South Africa. Other cultures have similar "tribal conclaves." In Afghanistan, the assembly, called a *jirga*, "is a standing local body, a tribal council of elder males that makes decisions that help guide and govern the tribe."[12]

Governance

In day-to-day administration and legislation, the chief rarely makes policy. When matters of serious consequence arise, the chief first discusses them with his inner or privy council for advice. Then he summons all the members of the council of elders for a meeting. Such matters might include additional tributes, market tolls, proposed new laws, the declaration of war, serious quarrels, and other matters of importance to the community. Adult males may sit in on such council meetings.

Traditionally, unanimity is the rule in most tribal systems, which means that the debate can go on for days. The primary reason for insisting on unanimity is the desire for tribal cohesion, unity, and survival. If a councilor, a head of a lineage, is irreconcilably opposed to a measure, he can leave the village with his lineage to set up settlement elsewhere. Generally, routine matters are resolved by acclamation. However, if the council is deadlocked and cannot reach unanimity on a contentious issue, the chief is obliged to convene a village meeting for a final verdict. Thus, the people serve as the ultimate judge or final authority on disputatious issues.

While such a village meeting would in general consist only of adult males, some ethnic groups allow the participation of women. At the village meeting, the chief begins by explaining the purpose of the meeting, stating the facts of the issue, and requesting that discussions begin. His advisers open the debate, followed by headmen or elders. Then anybody else, regardless of their station, who wishes to speak or ask questions may do so. If two men stand up together, precedence is given to the more elderly. Speakers stand, bow as a sign of respect, and face the chief. There is freedom of expression, but it must be exercised with reason and respect.

After everyone who wishes to speak has had the chance to do so, the senior advisers and headmen sum up and express their own opinions, after which the chief announces the decision. Most tribal laws are straightforward prohibitions, injunctions, affirmations, or adaptations of customary law to new and changing situations. For example, "No one may drive a wagon through the village on Sundays" and "No one may disturb the peace on this festival day."

Note that there are two fundamental requisites for the functioning of a political system geared toward consensus: freedom of expression and participation in the decision-making process by commoners. Dictatorship does not fit this model.

Stateless Societies

"I am convinced that those societies [as the Indians] which live without government enjoy in their general mass an infinitely greater degree of happiness than those who live under European governments."
—Thomas Jefferson[13]

"The most distinctive contribution of Africa to human history has been precisely in the civilized art of living reasonably peacefully without a state (or government)."
—Jean-François Bayart[14]

When Thomas Jefferson made the statement in a letter to Edward Carrington in 1787 that people who live without government enjoy an infinitely greater degree of freedom and happiness, he was probably referring to stateless societies. "Government" is a necessary evil; it is the leader who can be dispensed with, as in stateless societies.

A stateless society or "non-state" seems almost a contradiction in terms to Westerners, who may see the institution of the state as necessary to avoid tyranny while recognizing that a "bad" state can impose tyranny. They see the absence of the state as a recipe for chaos. On the other hand, "Africans who live in stateless societies tend to see the state as unavoidable tyranny; they seek and find order in other institutions."[15] These societies push the concept of liberty to its most radical extreme and fight fiercely against any hint of tyranny. The Igbo of Nigeria mince no words with *"ezebuilo,"* which means "a king is an enemy." This uncompromising stance explains why the Igbo fought a war (the Biafran War that began in 1967) to secede from Nigeria rather than submit to tyranny. It also underlies the current chaos in Somalia.

To guard against autocracy, many tribal societies have elected not to have chiefs or any centralized authority at all. Ecological factors and livelihood also play a role in the choice of political systems, especially among pastoralists. The nature of their livelihood makes centralized systems of government unfeasible. To govern themselves, they have devised viable social systems with their own values, skills, and wealth and have successfully maintained their societies. The Somali fall into this category, as do the Hmong. "During their history, there has not been any one Hmong leader who presided across borders even though the Hmong have a word for a Hmong national leader—*Hmoob tus vaj—tus coj ib haiv moob.*"[16] The Hmong can be found in northern Myanmar (Burma), Thailand, Laos, and Vietnam.

Political Organization

In stateless societies, there are only two units of government: the council of elders and the village assembly. There is no leader. The maintenance of justice as well as of cultural and territorial integrity are effected through the extended family organizations and the invocation of kinship behavior, not only in domestic but in wider spheres. A system of checks and balances is instituted in which two or more power centers are balanced against each other and applied on all levels of the community so that no single center predominates. There is a wide dispersion of this system across Africa, adopted by such ethnic societies as the Tiv and the Igbo of Nigeria, the Nuer of Sudan, the Somali, and the Bedouin Arabs throughout North Africa. Such societies reach compromises in conflict resolution rather than make judgments and apply sanctions.

Thus, in many acephalous societies, there is a clear separation between power (defined as the ability to influence events in a desired manner and direction) and authority (meaning the acknowledged or recognized right to exercise power). One does not necessarily flow from the other. The colonialists had great difficulty in dealing with this distinction in stateless societies. They sought leaders with "power" in such societies, and, finding none, they created them. But these leaders lacked authority since they were not part of the kinship group and were treated as external representatives of an alien government. Within the ethnic group, they had little legitimacy or authority, and what little they had was considered tyrannous by the people under them. In fact, the Somalis mocked the titles that the British and Italian colonialists created for the officials of the first central government: "The president of the Somali Republic, for instance, was called *madaxweyne,* which literally means 'big head.'"[17]

The Somalis push the concept of freedom to its most radical limit: they take orders from no one, but their country has been in chaos since 1991. They have not had any effective government since they ousted the late dictator General Siad Barre. To Westerners, the chaos in that country reflects the inability to establish a democratic order, but nothing could be further than the truth. Traditional Somali society is peaceful. It is governed by customary laws known as *xeer,* which come very close to natural law. Such societies are described as "near-kritarchies." Democracy is incompatible with kritarchy (defined as rule by judges); hence, the Somali have rabid contempt for "government," which they dismiss as *waxan* (the thing). The chaos seen in Somalia is due not so much to the inability to establish a democratic order but to the rejection of any attempt to impose a *waxan* on them. The Somali will fight any such "thing" imposed on them by the political elites, the international community, or Islamic extremists.[18]

Kingdoms

Beyond villages and chiefdoms, indigenous people have also organized themselves into kingdoms and empires. Kingdoms, ruled by monarchs, are more numerous in Africa, the Middle East, and Asia and may consist of chiefdoms of people of the same ethnic stock. Most are confederations of independent republics of chiefdoms—the Ashanti and Ga kingdoms, for example.

Although different tribal societies may have different conceptions of their kings, African natives have traditionally accepted their king as a necessary evil. He is necessary for the preservation of the social order, but he is a potential danger because he can abuse his powers and trample on the independence and freedom of his people. To resolve this dilemma, many African ethnic groups created, with various degrees of success, a "person" who is hidden from public view but whose awe-inspiring authority can be invoked to maintain order and harmony. This is akin to the tooth fairy or Santa Claus in Western culture, of which Western children are in awe. The equivalent in traditional African political culture is the divine king. He is secluded, and his everyday life is planned down to the minutest detail and loaded with socially useful taboos. His sex life, symbolically fused with his fertility and vigor, might be severely restricted. His most elementary physical functions, such as crying, eating, drinking, or defecating, are ritually controlled. And his movements are hemmed in by taboos. These taboos have applied to all African chiefs and kings.[19]

Most of these restrictions were designed to reduce the king to an executive nonentity, to curtail the discretionary use of political power, and to confine him to his palace, where he would keep his royal fingers out of people's business and private lives. As a remote, secluded, and utterly ritual figure, the king can also serve as a convenient scapegoat when things go wrong. As long as the king is prepared to obey these restrictions, some ethnic groups in fact do not care who the king is or where he came from. If he fails to perform his duties, he is disposed of. Regicide is imbedded in divine kingship, although it has been outlawed in most traditional societies since the beginning of the twentieth century. The custom stems from the belief in the unity of the king and the kingdom. The king is directly responsible for the prosperity or failure of the kingdom, and can thus be held responsible for conditions in the kingdom. Should he become ill or weak, the kingdom will be in danger; should conditions in the kingdom be bad, there must also be something wrong with the king.[20]

An understanding of the role of the king necessitates a brief discourse on traditional belief systems. Indigenes believe their universe is composed of three elements: the sky, the world, and the earth. The sky is the domain of spirits of both the living and the yet to be born as well as of powerful forces such as lightning, thunder, rain, and drought. The earth is the domain of the dead ancestors and other dead tribesmen as well as of the activities of the living, such as agriculture, fishing, and hunting. The world is peopled by the living, and is therefore the domain of war, peace, trade, and relations with other tribes.

Each of the three orders is represented by a god, each of whom must be in perfect harmony with the others. The sky god is often taken to be supreme. The king's role is to appease or propitiate the three gods and achieve harmony among them, thereby ensuring prosperity for his kingdom. If the sky god is angry, there will be thunder, heavy downpours, and flooding. And if the earth god is angry, there will be poor harvest, famine, and barren women. For comparative purposes, the kings of medieval Western Europe also had three fundamental duties: to ensure the spiritual welfare of their people by acts of piety and the protection given by the true faith; to defend their people against outside enemies; and to safeguard justice and peace at home. According to historian Basil Davidson, "The forms of kingship might be different: the content in Africa and Europe was essentially the same."[21] The difference, however, lies in the political roles. While African kings have little or no political role, medieval European monarchs had vast political powers. In ancient China, the people worshipped many different gods—weather gods and sky gods—and also a supreme god, named Shangdi, who ruled over the other gods. However, the ancient Chinese also had gods for misfortunes. Drought, for instance, was personified by the goddess Ba, the daughter of Heaven. Thunder and lightning were represented by the gods Lei-Kung and Lei-zi; disastrous floods by Gong gong.[22] By the beginning of the Zhou Dynasty (about 1100 BC), the Chinese were also worshipping a natural force called Tian, which is usually translated as "heaven." Like Shangdi, Tian ruled over all the other gods; it also decided who should rule China. "The ruler could rule as long as he or she had the Mandate of Heaven. It was believed that the emperor or empress had lost the Mandate of Heaven when natural disasters occurred in great numbers, and when, more realistically, the sovereign had apparently lost his concern for the people. In response, the royal house would be overthrown, and a new house would rule, having been granted the Mandate of Heaven."[23]

The king thus has two roles to play in a traditional society: political, as head of the kingdom, and spiritual, as the link to the universe. The king's role in governance is small, and his participation in the political decision-making process is insignificant.[24] He makes hardly any policy and delegates almost all of his political authority to other officials. His advisers and chiefs determine policies and present them for royal assent. The king's primary role is to maintain cosmological balance and, therefore, social order.

This emphasis on the spiritual function of the king means a separation of kingship and political leadership. In modern times, this tradition—the separation of the spiritual role from politics—has been maintained, for example, in the European kingdoms of Norway, the Netherlands, and Britain. In Asia, the Thai King stays out of politics. Notable exceptions to this separation of roles are Middle Eastern monarchs and two African kings: King Mohammed VI of Morocco and King Mswati III of Swaziland.

Most tribal societies seclude their kings in their palaces. The Yoruba king (*oni*) can only leave his palace under cover of darkness and appears in public only once a year. In some tribal systems, no one can see the king eat; he may not walk in cultivated fields, lest the fertility of the soil be affected. Among the Suku of the Democratic Republic of the Congo, "When the king drank, those present had to cover their faces while one of the attendants recited proverbs and sayings recapitulating historic events, praising the king for his good deeds and also hinting at those where he had shown himself to be unjust."[25]

Despite the puffed-up image of divinity, African kings, for example, are really scapegoat kings—blamed for any calamity that might befall the kingdom. If any of the three gods is "angry," and there is a famine, it means the king has not ruled well and has lost, as the ancient Chinese would have said, "the mandate of heaven." The Kerebe of northwest Tanzania deposed their *omukama* (kings) at the beginning of the nineteenth century: Ruhinda, who was unable to prevent an excessive amount of rain from falling, and his successor, Ibanda, who fell victim to an extended period of drought.[26]

Again note that despotism does not fit into this traditional kingship. With kings secluded in their palaces, seldom seen barking orders in public, there is no such thing as a despotic king. And traditional kings pay the ultimate price of accountability should a misfortune befall the kingdom. Today's despots, who leave such massive trails of destruction and chaos, don't know how lucky they are.

Confederacies

Politically, a large polity can be organized along three main lines:

1. A *unitary system* of government, in which decision-making is centralized in the capital city. This is the European model, where decisions are taken in London, Paris, Brussels, Madrid, and so forth.

2. A *federal system* of government, in which the constituent states retain some powers but the center is more powerful—as in the American and Canadian models.

3. A *confederate system* of government, in which the center is weak and the constituent states can break away if they choose to. This was the characteristic feature of ancient empires and of Switzerland today—a confederation of 26 cantons.

Historically, the unitary system probably emerged as the most suitable for Europeans because their nations consisted of citizens of single or homogenous ethnic stock. However, centralization of power and the decision-making process enhances the threat of despotism and is thus unsuitable for nations of multiple ethnicity. Wherever power is centralized in the developing world, it leads to competition among various groups—political, religious, ethnic, and professional—to capture it. This competition invariably degenerates into ethnic strife and conflict. Even in Europe, the unitary form of government is beginning to rupture with the Scots, the Walloons in Belgium, and the Basques in Spain seeking independence.

Early settlers in America rejected the European model because they saw the concentration of power as a source of tyranny and the state as necessarily tyrannous. They sought to write a constitution that protected the people from the state. Not finding such a constitution in Europe, the Americans looked elsewhere. "Immigrants arrived in colonial America seeking freedom and found it in the confederacies of the Iroquois and other Native nations."[27] As Frank Douglas Heath has affirmed: "The United States was originally organized under a set of articles of confederation that included many of the principles that work so well in the Emirates and Switzerland. Where these principles survive, people prosper."[28]

In ancient and medieval times, confederation was the most common form of political organization among different ethnic groups or nationalities. A confederation is formed when two or more nations or ethnic groups voluntarily come together and form a loose political organization to achieve a common goal—most often, mutual defense or blocking a rival group from gaining access to a particular trade route or the sea. The number of assenting nations can vary widely—from 6 in the Ga Kingdom in Ghana to 54 in the Mayan Empire in Mesoamerica.

The confederation may choose a capital, often peopled by the dominant tribe, and establish a council, to which each of the nations may send a deputy to deliberate on policies to achieve the common goal. Beyond that, the nations are left to govern and attend to own their affairs, as they did before the confederation. Obviously, this kind of political arrangement affords the constituent nations the greatest degree of autonomy and independence. As such, a confederation is characterized by decentralization of power and delegation of authority. If any nation or group is dissatisfied, it can pull out of the confederation at any time, and many did throughout history, explaining the tendency of confederacies to splinter. But the very looseness of that political arrangement enables it to meet the test of time. Confederacies have been the most durable of all the larger polities. The series of dynasties and kingdoms of ancient Egypt lasted for nearly 3,000 years. The Ghana Empire, a confederation, lasted for more than 800 years. Polities crafted by imperialism have seldom fared as well.

Volition is the key distinguishing characteristic of a confederation since the constituent nations come together voluntarily. This distinguishes it from an empire, which is the acquisition of foreign possessions (land, natural resources, and even labor) through the use of force (military) or deceptive and biased treaties. Imperialism involves conquest and subjugation.

Unfortunately, many ancient confederacies have historically been misclassified as "empires." Confederacies of the Americas such as the Inca Empire, the Mayan Empire, and the Aztec Empire are examples of these misclassifications. The Iroquois, Mixtec, and Zapotec confederacies have been properly classified. Pre-Columbian Latin America was the home of some very notable confederacies that had advanced civilizations and well-organized social structures, and which flourished in the arts, mathematics, astronomy, architecture, and engineering. What brought about the end of these empires was not so much the weaponry of the Spanish Conquistadors, but the diseases they brought with them.[29]

According to professor of Native American Studies Bruce Johansen, "Throughout eastern North America, Native nations had formed confederacies by the time they encountered European immigrants: the Seminoles in what is now Florida, the Cherokees and Choctaws in the Carolinas, and the Iroquois and their allies the Wyandots (Hurons) in upstate New York and the Saint Lawrence Valley."[30]

African confederacies include the Ghana Empire, the Songhai Empire, the Mali Empire, and Great Zimbabwe. This is the traditional way African societies form nations, although it is not limited to Africa. Examples of successful confederations include the United Arab Emirates and, as stated, the confederated cantons of Switzerland.[31]

In the Middle East and Persia, notable mention may be made of the Umayyad and Abbasid Caliphates, the Safavid, Seljuk, and Ottoman Empires, and the Sasanian-Parthian Confederacy of Iran. In Asia, the Maratha Confederacy of India was formed in the nineteenth century, and the Balochistan Confederacy stretched through Iran, Afghanistan, and Pakistan. Of course, the Mongol and Chinese Empires may also be mentioned.

The Swiss Confederacy

Switzerland is a confederation of 26 cantons that are built on its political heritage. The history of its system of cooperating cantons with extremely limited central authority arose during the fourteenth century. The Swiss of that era recognized the need for competing cantons to cooperate, specifically in matters of defense. In the Swiss canton system, "one person, one vote" is replaced by "one person, many votes." For example, to vote for candidates running for parliamentary elections, the voter is given several ballots with each corresponding to a different political party. The voter may vote for candidates selected by the party, substitute his own list, or make changes to the party's proposed list. For elections for the federal assembly, the voter is given a ballot with as many lines as there are positions to fill. The voter simply votes for the candidates he wishes to fill the posts. Further, citizens can act directly on specific policy issues; for example, by repealing a law through constitutional or legislative referendums. Every Swiss person can express his political authority in multiple contexts—the local community, the canton, and the nation as a whole. A wide diversity of political approaches is afforded by the dozens of cantons and half-cantons. Even though the different cantons of Switzerland have different languages, religious traditions, and cultures, their system works. According to one commentator, "Essential to making it work is the freedom of movement: the Swiss can vote with their feet and quit communities and cantons with ineffective policies and move to the ones that are organized in a way that is more to their liking. In short, the Swiss have severely limited the powers of their government."[32]

Empires

As noted above, an empire is the product of imperialism—the act of acquiring foreign possessions—land, resources, and people for slave labor or human sacrifice. It entails the subjugation of one or more groups of people who are culturally and ethnically distinct from the ruling ethnic group and its culture.[33] Often, coercion and military force are employed. It is different from a federation or a confederation in which autonomous states and peoples voluntarily associate. There were more than 175 empires in ancient and medieval times.[34] But, as we noted earlier, many of them were confederacies mischaracterized as empires.

In general, however, there have been differences in imperial rule in regard to the degree of independence or autonomy allowed subjugated people as well as in their flexibility and liberty to preserve their cultures. At one end of the spectrum are those empires that ruled the vassal states indirectly through their own local rulers, allowing the states extensive autonomy. At the other end are those empires where conscious efforts were made to supplant existing cultures and to force subjugated people to assimilate to a "superior" culture.

It is generally acknowledged that the first variety—indirect rule—was less harsh. As long as the vassal states were willing to obey orders and pay tributes or taxes, they were pretty much left alone to go about their business as before. This indeed was the case with the ancient Persian Empire, which allowed the locals to keep their own customs and religion:

> The empire was formed into provinces called satrapies, each of which was governed by a satrap on behalf of the king. A primary function of the satraps was to gather tribute; its presentation to the king is depicted on many of the stone reliefs at Persepolis. Other reliefs show the people supporting the king's throne, symbolizing the extent of his power but also the cosmopolitan nature of the empire.[35]

There was much tolerance of other peoples' cultures and religion. Indeed,

> Cyrus [the Great, sixth century BC] was the first Achaemenian Emperor of Persia, who issued a decree on his aims and policies, later hailed as his charter of the rights of nations. Inscribed on a clay cylinder, this is

known to be the first declaration of Human Rights, and is now kept at the British Museum. A replica of this is also at the United Nations in New York.[36]

Cyrus is also credited with promulgating "multiculturalism," a word coined to express the coexistence and peaceful cohabitation of peoples from different backgrounds and cultures in one land: "a doctrine which is the foundation of advanced societies especially in Australia and the USA and which was also Cyrus's claim to fame."[37]

Imperial rule of the direct assimilation type, however, had the potential to be repressive and cruel—and indeed often was. However, even in ancient and medieval times, there were limits to imperial rule; it was subject to three fundamental checks: reach, means, and geography.

By "reach" is meant how far military might could be projected to keep a subjugated people under control. The farther flung the empire, the more tenuous this reach; rebellious groups could make a break for it. Means of transportation and communication were poor or primitive in ancient times. By the time news of a rebellion reached the capital and warriors sent to crush it, it was sometimes too late. Language could also be a barrier when commands were issued that were not understood.

By "means" is meant the methods of coercion and population control. The imperial nation, presumably, was able to conquer and subjugate a group of people on account of its possession of "superior" weapons, efficient in their ability to kill. However, such superiority could be transitory, as the subjugated people could also, through trade with others, acquire similar or even more superior weapons. And even if a subjugated people could not secure weapons, they could simply pack up and vote with their feet. There was nothing the imperial nation could do to stop them as it had no means of controlling population movements. There were no clearly defined borders, no passport control or visa requirements.

By "geography" is meant the vast expanse of land that a subjugated group could escape to and settle on. The presence of large bodies of water, or even rivers, provided subjugated groups the opportunity to sail to freedom.

Improvements in transportation and communication and technological advances—especially in weaponry—and "improvements" in the means of population control, such as border guards and immigration control, vastly extended the "reach" and the "means" of imperial rule. As a result, it became more harsh and cruel—as was the case with the British, French, Spanish, and Portuguese colonial empires during the nineteenth century. But such types of harsh imperial rule did not endure either. Confederacies have outlasted them by far. Of course, most of the former colonies—nearly all in the developing countries—are today independent. But the "reach" and "means"—bequeathed by colonialism—are firmly in the hands of despots, who use them to terrorize their citizens. The oppressed fall back on their centuries-old defense mechanisms—uprisings or the feet—and become refugees, illegal aliens, or boat people.

CHAPTER 3

INDIGENOUS CURBS AGAINST DESPOTISM

"Despotism and kleptocracy do not inhere in the nature of African cultures or in the African character; but they are now rife in what was once called British colonial Africa, notably West Africa."

—P. T. Bauer[1]

DESPOTISM IS NOT A NEW PHENOMENON. It is a theoretical possibility in any political system that centralizes authority or concentrates power in the hands of a single ruler and is a construct that has engaged minds since ancient times. In the West, the writings of the classical liberals—John Locke, Alexis de Tocqueville, Thomas Paine, Voltaire, Adam Smith, James Madison, Baruch Spinoza, among others—railed against autocracy and state tyranny. For example, the English philosopher John Locke, often regarded as the father of liberalism, established the liberal ideas that governance may be regarded as a social contract and that government acquires consent to rule from the governed, not from supernatural authorities.

The liberals saw the state as a necessary evil and sought a world free from government intervention, or at least from too much of it. They believed that governments were cumbersome burdens that should stay out of the lives of people. The US Constitution, for example, is founded on the need to limit the powers of the state in order to protect the liberties of the people. The more power the state has, the less freedom its citizens have. Liberals also pushed for the expansion of civil rights, free markets, and free trade.

The American Revolution (1775–1783) and the French Revolution (1787–1799) used liberal ideas to justify the armed overthrow of despotic rule. The American rebellion was against the colonial power, Great Britain, while the French rebelled against the excesses of the ruling classes and King Louis XVI, an absolute monarch, whose predecessor, Louis XIV, had famously declared: "L'état, c'est moi" (I am the state). On January 21, 1793, Louis XVI was guillotined for "conspiracy against the public liberty and the general safety."[2] His was the first in a long string of executions, including that of his wife, Marie Antoinette.

It would be preposterous to assume that indigenous peoples have never considered the threat of despotism in their systems, have never had revolutions, and that present-day despotism is "acceptable" to them. Of course, they too had their "John Lockes," "Thomas Paines," "Adam Smiths," and other "classical liberals." However, their works and thinking are not available to all; they are transmitted not through books but by oral tradition, which is a poor means of communication over the ages since it relies on memory. Over time, some facts get mangled or lost forever. It usually starts like this: "Many moons ago . . ." Well.

Nonetheless, they had "revolutions" that resulted in many chiefs and kings not only being overthrown but also killed. There were many popular revolts in ancient China, Egypt, and elsewhere in the developing world. According to scholar Liu Junning: "What we now call Western-style liberalism has featured in China's own culture for millennia. We first see it with philosopher Laozi [Lao Tsu], the founder of Taoism, in the sixth century B.C. Laozi articulated a political philosophy that has come to be known as *wuwei*, or inaction . . . 'The more prohibitions there are, the poorer the people become,' he wrote in his magnum opus, the 'Daodejing.'" Junning also mentions others, such as Mencius, a fourth-century B.C. philosopher and the most famous student of Confucius, and Huang Zongxi (1610–1695), known as "The Father of Chinese Enlightenment."[3] The Gikuyu of Kenya had a revolution called *itwika*, derived from the word *twika*, which means "to break away from" and signified breaking away from autocracy to democracy.[4] The Yoruba king in Nigeria could be deposed from his office as a result of arbitrary or tyrannical action by a procedure known as *kirikiri*. "A mob would parade through the town or country-side loudly abusing him and ending at his residence, which was pelted with dirt and stones. If he did not leave the country or commit suicide within three months, then a select band of men seized and killed him."[5]

American revolutionaries overthrew the tyrannical colonial state, and French revolutionaries abolished the absolute monarchy and established a republic. The two revolutions, however, differed fundamentally in terms of their constitutional results. While both produced constitutions that sought to prevent state tyranny, the French saw the state as the ultimate guarantor and protector of individual rights, while the Americans saw the state as a threat to the individual and therefore wrote a constitution to limit the powers of the state.

Indigenous societies have no written constitutions, but many societies took measures to prevent state tyranny. Indigenous African political culture reveals an obsessive fear of state tyranny. In fact, most Africans regarded the state as necessarily tyrannous and structured their political institutions to provide an effective bulwark against this threat. As we saw in the previous chapter, some, like the Igbo, the Somali, and the Gikuyu, went to the radical extreme and abolished the state altogether, dispensing with chiefs or centralized authority. Recall the Igbo word *ezebuilo*—"a king is an enemy."

The burning fear of tyranny was also evident in those ethnic groups that chose to have chiefs. Their systems of government were highly decentralized, and the detailed devolution of authority, assignment of responsibilities, and the institution of a complex system of checks and balances were all designed to curb autocracy. The safeguards and measures—not written down, of course—were embedded in the slew of taboos and injunctions that a ruler had to obey. It is hard to imagine how a despotic king could function under a taboo that prohibited him from leaving his palace except under cover of darkness. Perhaps no other area of study is as fascinating as the checks and balances indigenous people built into their political systems to prevent or punish abuse of power or misuse of office.

The caliphate was the first system of governance established in Islam. It was a republic, and the rulers were bound by a set of laws that they could not break at a whim. Further, the people had the right to appoint their ruler through their local leaders and also had the right to remove him. This can be inferred from the inaugural speech of the first caliph, Abu Bakr:

> "O People! I have been put in authority over you and I am not the best of you.

"So if I do the right thing then help me and if I do wrong then put me straight.

"Truthfulness is a sacred trust and lying is a betrayal.

"As long as I obey Allah and His messenger, you should obey me, and if I do not obey Allah and His messenger, then obedience to me is not incumbent upon you."[6]

Despotism exists only in a political system that lacks effective checks and balances. The threat of deposition and recall has always kept potential despots in check. Where that threat does not exist, as in developing countries today, despots run amok. To most people in the developing world, despotism is alien and an affront to their own political heritage—a cultural perfidy. While traditional political systems are structured with safeguards against despotism, the modern systems imposed upon them lack these checks and balances. In the traditional systems, no one waving a bazooka can usurp power, declare himself a chief, sheikh, emir, or caliph, and rule without the consent of the elders and the people. This kind of rule—or despotism—is incompatible with the indigenous systems of governance. Two aspects of traditional systems militate against despotism.

The first is the traditional role of chief or sheikh. As a central figure in the village, he plays many other roles: he is the father figure to his people, an umpire and a guardian. The survival of his people is his imperative and, by dint of reason, as well as custom, consultation with his advisers and elders is mandatory. He must listen to as large a variety of viewpoints and proposals as possible. He mediates in disputes and thus has to be impartial, weighing all sides. As we saw in the previous chapter, the articulating principle of social organization and government in an indigenous society is kinship. A despot who brutalized and oppressed his own kinsmen would provoke clan leaders to rise up against him. Furthermore, because many traditional societies, including Native American nations, had no standing armies, a despot would have no coercive instruments such as the military or police to enforce his diktats. In Africa, out of over 2,000 ethnic groups, only a few African kingdoms, such as the Ashanti, Dahomey, and Zulu, had armies. In the Islamic empires, military officers were appointed as nominal provincial heads. But with these exceptions, the military played little or no role in government administration in traditional societies. Military rule is as alien as colonial rule.

The second aspect is the governing style and tradition of the indigenous systems. In these systems, kinship is traced back to the ancestors who laid down the moral code. The guardians of this moral code are the elders, who have authority because of their descent, age, and wisdom. Such a system may be referred to as a gerontocracy—rule by elders. As such, the style of governance stresses consultation with elders, unity, cooperation, and reaching a consensus. The system necessarily precludes despotism. A despot may have all the fire power (the biggest bazooka) but not legitimacy or authority, which is derived solely from having royal blood or ancestral descent, and the assent of the elders.

INSTITUTIONAL CHECKS AGAINST DESPOTISM

Most indigenous societies have institutionalized a whole battery of checks against tyranny and abuse of power by office holders.

Religious or Supernatural Sanctions

The office of chieftaincy is sacred, for it is the repository of ancestral spirits. These spirits watch the living constantly and reward good rulers, but punish wrongdoing with epidemics, calamity, and other catastrophes on the earth, and ostracism of the souls after death. An occupant who defiles the office incurs the wrath of the ancestors. The Temne of Sierra Leone took their spiritual injunctions a step further. The corpse of a bad chief was dragged along the ground and mocked by those who hated him. "By defiling the corpse, the Temne believed they would prevent his soul from joining the spirits of the ancestors. Most often, that indignity of such a funeral ceremony acted as a check on bad chiefs."[7]

Private and Public Admonitions

A bad chief always causes disaffection among the people and brings shame to the royal lineage. Those who chose or appointed him also have the power to recall or depose him if he fails to perform satisfactorily. Before a despotic ruler is removed from office, however, most indigenous systems give him ample opportunity to reform. He is reminded of the oath he swore upon assumption of office, which might have required him to listen to advice, not abuse his power, not act autocratically, not abuse his people, and not go after other people's wives, among other things. A reminder of his own oath often serves as an effective deterrent.

Prohibitions against the Office of Chieftaincy or Kingship

Various restrictions have been applied against the office of chieftaincy to ensure that whoever occupies the "stool" or throne acts properly. For example, the king is forbidden to speak directly to the people in public. Some of these injunctions are cleverly designed to check despotic tendencies and the misuse of power. Of particular interest is the prohibition against property holding. To prevent a ruler from using his position to amass wealth for himself, the king may not, except in a few circumstances, own any personal property while in office. Everything that the ruler acquires while in office automatically becomes "stool property" or property of the office—unless the elders consent to its becoming the personal property of the king. That rule applies to the wives of the chief as well. To make the rule effective, the administration of tribal funds and property is put in the hands of someone else other than the chief, who is barred from any close contact with the stool finances. This prohibition is akin to requiring an American president to place private holdings of stock in a "blind trust."

Institutional Checks against Autocratic Chiefs

The Royal Family

Recall that the chief is *chosen*. The queen or clan mother or the clan chiefs consult with elders and dignitaries of the royal family and make a selection, which must be ratified by the council of elders. If the chief drifts toward despotism or shirks his responsibilities, he brings shame to the royal family. It is the duty of the queen mother to scold, reprimand, and rebuke such an errant chief. If she fails in this duty, she herself could be deposed in some tribal systems. This is often the first line of defense against despotism.

The Inner Privy Council

The second check against despotism is the privy council of advisers, a small group drawn mainly from the inner circle of the chief's relatives and personal friends who may include influential members of the community. The duty of the advisers is not only to serve as a sounding board but also to keep a check on the chief's behavior. If he errs, the advisers speak to him privately and, if necessary, reprimand him. If the chief persists in his despotic ways and refuses to listen to his advisers, they might abandon him. And if this check fails, there is a third, which is the most important: the council of elders.

The Council of Elders

The council is the representative body of the commoners and must be consulted in crafting any law. Without this council, the chief has no power; he can make no laws by himself. Council approval or unanimity is needed on all matters affecting the community. If the chief acts autocratically, the elders might ask the queen mother to recall him and select another chief.[8]

Indigenous societies have also provided avenues for rulers to interact with the people directly. The Akan, for example, provided their people with an opportunity to admonish their rulers at certain festivals. The Ashanti had the *odwira* festival at which the ruler gave a public account of himself. The people could express displeasure at his misrule by boos and hisses. In fact, they could do more: they could take legal action against the oppressive ruler.

This practice also existed in the ancient Persian Empire. When the Persian king granted public audience in the open to all of his subjects at the Nowruz and Mihrigan celebrations, anyone could make petitions or complaints—including ones that were against the king himself.

> If a complaint was presented against himself, he immediately got down from the throne upon reading it, took the crown from his head and placed it on the empty throne, and turning to the Supreme Spiritual Lord who sat beside him, handed him the complaint on knees and begged him to hold inquiry in the case and pronounce an impartial judgment. If this was pronounced against the Great King he immediately had to make amends to the wronged party before wearing again the crown and resuming the throne.

This example was intended to serve as a warning to all officials in the empire to behave justly toward those under them, and to remedy promptly any wrongs brought to their notice. Indeed, there were instances where prominent officials failed to do so. Such was the case of the grand marshal of the marches in Azerbaijan, who had been appointed to rule that province in the days of Xosore the Great. An old woman had brought a petition against him. "It was found on a careful inquiry that that governor had amassed a huge fortune by a tyrannous and unjust rule. At the instances of the Great King, the Grand Senate sat in judgment on that ruler, and finding him guilty, pronounced on him the capital punishment, which was forthwith executed."[9]

The Final Defense—The Feet

If a tyrannical chief or a ruler manages to overrun the various lines of defense, the people might exercise the "exit option"; that is, they vote with their feet to go and settle somewhere else. The chief cannot stop them because he has no instruments of force or coercion to do so. The history of the world is full of such migrations of people, which still continue today, evidenced by the millions of political and economic refugees.

Institutional Checks against Despotic Kings

As we saw in the previous chapter, very few kings in traditional societies have had absolute power. The exceptions include the monarchs of the Middle East and the pharaohs of ancient Egypt, who were regarded as living gods. It may be suspected that divine kingship and the panoply of government would tend to authoritarianism, but several institutions have militated against this in African states. First, African kings played an insignificant political role in government. Their traditional role was spiritual. Second, they were not only enclosed in their palaces but also cocooned in a web of taboos. Third, most of the king's powers were delegated to subordinate chiefs under him. As anthropologist Paul Bohannan says, "almost all African kingdoms have institutionalized means to keep [the ruler] from abusing his power."[10] Scholar James Vaughan notes: "In many instances, the dependence upon the *rule of law* and a respect for law seems to have inhibited ambitious rulers. Nor should it be forgotten that regicide itself was an ultimate check upon the excesses of a king."[11]

Since the abolition of regicide, kings are simply dethroned. The *oba* Samuel Aderiyi Adara of the Ode-Ekiti community of Ekiti State in Nigeria was dethroned for not contributing enough to the development of his community. Unable to answer the charge at a meeting, he was asked to vacate the throne to allow a more progressive-minded person to occupy it:

> While the meeting was still going on, some youths in the town invaded the venue, removed the dress of the traditional ruler, including his royal beads and crown, and chased him out of the town. Shortly after, traditional trees in strategic shrines were cut down, symbolizing the demise of the *Oba*.
>
> The spokesman for the community said it was the collective decision of both the old and young to dethrone the monarch, saying his reign was "disastrous, woeful and sorrowful."[12]

Institutional Checks against Imperial Rule

As we saw in the previous chapter, many empires in ancient and medieval times were actually confederacies in which tyrannical rule was not a possibility as, by definition, a confederacy is a voluntary association. Imperialism implies aggression against *other* tribes or ethnic groups and involves coercion or the application of force. Therefore, the term is not applicable to voluntary associations or to one's own people.

Imperial rule proper was of two types: indirect and direct rule. The indirect rule was generally less harsh. Subjugated groups were allowed to keep their customs and religion and governed themselves as before—as long as they were willing to pay tributes. The ancient Persian Empire was of this variety. In the case of direct rule, there were a number of factors that inhibited harsh rule and rigid central control. The first was, of course, the language barrier. This difficulty constrained rapid assimilation of the subjugated group. The second factor was the fact that lines of authority in indigenous societies were based upon kinship and ancestral connections. It was difficult to supplant these and substitute authority from imperial officers who lacked kinship relations and, thus, legitimacy or authority.

The third check was geographical. In ancient and medieval times, continents were sparsely populated. Ethnic groups that found themselves under alien tyranny always moved into the great expanses of unoccupied land to uphold their independence and protect their cultures.

The fourth check against imperialism was logistical. Despotism necessitated the possession of efficient population control instruments.

These were unavailable due to the underdeveloped state of technology, transportation, and communication networks in the early days. When a subjugated people on the outer reaches of an empire broke away, it often took several weeks for the information to reach the capital. Talking drums reduced the informational lag somewhat but not by much.

In the seventeenth and eighteenth centuries, the main weapons in traditional societies were the bow and arrow, or the spear, which everybody could make. They were, in that sense, democratic weapons. "No man [could] be a despot for long, especially where the technology [was] relatively primitive. It was only in the latter part of the last century, after the introduction of guns, that the *kabaka* [of Buganda] had even a small standing army."[13] Most societies that had standing armies disbanded them after a war, or had them cultivate food to feed themselves, so that the armies did not become a drain on tribal treasuries or terrorize the people. In fact, P. T. Bauer put it succinctly: "Despotism and kleptocracy do not inhere in the nature of African cultures or in the African character; but they are now rife in what was once called British colonial Africa, notably West Africa."[14] Analysts would probably do well to look for the causes of despotism and kleptocracy elsewhere than in indigenous African culture and character.

Very few African empires had rigidly centralized administrations. Historical evidence suggests that those empires that were characterized by strong, centralized administrations were inherently unstable and chronically threatened by internal revolts. Although a superior military might have kept rebellious vassal states in check, it was only a matter of time before the subjugated states successfully asserted their independence or bolted for freedom.

In fact, the traditional African political system was fundamentally and structurally anti-empire. According to sociologist Chancellor Williams, "The very circumstances of the endless process of segmentation, of forever splintering off to form small independent mini-states, developed a built-in factor of disunity, reinforced by the attending growth of different languages. Self-government or chiefdom was the inevitable way of life, not a theory."[15] The cultural imperative was independence, and the assertion of central control often led to rebellions and the break-up of kingdoms and empires. Economic historian Peter Wickins is emphatic in his conclusions: "Strong centralized government was the exception rather than the rule in sub-Saharan Africa. Poverty of communications made it difficult to prevent states from breaking up . . .

Secondly, even relatively wealthy rulers, like the Mwene Mutapa, could not maintain a professional army of any size to enforce commands. Executive weakness and bad communications, together with total or general illiteracy, necessitated devolution of powers of administration, either to appointed officials or to subordinate rulers."[16]

Summary

Painstaking efforts, though not conclusive, have been made here and in the preceding chapter to demonstrate that despotism is not an integral feature of indigenous political systems. These systems were based upon kinship, consultation, and consensus-building. Despotism, of course, was always a theoretical possibility, but it seems that, after encountering it, measures were put into place to prevent its reoccurrence. Rulers were certainly not elected by ballot but were chosen by a clan mother, a queen mother of a royal family, or a council of elders. Those who chose the ruler also had the power to remove him. Further, as noted earlier, the rulers were cocooned in webs of taboos and injunctions, a breach of any of which could result in removal from office. The very possibility of deposition in itself served as a deterrent to autocracy. In addition, the rulers were surrounded with councils upon councils, without which they could not initiate any action or laws. Nor did the rulers have instruments of coercion—military and police forces—under their permanent control to enforce any diktats. It did not make sense for a ruler to brutalize and oppress his own people; he would be decapitating his own tribe for the benefit of a stronger neighbor. And even if he did, clan leaders would rise up against him. The people always had the final say: the exit option. A ruthless ruler simply found himself abandoned. This discussion naturally begs the question: Why has despotism become rife in the developing world in modern times? We now turn to this question.

THE REAL CAUSES OF DESPOTISM IN MODERN TIMES

In general, various factors have conspired to enable despotism to flourish in the developing world in modern times:

1. The unitary system of government
2. Western-style multiparty democracy

3. Means and reach
4. Other factors such as the Cold War and foreign aid.

Nearly all the developing countries were at some point colonies of European powers that bequeathed the unitary system of government to the newly independent countries. The nationalist heroes who endured hardships, indignities, and even jail to bring freedom to their people should have jettisoned that model of government as the Americans did, but they retained it. The unitary system, in which all decisions and power are centralized or concentrated in the capital city, may be suitable for homogenous, single-tribe European nations, but it is deeply flawed and fundamentally unsuitable for polyethnic developing nations. Recall that in the larger traditional polities, confederation was the norm. Even kingdoms composed of the same ethnic stock were often confederacies.

In centralizing decision-making and concentrating power at the center, the unitary model of governance increases the threat of despotism exponentially. In fact, despotism will emerge in *any* political regime that centralizes power and lacks an effective system of checks and balances. Furthermore, concentrating decision-making and power at the center transforms the state into a "prize" or a "gold mine." Now graft onto this system the Western-style multiparty "winner takes all the gold" democracy, and the explosive potential becomes apparent. First, all sorts of groups (ethnic, political, religious, and professional) compete ferociously to capture this pot of gold, and this competition often degenerates into civil war. Naturally, in this competitive sport, the group with the biggest bazooka comes out on top, which explains the reign in the 1970s and 1980s of the *caudillo*s in Latin America and military vagabonds in Africa.

Second, whoever or which group captures that pot of gold will never relinquish it. One man, one vote came to many African countries one time. And once captured, this centralized power is used to settle old scores, loot the treasury, squash any opposition, and perpetuate oneself in office. Presidents use their power to enrich themselves and their cronies and to advance the economic and political interests of particular groups while excluding others—the politics of exclusion or quasi-apartheid. The richest persons in Africa are often heads of state and ministers. Recall that "Sudanese President Omar al-Bashir has been accused of siphoning off up to $9 billion of his country's funds and placing it in foreign accounts, according to leaked US diplomatic cables."[17] Also recall that the late General Sani Abacha of Nigeria, General Ibrahim Babangida of Nigeria, the late Felix Houphouet-Boigny of Ivory Coast, and Mobutu Sese Seko *each* stole more than the net worth of all 43 US presidents *combined* (which is $2.7 billion)![18] Why would any head of state want to give up power?

With Western-style liberal, multi-party democracy, incumbent despots don't lose elections; to do so would amount to political suicide. Thus, they use every trick—fair and foul—to ensure a "win" with "comfortable" margins. Forget about free and fair elections and foreign election observers. President Hamid Karzai stole the November 2009 election right under the noses of NATO forces and UN observers in Afghanistan.

Witness the 2009 and 2010 elections in Bahrain, Burkina Faso, Burundi, Egypt, Ethiopia, Iran, Ivory Coast, and Rwanda. No coconut lost. The international community kids itself if it thinks the presence of a handful of foreign observers can ensure fairness and transparency. In many cases, the elections are stolen even before the foreign observers arrive. The usual trick is to permit a certain number of foreign observers and closet them in five-star hotels in urban areas, then chauffeur them to pre-selected polling stations, where voting is conducted peacefully, freely, and fairly. But the skullduggery takes place in rural areas, from which the foreign observers are frightened away with tales of high HIV infection rates, nasty man-eating crocodiles, and lack of toilet facilities and social amenities. Such was the case in Ghana's 1992 elections: a tiny village in Northern Ghana, with a population of 5,000, managed to cast 54,000 votes for the incumbent regime.

Third, the danger of despotism has been enhanced by "means" and "reach." The departing colonialists left behind standing armies, police, and security forces, so that despots have at their disposal a lethal arsenal with awesome firepower and brutally efficient weapons. They can mow down a crowd of thousands in an instant. Improvements in communication and transportation have enormously extended the reach of despots. Witness the brutal crackdowns on street protests in Egypt, Libya, and Tunisia with tanks, helicopters, and fighter jets in February 2011. The crackdowns in Bahrain, Syria, and Yemen were even more vicious.

Finally, today's international environment fosters despotism because a despot can easily find foreign patrons. During the Cold War, despots peddled their ideological credentials and secured billions in aid from both the East and the West. Today, they only need to have oil or strategic minerals or profess to be fighting terrorism. Anyone who opposes them is a "terrorist"! Said President Alexander Lukashenko of Belarus in August 2003: "Anyone joining an opposition protest would be treated as a 'terrorist.' We will wring their necks, as one might a duck."[19] Similarly, former Tunisian president Ben Ali, under siege in January 2011, denounced the street protests against his regime as an "act of terrorism."

INDIGENOUS VERSUS WESTERN INSTITUTIONS

Autochthonous Democracy

It is important to draw distinctions between indigenous and Western institutions. There are different forms and different varieties of democracy.[20] Again, the absence of one particular form does not imply the non-existence of the institution. The absence of voting does not mean that despotism is the norm for the people of the developing world. In traditional systems, rulers are chosen. Prior to the advent of colonialism, governance in many tribal or traditional societies entailed consultation and decision-making by consensus—a different form of democracy.

Markets

The market is another institution that was not invented by the West. Markets evolved naturally as traders met at a designated spot—often where two bush paths crossed—to exchange goods. As business blogger Christopher Locke describes it, "Traders returned from far seas with spices, silks, and precious, magical stones. Caravans arrived across burning deserts bringing dates and figs, snakes, parrots, monkeys, strange music, stranger tales. The marketplace was the heart of the city, the kernel, the hub, the omphalos."[21]

In the days of barter, goods were exchanged directly for other goods. This required searching for someone who had what one wanted and also wanted what one had—a double coincidence of wants—a cumbersome and time-consuming process. A marketplace emerged to save time and effort—a central place where anyone with anything to barter could go. Then, at the marketplace, people made an important discovery. Certain commodities that were in greater demand, say, salt, were trading more readily than others. So, instead of trading a goat directly for bread, which might be difficult, one traded the goat for salt and then, later, the salt for bread. The salt then served as a "medium of exchange" and therefore "money." It was also "a store of value" since the value of the goat could be stored in the salt and spent later—exchanged for bread the next day or week.

The function of money is to serve as a medium of exchange and a store of value. Prior to contact with European colonialists, the people in the Third World used various commodities as money: amber, beads, cowries, drums, eggs, feathers, gongs, hoes, ivory, jade, kettles, leather, mats, nails, oxen, quartz, rice, thimbles, vodka, wampum, yarns, and zappozats (decorated axes) in addition to salt.[22]

In many traditional societies, the shade of a big tree was good enough to serve as a marketplace. Hundreds of examples can be given from Asia through the Middle East (bazaars) to Africa (village markets) to Latin America. The European colonialists introduced into these societies super-markets and malls, which are just different forms of the same institution—the market. Similarly, the Europeans introduced paper currency, which, of course, is more efficient than salt when purchasing a cow. But that does not mean the Europeans invented the institution of money or the market.

Peasant Capitalism

The West and Europeans did not invent the institution of capitalism either. Again, there are different forms of it. Capitalism is an economic system in which private actors—rather than a central government bureau—solve the economic problem of what to produce, how much, and for whom. Private actors employ resources—land, labor, capital, and their own entrepreneurship—to produce goods and services, which are then sold on markets for profit. Markets and profit are thus essential elements of capitalism.

As we have seen above, markets were ubiquitous in traditional societies in developing countries. So too was the notion of profit—a term known in virtually all peasant societies and for which there were hundreds of local terms. The Ashanti of Ghana, for example, call it *mfaso* while the Ga call it *seenamo*. Moreover, the mode of production in peasant, nonfeudal societies was essentially capitalistic. However, there are five notable differences between peasant capitalism and Western capitalism.

1. **The Economic Unit:** Whereas in the West, the basic economic and the social unit is the individual, in peasant societies it is the collective. The extended family is a "corporate unit" and owns the means of production. Whereas an American individual may set out to start a business on his or her own, in Africa the extended family may do so.
2. **The Scale:** Whereas Western capitalism can produce vast quantities of goods and services, the scale is brutally limited under peasant capitalism.
3. **Profit:** Whereas under Western capitalism profit is appropriated by the owner(s) of the business, in peasant societies the profit is shared among family members or with workers.
4. **Institutional and Infrastructural Support:** Whereas the American businessman may pick up the phone and call potential investors, or float the company on the stock exchange, a peasant businessman lacks these facilities.
5. **The Use of Capital Goods:** "Capital," in contrast to popular usage, is not money, as in "business capital." It is defined in economics as anything that is not wanted for its own sake but is desired in the production of further goods. For example, a tool, equipment, a piece of machinery, and even a fishing net are all "capital goods." The use of capital goods is very productive and efficient. Catching fish with a fishing net is more efficient than doing so with bare hands. In peasant economies, the amount of capital goods is limited, consisting of simple tools such as hoes, machetes, dug-out canoes, etc. In the West, there are large quantities of capital goods and, thus, Western capitalism can produce vast quantities of goods and services. In peasant economies, production is labor-intensive, and portage means carrying things on the head.

Regardless of these differences, the mode of operating a business is essentially the same. Peasant families, acting as corporate units, employ their own resources to plant certain crops on their land. They do so of their own volition—not at the behest of their chiefs or traditional rulers. The harvest is used to feed their families and the surplus is sold on markets. Profit made is used to improve their living conditions and send gifted children to school. These peasant farmers are free enterprisers. If the cultivation of corn is unprofitable, they switch to other crops. Sculptors, various artisans, hunters, fishermen, woodsmen, craftsmen, food vendors, and so forth are also free enterprisers. They all engage in their various economic activities of their own volition. They do not rely on the tribal or traditional government for sustenance. They sustain themselves from the profit made from their enterprises. They do not operate their businesses for altruistic reasons.

Thousands of examples can be given from history in Asia, the Middle East, Africa, and Latin America. There were also cottage industries before contact with the West: metalware, pottery, glass, iron working, gold, silver mining, basketry, leatherworks, woodwork, clothing, and others. Arab merchants who drove long caravans across Asia and the Sahara in the days of Marco Polo were free enterprisers.

The city of Hanoi, Vietnam, has a tree-shaded Ancient Quarter with 36 narrow streets, each named after the guild that once controlled it: Fan Street, China Bowl Street, Sweet Potato Street, Commercial Hat Street, Blacksmith Street, etc. The *New York Times'* Seth Mydans reports,

> There are still jewelry shops on Silver Street, sweets and pastries on Sugar Street, votive papers and toys on Votive Paper Street and pots and pans on Tin Street. . . . Traders have done business on this since the 9th century, according to Nguyen Vinh Phuc, a leading historian of Hanoi. The 36 guilds established themselves at the start of the 19th century. The outside world first made an impact when traders began arriving from around Europe and other parts of Asia, bringing with them gemstones, telescopes, clocks and weapons. They took home sugar, silk, spices, precious wood, rice and ceramics.[23]

As Edward Wong wrote in the *New York Times,* centuries ago, the term "silk" was synonymous with China, and the town most associated with it was Jili. Since the climate and water were ideal for sericulture, "Every home in Jili once had hand tools that the residents used to spin silk thread. In the Qing Dynasty, founded in the 17th century, Jili silk was used to fashion the clothing of the imperial court in Beijing and of the emperor himself."[24] In 1851, at the London Great Exhibition, a Chinese businessman displayed Jili silk. It won prizes handed out by Queen Victoria, and was later presented to her as a birthday gift.[25]

After the industry boomed with the opening of Shanghai to foreign companies, the silk-trading houses of four families—nicknamed the Four Elephants—became dominant in the area. Their combined wealth supposedly equaled the annual tax revenue that the Qing rulers collected from all of China. The trading families built lavish mansions. One such home in Nanxun still stands—built by Zhang Shiming between 1899 and 1905, it had a ballroom and held 600,000 volumes of books, one of the most extensive collections during the Qing Dynasty.[26]

This was just pure peasant capitalism. What often limited the scope were access to land, business, or start-up capital, and foreign competition. But the peasants coped in various innovative ways. Starting any business under capitalism requires start-up capital, which was scarce in indigenous societies. Banks during the colonial era refused to lend to peasants who lacked collateral, so the peasants turned to two traditional sources of finance. One was the "family pot"—a fund maintained by each extended family into which members made contributions according to their means. Members could borrow from this fund to establish a business.

The second source of finance was a revolving credit scheme that was—and still is—widespread across the developing world. In Africa, it was called *susu* in Ghana, *esusu* in Yoruba, *tontines* or *chilembe* in Cameroon, and *stokfel* in South Africa. Elsewhere in the developing world, there was *hui* in China and Vietnam, *keh* in Korea, *tandas* in Mexico, *pasanaku* in Bolivia, *san* in the Dominican Republic, "syndicate" in Belize, *gamaiyah* in Egypt, *hagbad* in Somalia, *xitique* in Mozambique, *arisan* in Indonesia, *paluwagan* in the Philippines, chit fund in India and Sri Lanka, *pia huey* in Thailand, and *ko* in Japan. Typically, a group of, for example, ten people would contribute $100 into a fund. When it reached a certain amount, say $1,000, it was handed over to the members in turn. For many businesses in the traditional and informal sector, the loan club was their primary source of capital. If the same tontine scheme were organized in the United States, it would be called a credit union! A credit union is simply an association of individuals who pool their savings together to lend only to themselves (the members).

In commerce, middlemen or agents are able to secure trade credit solely on the basis of trust. A producer or an importer advances some goods to a trader for repayment to be made in a few months in a medium acceptable to the supplier. In nineteenth-century Senegal, for example, 30 barrels of flour were payable in four months; bars of iron had five months' credit in the nineteenth century.[27] In West Africa, much of the palm oil trade operated on the trust (credit) system.[28] The trust system works because of the extended family system: default would bring shame to one's clan and besides, the clan could be held liable.

If a profitable opportunity presents itself, peasant traders exploit it. Profit made is private property; it is for the traders to keep, not for the chiefs or rulers to expropriate. What peasants do with their profit is for them to decide. The traditional practice was to share it. Under the *abusa* scheme devised by the cocoa farmers of Ghana at the beginning of the twentieth century, net proceeds or profit are divided into thirds: one third goes to the owner of the farm, another third goes to hired laborers, and the remaining third is set aside for farm maintenance and expansion. Under the less common *abunu* system of Ghana's market traders, profits are shared equally between the owner and the workers. Variants of this profit-sharing scheme have been extended beyond agriculture to commerce[29] and fishing.[30]

Of particular note are the women traders of West Africa who have dominated market activity for centuries. They are particularly adept at price discrimination—charging different prices to different customers for the same commodity. One bargains with them to secure the best price, but they are skillful in extracting the highest price from most customers. They used profits from their market activity not only to send their children to school, but also to fund the struggle for independence from colonial rule in the 1950s. In fact, the mothers of many of the liberation heroes, such as Kwame Nkrumah of Ghana and Nelson Mandela of South Africa, were market women.[31]

THE INFORMAL SECTOR:
A DYNAMIC ENGINE OF GROWTH

Today, peasant capitalism is very much alive in the rural areas and informal sectors of all developing countries.[32] In the rural areas, peasant or small-scale farmers are still a fixture in today's globalized world. It is in the informal sectors where the vast majority of the people in developing countries live that peasant capitalism still flourishes spectacularly.

Any visitor to the outskirts of a city in a developing country will attest to an informal sector bustling with economic activity. The vibrancy, buoyancy, and even the chaos are particularly eye-catching. There are street hawkers, peddlers, food vendors, repairmen, and others. Some cry out to advertise their wares or announce their arrival. Some hawkers and peddlers arrive after traveling long distances on foot and perform a delicate balancing act, carrying basins or baskets on their heads while handing out change to customers. Some come pushing small handcarts laden with vegetables, yams, potatoes, etc. The occasional bleating goat on a leash is dragged by. Fresh eggs, fruits, and vegetables of all types in sacks or canework baskets are available. An old truck, overloaded with goods, lists to one side. It is pointed sideways but groans forward in a perfectly straight line. Then there are tailors, artists, sculptors, and artisans who make various items such as carvings, iron gates, furniture, sweeping brushes, and clothes in their homes or outbacks and then bring them to the roadside to set up shop.

The size of the informal sector in developing countries is quite large—larger in many countries than the formal economy itself—and accounts for a greater percent of total employment. According to economists Friedrich Schneider and Dominik Enste,

> On average the size of the informal economy in Africa (in percent of GDP) was 42% for the years 1999/2000. Zimbabwe, Tanzania and Nigeria have with 59.4, 58.3 and 57.9% by far the largest informal economy . . .
>
> Thailand has by far the largest informal economy in the year 1999/2000 with the size of 52.6% of official GDP. Followed by Sri Lanka with 44.6% and Philippines with 43.4%.
>
> In Latin America, the largest informal economy has Bolivia with 67.1%, followed by Panama with 64.1% and Peru with 59.9%.[33]

The informal sector is the focus of *The Mystery of Capital* by Hernando de Soto, who describes the buzz of hard work, enterprise, and ingenuity:

> Street-side cottage industries have sprung up everywhere, manufacturing anything from clothing and footwear to imitation Cartier watches and Vuitton bags. There are workshops that build and rebuild machinery, cars, even buses. There are even dentists who fill cavities without a license . . . These new entrepreneurs are filling gaps in the legal economy as well. Unauthorized buses, jitneys, and taxis account for most of the public transportation in many developing countries. Vendors from shanty towns

supply most of the food available in the market, whether from carts on the street or from stalls in buildings they construct.[34]

According to de Soto, in Egypt, "To open a small bakery, our investigators found, would take more than 500 days. To get legal title to a vacant piece of land would take more than 10 years of dealing with red tape. To do business in Egypt, an aspiring poor entrepreneur would have to deal with 56 government agencies and repetitive government inspections."[35] De Soto's complaint is that the poor have assets but, because they have no legal title to them, they cannot be used to secure capital or loans from commercial banks. He estimates this "dead capital" to be $9.3 trillion. If only the informals could be brought into the formal legal property system, this dead capital could be unleashed. De Soto's campaign, then, is to get governments in the developing world to undertake legal reform and extend property rights to the informals. But the ruling vampire elites can't be bothered because they hold the informals in such rabid contempt: they are "filthy," they live in the "slums," their activities are such an "eyesore," and—most important of all—the informals do not pay taxes for the ruling elites to loot. As de Soto discovered in Egypt, "Hidden forces of the status quo blocked crucial elements of the [legal] reforms."[36]

These informals are very hardworking and entrepreneurial and must be admired. They toil, breaking their backs pushing carts, carrying goods on their heads, and walking long distances. Again, it is important to emphasize that the economic system here is peasant capitalism. They raise capital to run their small businesses, which are mostly household- or family-owned. Again, they do so of their own volition, not under orders from a tribal government. Further, they are not wards of the government, nor do they depend on it. Theirs is a daily struggle for survival. If these strictures about peasant capitalism and the informal sector are being belabored, it is for a reason.

All too often in the developing countries, some culturally and economically illiterate ruling vampire elites emerge, aided by some crackpot despots, to denounce markets as "Western institutions" and set out to ban or destroy them. Rather than being banned, the markets should be cleaned up and better organized. This is exactly what Dr. Muhammad Yunus did with the Grameen Bank in Bangladesh in 1978, igniting a revolution in microcredit finance and earning a Nobel Peace Prize.[37]

More importantly, the informal sector has always existed in the West, where great inventions and technological strides were made. In garages, basements, and backyards, inventors tinker with their gadgets and contraptions, and entrepreneurs craft new products, produce prototypes, and improve upon them. They then test-market them among relatives and friends before releasing the products to the market. Basement tinkering, garage sales, backyard sales, flea markets, farmers' markets, and fish markets are all part of the informal sector in the West, and hundreds of thousands of inventors, entrepreneurs, manufacturers, and computer scientists started out this way. A few examples:

- George Stephenson, who invented the first steam locomotive
- Alexander Graham Bell, who invented the modern telephone
- Henry Ford, who produced the Model T automobile
- Bill Gates and most of the Silicon Valley computer wizards.

All these great men started out tinkering with ideas and gadgets in the informal sector and then test-marketing them. Henry Ford did not start out by setting up a large corporation with a stellar board of directors and a listing on the New York Stock Exchange. He started out doing small experiments and testing small internal combustion engines in the informal sector.

The despots and the ruling elites in many developing countries have not only set out to destroy the informal sector but also to obliterate their own cultural heritage. Here is the cultural rap sheet against these despots. There are no Western criteria, concepts, or precepts employed in this indictment. It is all *cultural* because despots are cultural ingrates and traitors.

1. They denied their people their own cultural freedoms, such as freedom of expression, assembly, and movement.
2. They imposed an alien political system on their people. Participatory democracy, decision-making by consensus, confederacy, decentralization of power, political freedoms, and checks and balances, which characterized the so-called primitive traditional system, vanished under dictatorships.
3. They imposed an alien economic ideology and systems on their people. The traditional economic system was peasant capitalism. Marxism, socialism, or any hybrid is flat-out alien. In peasant capitalism, means of production are

privately owned by lineages or extended families, not by tribal governments. There are free markets, free enterprise, and free trade. Prices on traditional markets were not fixed by price controls. Family-owned businesses operated freely, and profit made was theirs to keep. People conducted their businesses of their own free will, not at the behest of the chief. Centralized government control and direction of economic activity are the exceptions, rather than the rule. State intervention in the economy is not the general policy except in a few kingdoms. And Marx and Lenin were not black Africans.

4. They sought to destroy the traditional institutions. Chiefs, sheikhs, and sachems, for example, were marginalized and stripped of much of their traditional authority.
5. They oversaw the senseless destruction of the informal sector—the dynamic engine of growth.

War on the Informal Sector

Most perfidious has been the declaration of war on the informal sector by ruling elites—the very sector that could provide an impetus or engine for economic growth. Fancy these acts of cultural and economic insanity: in many parts of Africa, markets were denounced as capitalist institutions and destroyed by Marxist and socialist leaders in Ethiopia (under Mengistu Haile Mariam), Ghana (under Fte./Lte. Jerry Rawlings), and Guinea (under Sékou Touré). On May 18, 2005, paramilitary units in the Zimbabwean capital of Harare, armed with batons and riot shields, smashed up the stalls of street traders, targeting the huge informal sector in a police operation. The official statement claimed that the raids were aimed at black-market profiteers who were hoarding commodities. In what President Robert Mugabe dubbed "Operation Murambatsvina" (which the state-owned press translates as "Operation Restore Order" but which in Shona translates as "Operation Drive Out the Rubbish"), according to a UN special envoy, the police "destroyed 34 flea markets, netted some Z$900 million ($100,000) in fines, and seized some Z$2.2 billion of goods."[38] At least 22,000 street traders were arrested, and 700,000 people were left homeless.[39]

In North Korea, harsh currency reforms confiscated the savings of small businesses and forbade the use of foreign money. The result was runaway inflation fueled by food shortages when traders withheld goods from the markets. The *Washington Post* reported that

> Currency reform is part of an aggressive crackdown on free markets by North Korean leader Kim Jong Il. His government has ordered the closure . . . of a large wholesale market in the northeastern port city of Chongjin. Another major wholesale market near the capital, Pyongyang, was shut down in June 2009 . . .
>
> Recent surveys of defectors have found that as many as 75 percent of them were involved in market activities before fleeing the country.[40]

On December 17, 2010, a young unemployed university graduate tried to sell fruits and vegetables by the side of the road. Africans have been doing this for centuries; they don't need a permit from the chief or the sheikh. But a police officer ordered this young man to stop his informal sector activity because he did not have a permit. When he protested, the officer spat in his face, and the police seized his cart. He set himself on fire and later died of his injuries. That young man was called Mohamed Bouazizi, and he lived in Sidi Bouzid, Tunisia. His story has forever changed the face of North Africa and the Middle East.

Two lessons can be drawn from the self-immolation of Bouazizi. First, building upon the indigenous and the informal sectors—instead of destroying or holding them in contempt—can at least provide employment for the Bouazizis. Politically, the principles embedded in traditional institutions can be extracted and incorporated into modern governance: principles of confederation, consensus, participatory democracy, freedom of expression, accountability, checks and balances, rule of customary law, free markets, free trade, and free enterprise (the Swiss, for example, did not repudiate their political heritage; their canton system is based on an ancient confederacy principle). Second, the ruling elites who deprecate the dignity of their people and hold their cultural heritage in contempt will be swept away in popular revolutions.

CHAPTER 4

THE MODUS OPERANDI
OF DESPOTIC REGIMES

"If they gathered without sanction, they will be bashed on the head with a club. A softer government position would only embolden them. If the objective is forcing concessions on the powers that be, and if the powers that be do buckle under, then provocations will be endless. They will be staged again and again."

—Russian premier Vladimir Putin, about
groups demonstrating for their right
to free assembly as guaranteed by
Article 31 of Russia's Constitution[1]

IN THE TRADITIONAL SYSTEM, power is vested in the chief or sheikh. Legitimacy as a ruler requires having "royal blood" or descent from the ancestors (the founders of the community) or, for Shia Muslims, from the Prophet Muhammad, and authority is conferred by a council of elders that represents the people. In a democracy, power is vested in the president or prime minister, legitimacy requires an electoral mandate, and authority is conferred by a parliament that represents the people. A dictatorship respects no such basic distinctions. Power is usurped, legitimacy can be manufactured or purchased, and authority is conferred by the possession of instruments of coercion.

Despots come in three forms: civilian, paramilitary, and military. The military variety tends to be the most vile and vicious. Their general motivation for intervening in politics is often "to save their countries" from some catastrophe: a perceived morass of injustices, rampant corruption, abuse of power, and lack of freedom. Their scale of repression tends to be total, with restrictions on almost every type of freedom: expression, movement, and assembly. Further, the institution of repression tends to be immediate, with draconian measures frequently issued by fiat or decree to take immediate effect. Next are the paramilitary despots. In this category are former rebel leaders who either led an insurgency or rose to power on the crest of a popular revolution against an illegitimate and tyrannical regime. Of particular significance is how these revolutionary/rebel leaders or so-called freedom fighters betrayed the cause of their own revolution.

The civilian variety of despot tends to evolve over time. Many in this category took up the reins of power in an already autocratic state, as was the case with Africa's postcolonial leaders. It is hard to argue that they were born despots; they all fought for freedom from colonial rule, but over time, they succumbed to the trappings of power and evolved or transformed themselves into despots by circumstances or political opportunism.

Many despots, including even some military ones, start out as genuine popular heroes. They are initially hailed as "saviors" or "heroes" amid euphoria and are revered and deified. Easily winning popular elections, they are swept into office with huge parliamentary majorities. A vision is set for their countries, with a rigid regimen that everyone must follow. But the public adulation eventually goes to these leaders' heads, and they succumb to delusions of grandeur. Advisers whisper praises in their ears: that they are the "messiah" or the "real Muhammad." Then, self-immortalization begins. Statues of these leaders are built, currencies bear their portraits, their pictures hang in every nook and cranny of their states, and all important monuments are named after them. Every word they utter must be heralded with praise. Turkmenistan's late despot, Saparmurat Niyazov, who died in 2006, even named months after himself.

Since they are semigods, saviors, or fathers of their respective countries, it is sacrilegious to criticize them. Fraudulent conspiracies, assassination plots, and national emergencies are constantly invented to deal with critics and to accumulate more power. On November 13, 2010, President Hugo Chávez of Venezuela claimed that private bankers and insurance firm bosses were raising money to pay someone to kill him. "I have proof of new conspiracies . . . I prefer death than to sell myself to this exploitative bourgeoisie."[2]

Critics are often labeled "colonial stooges," "imperialist lackeys," "contrarevolutionaries" (contras), or agents of foreign saboteurs. With huge parliamentary majorities, despots subvert the constitution and grab even more power as their parliaments rubber-stamp their legislation. Constitutional term limits have been repealed in Cameroon, Chad, Uganda, and many other countries. In power since 1979, President José Eduardo dos Santos of Angola introduced constitutional changes in 2010 that eliminated presidential elections; he can stay in office until 2022 without having to face direct presidential election. In addition, enormous power is concentrated in the president's office. It controls all budgets and appoints judges, prosecutors, generals, state governors, and election commissioners.[3] Robert Mugabe of Zimbabwe has taken similar actions.

Despots then ignore with impunity those sections of their own constitutions that guarantee individual rights and freedom. Consider sections of the following constitutions:

- **Article 35.** Citizens of the People's Republic of China enjoy freedom of speech, of the press, of assembly, of association, of procession, and of demonstration.[4]
- **Article 20.** Protection of freedom of expression is assured in Zimbabwe's Constitution.[5]

Robert Mugabe of Zimbabwe once contemptuously dismissed his country's constitution as "that dirty piece of paper." In fact, individual rights and freedoms have been proscribed by many postcolonial African leaders who outlawed opposition parties and declared their countries "one-party states" and themselves "presidents-for-life." In Myanmar (Burma) and China opposition parties are not allowed. In Uganda, political parties are allowed to exist, but a political rally of more than six people is illegal. Imagine.

Each insidious step taken toward tyranny is defended by the need to achieve some utopian objective or fight some external or imaginary enemy. In Zimbabwe, shortly after independence in 1980, freedom of expression was squelched when Robert Mugabe's government took over the country's newspapers, arguing that the newspapers—owned by the South African Argus newspaper group—were racially biased. As elsewhere in Africa, each repressive measure was dressed in either anticolonialist or antiracist garb.

THE DECISION-MAKING PROCESS

Regardless of their stripe, the modus operandi of all despots is strikingly similar. Despite their economic illiteracy, dictators insist on making all important decisions themselves. The decision-making process is closed and centralized—even under the so-called revolutionary regimes that tout "consultation with the people" and in countries that have parliaments. In the highly personalized systems, the head of state makes all final decisions with the aid of a tiny cabal of advisers, cronies, and trusted lieutenants. Advisers may be renowned in their own fields of work and brought in to assist the leader. However, they are frequently dismissed or replaced when the need or the whim arises. The leader often creates a coterie of followers with personal loyalty to himself and to the ideology he espouses. Said ex-President Daniel arap Moi at Kenya airport after returning from a trip to Ethiopia in 1984: "I would like ministers, assistant ministers and others to sing like a parrot after me. That is how we can progress."[6]

For parrots, sycophants, and "followers," it is not dedication to the despot's ideology but the expectation of sharing in the spoils of office that keeps them faithful. The spoils must be jealously protected. Rivals are systematically crushed, imprisoned, or exiled. Most of the population does not benefit from the spoils and is subject to repression. Popular participation, as in village meetings in traditional societies, is rare. Where parliaments exist, they merely rubber-stamp decisions that have already been taken. In this mode of operation, decision-making is politicized: the test of inclusion is fealty to the leader, ethnicity, and the strength of their "conviction" regarding his precepts. But since these are difficult to assess, the politics of court intrigue flourishes in such settings: conspiracies, rumors, intense jostling for positions, plots, purges, and reshuffling become the defining characteristics of despotic regimes.

Insecurity breeds a craving for support and drives all the strongmen to place a premium on trust. Thus, the bulk of key positions in the political, bureaucratic, police, and military establishments are filled with personally loyal individuals: brothers and cousins, friends and classmates, kinsmen and tribesmen. Colonel Qaddafi's main support was the elite security brigades that were designed to ward off a coup by army conscripts. One of his sons, Khamis, led the 32nd Brigade, which was Tripoli's main defense.[7] In Yemen, Ahmed Ali Saleh, the son of the dictator, Abdullah Saleh, is in charge of the Republican Guard, the best-trained and -equipped unit.

In general, the mode of operation of despotic regimes is designed to achieve three fundamental objectives:

1. Secure and nurture a support base to carry out their vision
2. Seek legitimacy
3. Maintain social control

THE SUPPORT BASE

To advance their vision and maintain social control, despots must find ways of constructing alliances to carry out their decisions, to extract resources, and to maintain their support base. In general, they rely on patron-client and patron-patron relationships. Sycophants may be employed as clients to sing praises and execute the diktats of the strongmen. Hatchet men and ruthless thugs are hired to carry out dastardly deeds such as "eliminating" a political rival or dissident. For a more worthy goal, however, a direct appeal to the populace may be made. For example, to garner support for the struggle for independence, the nationalists promised to distribute the benefits of independence—free education, health care, affordable housing, and jobs—to the people. Strongmen may also court the support of local leaders, such as chiefs and market traders, with promises of personal gain, public office, or local development.

Solidarity ties, such as ethnicity, religion, or racial group, are exploited to secure support. Despots channel resources and funds to members of a particular group in exchange for the group's support and loyalty. Thus, one finds despots surrounding themselves with such kinsmen, who are placed in key positions in ministries and government posts, not on the basis of qualifications or merit but for reasons of political loyalty and tribal solidarity. In Saddam Hussein's Iraq, the Sunni were the favored ones. When people are employed or promoted not because of merit but for political or ethnic reasons, efficiency suffers, professionalism declines, and government institutions become dysfunctional.

The despot makes every effort to co-opt leaders of important organizations such as the Trade Union Congress, the teachers' association, student unions, and other ethnic groups to expand his support base. The result is a grand coalition of interest, religious, and ethnic groups competing for access to the despot and for scarce resources from the state. The despot may play one group against another in order to maintain control. He may also cruelly punish a "disloyal" group in order to keep the others in line. Like Saddam Hussein during his dictatorial reign, Qaddafi has cunningly played the tribal game. He offered economic privileges to tribes loyal to him—his own Qaddafi tribe and the Warfala and Tarhuna tribes around Tripoli and the western part of the country. Less favored were the Zawiya, the Zentan, and the Obeidat tribes.

A despot is always looking for political support to accord him some legitimacy. He may hijack the dominant party in the country—by clever design or chicanery—then subvert the constitution of this party to achieve his vision, which in most cases amounts to self-aggrandizement. Cronies or allies are placed in the key positions of the party to ensure that the despot is always nominated as the party's presidential candidate. Where a dominant party does not exist, either because all political parties have been banned or because the dominant party refuses to be taken over, a new political party or movement may be created—especially by military despots. Such a movement may be founded on some lofty ideal, such as national redemption, reconciliation, and justice. The youth—especially university students—are recruited for such movements, which are later turned into political parties.

The support base is maintained by dispensing patronage or other spoils of power. Spoils, also used to buy political support, come in a variety of forms. Strongmen reward their followers with access to state resources, scholarships, "jobs for the boys" in the civil service, government boards, and public corporations. But the "boys" become unproductive charges for the state, and the state bureaucracy becomes bloated with redundant staff. Soldiers can be bought with pay increases, subsidized housing, commodities, and faster promotions. State workers may be provided with subsidized housing and subsidized transportation. Some despots may provide clients with opportunities for illegal gain from public office. Corruption—accepting or extorting bribes for decisions or actions taken in a public capacity—is one such opportunity. Others include public property theft, appropriation of public revenues (fraud), and nepotism.[8]

Strongmen also reward their clients by granting special privileges. For example, they may grant preferential access to resources subject to government regulation, such as favorable allocation of import or other licenses and tax waivers. As political scientist Richard Sandbrook notes, "All these allocations of non-governmental benefits can become counters in the game of factional maneuver."[9]

Essentially, the model of governance is based on the monopolization of political power by one individual or group and the dispensation of patronage to cronies, loyal supporters, and tribesmen. This support base provides the legitimacy the despot craves. The result of this political machine, sometimes called clientelism, is that politics is viewed as extractive: the state sector is seen as a source of wealth from which the favored extract as much as possible.

This support base should never be underestimated or discounted for two reasons. First, the fiercest resistance to calls for change or reform is most likely to come from this support base as it benefits from the rotten status quo. It stands to lose patronage, privileges, perks, and wealth if the despot is replaced. Robert Mugabe of Zimbabwe was willing to pack up and go into exile when he lost the March 2008 election. But the military chiefs, fearful of losing their perks and ill-gotten wealth, forced him to stay on, thus making him a "hostage president." Obviously, opposition groups or freedom activists need to devise strategies of neutralizing the resistance from the support base.

Second, no matter how despicable and unpopular a despot might be, he still has his support base. It may be 30 percent, meaning that the overwhelming majority of the people are fed up with him. But if seven opposition parties challenge him in an election, they divide the opposition vote among themselves. If each wins 10 percent, none will be able to unseat the despot.

Regardless, the dispensation of patronage to buy political support has resulted in soaring government expenditures and bloated, inefficient bureaucracies that waste scarce resources. But trimming these bureaucracies, as demanded by the imperatives of economic reform (or structural adjustment), has been anathema to the ruling elites since it cripples their ability to maintain their political support base.

CONTROL OVER KEY STATE INSTITUTIONS

To facilitate the dispensation of patronage and reduce any threat to his power, the despot usurps control over all key state institutions: the army, police, civil service, state media, parliament, judiciary, central bank, and educational system. Each of these must serve his dictates. To ensure this, he packs these institutions with his own supporters or tribesmen. Those who remain must sing his praises in order to keep their jobs. Professionalism in these institutions is destroyed and replaced with sycophancy.

The first order of business for any dictator is to grab control of the security forces—the military, police, and paramilitary. The tactical objective here is to secure the survival of his regime by neutralizing or crushing any potential threat. In much of the Middle East, autocrats depend on the support of the army, the security forces, and the intelligence services. A despot may employ a whole range of tactics to secure their loyalty. First, upon ascending to power, he systematically purges the security forces of personnel whose loyalty is questionable and replaces them with officers of the dictator's ethnicity or religion. Second, he may buy the loyalty of the officer corps with salary increases, the purchase of new weapons, large emoluments, cars, and other gifts. Saddam Hussein "routinely doled out new cars, Rolex watches and cash to senior generals, according to several general officers who acknowledged receiving such gifts."[10]

In much of Africa, the security forces are privileged elite. Soldiers and policemen are often accountable to no one—not to politicians, not to the press, not to the public they say they serve. They are clothed, comfortably housed, and well fed at government expense. They are issued guns and bullets, which they often use to suppress the people.

Even then, dictators—always paranoid—do not often trust their own military. Because of their weak legitimacy and the narrow base of lieutenants with access to the spoils, the strongman must increasingly rely on threats and coercion for his survival.[11] But he cannot trust the military; it could overthrow him. So he creates a special battalion and equips it with weapons that are far superior to those of the military. But even then, the loyalty of this special battalion may not be a certainty. So he creates an elite presidential guard with troops drawn from his own tribe or from a foreign country to ensure reliability. In this way, the strongman creates layers upon layers of security organs—to watch not only the populace but also each other. In this obsession with security, simple basic principles are routinely flouted.

The basic function of the military and the police is to protect the territorial integrity of the nation as well as the lives and safety of its citizens. But many of Africa's soldiers and policemen have completely abandoned their traditional functions and roam the continent like hyenas, inflicting injury on innocent, unarmed civilians and causing wanton carnage. In *We Wish to Inform You That Tomorrow We Will Be Killed with Our Families*, Philip Gourevitch writes, "Across much of Africa, a soldier's uniform and gun had long been regarded—and are still seen—as little more than a license to engage in banditry."[12] As they grow increasingly insecure and paranoid, autocrats spend enormous sums on the military and security forces, consuming large chunks of their budgets. In Africa alone, military expenditures exceed $20 billion a year—resources that nearly equal the total amount Africa receives in aid from all sources and that could be devoted to development. Ironically, all those expenditures on the military do not buy a despot an iota of security. In the end, despots are often hoisted by their own petard and are ousted by officers from their own security apparatus, as we shall see in chapter 5.

The next key institution of which a despotic regime seizes control is the media. Most Westerners take their freedom of expression for granted and fail to realize the critical importance of free and independent media. As Joseph Stalin once remarked, "Control the media (cinema) and you control the minds of the people."[13] A despotic regime may seek to control the flow of information for a variety of reasons:

1. To keep movements of top officials or army commanders or military exercises from being reported, especially if the regime perceives a threat to its survival.
2. To use the media as a tool for indoctrination to advance a certain political ideology, religion, or the personality cult of the leader.
3. To use the media as a propaganda mouthpiece of the government, praising government policies and lambasting its critics.
4. To keep the people in the dark. The regime may not want embarrassing lapses in judgment, competence, or governance—such as waste of state resources, graft, embezzlement, and corruption—exposed as this might incite public outrage.
5. To keep the outside world in the dark regarding events in the country. The regime may not want flagrant violations of human rights, brutal repression, and government malfeasance exposed to the outside world. A despot does not want the

world to know of the skulls of dissidents being crushed in his torture chambers, or of the women being raped in prison (as occurred in Iran in June 2009) and in broad daylight (in Guinea in September 2009).

6. To silence the opposition, dissidents, and critics of inane government policies.

A despotic regime has at its disposal a whole battery of measures to control key state institutions—ranging from the mild to the cruel and barbaric.

Licenses and Censorship

Radio and television stations may be denied licenses to operate if they are deemed to be anti-government, and the licenses of existing stations may be yanked if they are perceived to be critical of the government. In Venezuela, "the Chávez government declined to renew RCTV's license to broadcast on the public airwaves in 2007, forcing the station onto cable. Seven stations were also suspended for not complying with regulations."[14]

Censorship of the print media is another tool used to suppress dissenting opinion. Newspapers and magazines are required to submit articles intended for publication to a censorship board for preapproval; where such boards do not exist, journalists and editors must practice self-censorship. A series of violations of censorship laws may result in imposition of fines, jail term, or the permanent suspension of a publication license. Another method is to deprive the publication and its staff of funds. For example, private newspapers that criticize the government may lose advertising revenue from state corporations. Vendors and journalists who write for such "opposition" newspapers may be blacklisted.

Dismissals, Arrests, Detention

This is the standard tactic, whereby journalists or editors are arrested by security agents—sometimes in the dead of night—for writing stories that displease the authorities.

- **China:** "Zhang Hong, a top editor of a weekly newspaper who recently called for the reform of China's onerous household registration system that restricts where people can live, was forced out of his job in a fresh warning that journalists who boldly challenge government policy face retribution."[15]

- **China:** A former literature professor and relentless critic of China's single-party political system and censorship, Liu Xiaobo, was detained in December 2008. He had helped to draft a petition known as Charter 08 "that demanded the right to free speech, open elections, and the rule of law." He was released, tried, and sentenced to 11 years in prison for subversion. When he was awarded the 2010 Nobel Peace Prize, Chinese authorities were irate. They described the award as "blasphemy," placed his wife under house arrest, and blocked him from attending a banquet called by his supporters to celebrate news of the award.[16]

- **Iran:** "More than 90 journalists were rounded up to suppress dissent in the aftermath of the disputed June presidential election. When the Committee to Protect Journalists (CPJ) conducted its annual census of imprisoned journalists on Dec 1, 2009, Iran still held 23 writers and editors, a figure second only to China."[17]

- **Venezuela:** President Hugo Chávez of Venezuela is waging an insidious "media war." In August 2009, he ordered 34 radio stations shut down. In September, his government pushed along plans to shutter an additional 29 radio stations.[18]

Murders and Disappearances

According to the Committee to Protect Journalists (CPJ), in 2009, 25 journalists were killed; in 2010, this number shot up 71.[19] Among the killings were:

- **Kyrgyzstan:** "A prominent opposition journalist died after being thrown from a sixth-story window, his arms and legs bound with duct tape. . . . The journalist, Gennady Pavlyuk, was on a business trip in Almaty, the commercial capital of neighboring Kazakhstan, when he was attacked on December 16, 2009. He was in a coma before dying of severe trauma. His colleagues said he was 40 years old, with a wife and son."[20] In March 2010, the despot Kurmanbek Bakiyev was overthrown in a popular revolt.

- **Russia:** Anna Politkovskaya, a courageous journalist who exposed appalling human rights offenses in Chechnya, "was shot five times as she entered her Moscow apartment building on October 7, 2006." Since her death, at least seven journalists and human rights activists have been killed in Russia, including Anastasia Baburova, who also worked for Politkovskaya's newspaper, *Novaya Gazeta.* Baburova died hours after being shot on January 19, 2009.[21]
- **Bahrain:** Ali Abdulemam is a Bahraini journalist, blogger, and former prisoner of conscience. In 1999, he created the website Bahrain Online to share ideas and strategies for political change. He was incarcerated in 2009 for nearly six months for his activism, subjected to abuse while imprisoned, and released in February 2010. He was invited to speak at the Oslo Freedom Forum on May 10, 2011 on "The Dawn of a New Arab World." He never made it. The president of the Forum, Thor Halvorssen, said he had "disappeared."[22]

Criminal Defamation and Libel Suits

Owing to the explosion in the number of satellite dishes and electronic communications (fax machines, the Internet, e-mail, etc.), much more information is now available in the developing world. The new technology has severely crippled the ability of despots to control the flow of information and keep their people in the dark. In their desperate attempts to retain control, defamation or libel suits, heavy fines, and murder have become the choice tactics of corrupt despotic regimes.

A newspaper can be hauled into court for defaming the despot, for example, for reporting that he is not well. A senior government official can also bring legal suit against a newspaper for libel, for example, for publishing stories alleging corruption or incompetence. A pliant judge or court may impose a large fine that the struggling newspaper may be unable to pay, forcing it to shut down. The chicanery employed here is that the despot may claim there is freedom of the press, but criminal libel suits effectively preclude the possibility of a free press. Here are some examples.

- **Bahrain:** According to Article 19, an organization that promotes freedom of expression, "Bahrain and Lebanon have the highest number of civil defamation cases out of all the countries surveyed. Cases in Bahrain are particularly high comparative to the small size of the population. Moroccan courts awarded the largest damages during the period, with its highest compensation of US$354,000 or almost 100 times the per capita GDP. The lowest damages awarded were in Egypt, Libya and Algeria."[23]

- **Belarus:** In August 2005, authorities slammed Pavel Marozau with a criminal libel suit for short satirical animated Internet cartoons that featured caricatures of President Alexander Lukashenko and his administration and poked fun at him for his Soviet style of leading the country. Security agents questioned him and two others, accusing them of insulting the honor of Lukashenko and charged them under Article 367 of the Criminal Code, which provides for punishment of two to four years in jail. However, the EU Human Rights commission intervened and they were set free.
- **Tajikistan:** On September 3, 2010, "journalists Kamar Ahror and Tilav Rasulzoda were detained by security officials in Khujand while reporting on an attack on a police station. Photos they had taken in Khujand were also deleted. There are libel cases against *Asia Plus, Farazh, Ozodagon, Paikon,* and *Millat* for publishing articles critical of the government."[24]
- **Russia:** "*The Kommersant* daily newspaper was ordered by a Russian judge to pay US$34,274 to Andrei Lugovoy for offending his honor and business reputation. The newspaper had reported the United Kingdom's attempts at extraditing Lugovoy for the murder of Alexander Litvinenko, who was poisoned with radioactive polonium in London in 2008."[25]

Curbs on the Internet and Radio Jams

Domestic sources of information under a despotic regime are tightly controlled, but foreign sources are not, and they can provide invaluable information about events within the country. As such, a despotic regime seeks to block access to foreign sources by using a variety of techniques. Ownership of satellite dishes may be banned. Broadcasts from certain foreign stations may be jammed. During the street protests in Iran after the fraudulent elections in June 2009, BBC broadcasts were jammed, and access to popular sites such as Twitter and Facebook was either blocked or slowed to a crawl. During Ethiopia's May 2010 elections, broadcasts from the Voice of America (VOA) were jammed. Meles Zenawi's ruling party won 99.6 percent of the vote. The Zenawi regime also uses selective and irregular jamming to wear out opposition broadcasters and force them off the air. In 2006, the Uganda government jammed radio stations that were airing election results, forcing people to rely solely on the electoral commission (EC) tally center. Those elections were generally regarded as fraudulent. During street protests in Tunisia, Egypt, Libya, and Yemen, governments repeatedly blocked Internet access and text messaging.

Access to the Internet may be controlled by a government-owned server. Certain websites or blogs that promote freedom are "forbidden" and blocked. Government agents may even hack into discussion forums to spy on who is saying what about the despotic regime. After street protests following the fraudulent June 2009 elections, Iranian authorities went further in their crackdown on the opposition. They tracked the Facebook, Twitter, and YouTube activity of Iranians around the world, identifying them at opposition protests abroad.[26] Then they sent warnings to their families at home. China's sophisticated Internet-filtering system, unofficially dubbed the "Great Firewall," blocks access to a range of foreign content, from negative comments about China's leaders to details about sensitive historical events.[27] China blocked access to Twitter during the bloody ethnic riots in the far western region of Xinjiang in July 2009, fearing "troublemakers" might use it to foment unrest. After the Jasmine Revolution in Tunisia in January 2011, China scrubbed the word "jasmine" from Internet search engines.

Bloggers are also being hounded and persecuted for posting critical articles. According to Reporters Without Borders, a Paris-based watchdog group, "at least 17 'netizens' are in jail across the Middle East: eight in Iran and the rest in Bahrain, Egypt, Morocco, Saudi Arabia, Syria, and the United Arab Emirates. China may be the biggest online oppressor, but the Middle East is not far behind."[28]

Africa, which has more despots per capita than any other continent, is the region where the flow of information is most severely restricted. Societies that advance are those that permit freedom of expression and the free flow of information. Of Africa's 54 countries, only 10 had a free press in 2010. Most galling, the public's right to information and the right to hold and express opinions and ideas are guaranteed under both Article 19 of the UN Charter and Article 9 of the African Charter on Human and People's Rights, to which most African countries are signatories.

Ethiopia, with a population of 83 million in 2009, has only one radio station, and that is owned by the state. The repression of the media has been sustained with mass imprisonments of journalists and stiff penalties for libel. The threat of jail has forced Ethiopian journalists to flee into exile. In 2009, antiterrorism legislation set prison terms of up to 20 years for anyone who "writes, edits, prints, publishes, publicizes, or disseminates" statements that the government vaguely describes as advancing terrorist interests.

However, no government has decimated the press corps as thoroughly as that of Eritrea, whose president, Isaiah Afwerki, doesn't even understand what a free press is: "What is free press? There is no free press anywhere. It's not in England; it's not in the United States. We'd like to know what free press is in the first place," he once asked.[29] He closed all the independent media, rounded up critical editors and reporters, and jailed them without trial, quashing calls for democratic reforms. Belarus, Gambia, North Korea, and Venezuela are among other countries where the independent media are brutally suppressed. Editors and reporters are routinely jailed on trumped-up charges of sedition, defamation, and false reporting.[30]

Wresting control of the media from the hands of a despotic regime, or at least securing the establishment of independent media outlets alongside the state-controlled ones, should be a particular focus of opposition groups.

Cowing the Judiciary

A despot needs the judiciary for several reasons:

1. To enforce his diktats or decrees, even when they make little sense
2. To give an appearance of the "rule of law"
3. To block or repulse any legal challenges brought against his regime
4. To jail opponents of the regime.

To achieve these objectives, the despot may dismiss, jail, or order the murder of judges who dare think "independently." In Zimbabwe, judges can be discharged or transferred for political reasons. For example, in February 2002, Justice Benjamin Paradza was arrested after an unfavorable ruling against the Mugabe government.[31]

Other examples of intimidation of the judiciary follow.

- **Kyrgyzstan:** Five Kyrgyz judges were fired for a variety of misdeeds—ranging from bribery to gross violations of the law—by the despot, Kurmanbek Bakiyev, on November 12, 2008.[32]
- **Venezuela:** When Judge María Lourdes Afiuni issued a ruling in December 2009 that displeased President Hugo Chávez, he did little to hide his anger. The president hinted on national television that in earlier times she would have been put before a firing squad, and he sent his secret intelligence police to arrest her. They put the judge in a cell near more than 20 inmates whom she had sentenced on charges like murder and drug smuggling.[33]

Pakistan is one country where the judiciary has fought back ferociously. Its governments—especially the military ones—have a particular dislike for the judiciary, falsely believing that judges are always engaged in conspiracies to undermine and weaken them. But their attempts to cow the judges have invariably failed. The former military dictator, Pervez Musharraf, sacked more than 60 judges under an emergency order on November 3, 2007, as the Supreme Court was set to rule against his election to a second presidential term. But that move "triggered a political uproar, forcing him to resign in August 2008 to avoid impeachment in parliament by parties in the coalition government."[34] The sacked judges were reinstated later.

Fixing the Electoral Commission

A despot may, of his own volition or under pressure from foreign donors, domestic opposition, and civil society groups, decide to hold elections to give a veneer of legitimacy or democracy to his regime. But in most instances, despots employ various tricks to rig elections and ensure their "re-election." As noted earlier, Rwanda was set to vote on August

7, 2010, but even before the vote, preparations were being made for the September inauguration of President Paul Kagame.[35]

A free vote means that those eligible to vote are allowed to vote without any hindrance, intimidation, or violence. But despots can't allow this because they know they can't win a free vote. So every effort is made to game the electoral process and frustrate the opposition. Its supporters may be intimidated, beaten, and prevented from voting by government-sponsored thugs. They may also find that their names are not on the electoral register, and that they are therefore disqualified from voting.

A fair vote means that all parties, even those opposed to the despot, are given a fair chance to participate or compete. Again, the despot fears giving anyone a fair chance or a level political playing field because he knows he will lose. State-owned media may refuse to carry opposition ads. Even political rallies may be disrupted by government-paid goons. In some countries, such as Myanmar (Burma) and Uganda, political rallies of more than six people are banned. In addition, the names of opposition supporters may be purged from the voters' register, and the register itself may be padded with ghost names.

There are more than 200 ways of rigging an election. Even if the despot allows a free and fair vote, he always wins—even though the vast majority of his people are fed up with him. As Stalin once said, "The people who cast the votes decide nothing. The people who count the votes decide everything."[36]

The people who count the votes are the electoral commission—often appointed by the despot himself and packed with his allies. Needless to say, ballot boxes stuffed with pro-dictator votes are taken to the polls even before they open. Opposition strongholds are denied ballot papers or the papers are sent there late in the day. The vote count is not transparent. Figures are manipulated to ensure that the despot "wins." In a 2002 referendum on whether he should rule for another seven years, Saddam Hussein of Iraq won 100 percent of the vote. "There were 11,445,638 eligible voters—and every one of them voted for the president, according to Izzat Ibrahim, then vice chairman of Iraq's Revolutionary Command Council. The government insisted that the count was fair and accurate."[37]

For the November 7, 2010, election in Myanmar (Burma), the constitution was largely written by the military leaders to ensure that they would remain in control. As the *Financial Times* reported, "A quarter of the seats in national and local assemblies [were] to be filled by military appointees, allowing the army to suspend democracy almost at will, and [to] retain a veto on any constitutional changes. The junta also sought to limit voters' choice, in that 80 percent of the candidates up for election belonged to two parties broadly aligned with the government": the Union Solidarity and Development Party (USDP) and the National Unity Party (NUP).[38] In 153 constituencies, there were no opposition or independent candidates. The junta warned groups of workers in such places as factories that voting for candidates not aligned with the government could mean the loss of jobs. Others were threatened with "relocation" by the Burmese Tatmadaw—army—unless they voted USDP.[39] Three days before the vote, the military even claimed to have "won" its first vote in 20 years. Burmese authorities barred most international monitors and journalists from observing the elections. A group of diplomats invited by the government to observe the process was led by the North Korean ambassador—of course.

States of Emergencies and Martial Law

A despotic regime is always looking for some excuse to divert attention from economic failures and grand-scale looting of the treasury, and to decimate opposition to its rule. It may invent a "national crisis," declare a "state of emergency," and suspend the constitution and civil liberties in order to mobilize the people and resources to deal with the "national crisis." Normally, a state of emergency is a governmental declaration that suspends one or more normal functions of executive, legislative, and judicial powers. It may also suspend some civil liberties and advise citizens to change their normal behaviors. In addition, some government agencies may be ordered to implement emergency preparedness plans. Such a declaration can be made in times of a natural disaster, such as droughts or floods, or during periods of civil unrest, war, or armed conflict. But despots often use these declarations (martial law in the case of military regimes) for nefarious purposes. States of emergency have been widely used by such despotic regimes as those of Hosni Mubarak of Egypt (repealed after he was ousted in February 2011) and Robert Mugabe of Zimbabwe. North Korea's dictator, Kim Jong Il, constantly keeps his people on a war footing, largely to hide his failures and/or divert their attention from their economic woes. The occasional saber rattling and harmless firing of a missile into the ocean achieved this sinister purpose.

DEALING WITH THE OPPOSITION

Opposition to despotic rule originates from several quarters: parliament, if one is allowed to exist and has not yet been turned into a "rubber stamp," the intelligentsia (professors, writers, novelists, editors, students, etc.), civil society organizations, and churches or mosques. In each case, the despotic regime uses a carrot-and-stick approach to neutralize the opposition. Opposition MPs may be enticed with cabinet positions or government appointments. If they refuse, life can be made difficult for them. Dissidents and opposition leaders are always kept under heavy surveillance.

Surveillance, however, can morph into abduction. Chinese rights activists still "worry about the fate of Ding Zilin, the head of a group of relatives of victims of the 1989 Tiananmen Square crackdown and who disappeared along with her husband, Jiang Peikun, on October 14 [2010]. In Shanghai, activist Feng Zhenghu was taken away by police [in October 2010] and has not been heard from since."[40]

The universities are often hotbeds of opposition to tyrannical rule as they are places for the free exchange of ideas. University students have often started street protests that turn into a people's revolution, as in Indonesia, Tunisia, Egypt, and Sudan. The free exchange of ideas at universities is anathema to a dictator, who may deal with them in several ways:

- He may buy off the professional elites with a ministerial post, a diplomatic posting, a directorship of a state corporation, a Mercedes-Benz, or a government bungalow. The worst of the lot are probably the intellectuals—in particular, the university professors, lecturers, or the highly educated. They are supposed to understand such elementary concepts as freedom, democracy, and rule of law. Yet, for a pittance, some are too willing to serve as intellectual prostitutes—selling their conscience, principles, and integrity to hop into bed with despicable despots.
- He may infiltrate the universities with bogus student "revolutionary" organs, such as "university guards" in Iran,

whose sole purpose is to spy on professors, lecturers, and students opposed to the regime. Professors may be intimidated, hounded, harassed, jailed, or even killed. Thousands of professors and intellectuals have fled China, Iran, Myanmar (Burma), and many African countries.

- He may also reduce funding to the universities. This was the tactic of military regimes in Liberia and Nigeria. In country after country in Africa where military rule was entrenched, universities and colleges decayed because they were starved of funds by the military.

Although the official excuse is invariably lack of funds, the military predators always find the wherewithal to purchase shiny new bazookas for their thugs. But the *real* reason is that educated people are a threat to semi-illiterate military brutes because they know their rights and can challenge them.

Autocrats employ a variety of techniques, ranging from the subtle to the ruthless, to frustrate opposition leaders and prevent them from winning power. Despots may defang or neutralize opposition parties in several ways. They may ban them outright or severely restrict their activities by requiring them to secure police permits before holding rallies, or restricting the number of people who can attend such rallies. Where permits are required, several days' advance notice may be demanded, giving the despotic regime sufficient time to organize a counterdemonstration or hire thugs to disrupt opposition rallies.

Incumbent advantage is ruthlessly exploited to ensure that the political playing field is never level for the opposition. The despot controls the transition to democracy, writes the rules of the game, and appoints the electoral commissioner, as well as the constituent body that will write the constitution to his liking. The electoral law of Zimbabwe, for example, gives President Mugabe the power to approve or invalidate the results of any general election.

Beyond this rigged system, there are other ways of neutralizing the opposition. Co-optation may be tried first. A harsh government critic may be offered a high-level appointment to silence him. Cases abound, for hundreds of intellectuals and opposition leaders have fallen prey to this tactic and joined despotic regimes.

If a political party refuses to cooperate with the despot, it may be infiltrated and destroyed from within. A mole who reports on the movements of key opposition party officials may be planted. Then a plot may be hatched to waylay an opposition leader during travel, and some "mysterious road accident" puts him away. An attractive female decoy is often used to infiltrate opposition parties and organizations. If an opposition group is dominated by one ethnic group, a despot may recruit another ethnic group to battle the first in the classic "divide and conquer" tactic.

Similar tactics may be employed against civil society organizations. They may be banned, denied registration permits, or infiltrated. Churches, which are often vocal critics of dictatorships, are usually warned to stay out of politics. If the elites cannot be bought, a silent and effective method is to pauperize them by blacklisting or depriving them of revenue. No state establishment or a private business concern, for fear of being blacklisted itself, will offer an ex–government critic a job.

When subtle tactics fail to work, dictators may resort to terror and intimidation. The secret police or paramilitary organizations are another way to suppress any signs of dissent or revolt and ruthlessly pursue critics, who may be arbitrarily detained or even killed. A civilian or military agency, or often both, conducts intelligence and surveillance to sniff out conspiracies. Such an agency may also infiltrate opposition organizations to report on their activities, plant malicious disinformation, or even destroy the organization from within. Moles are generously rewarded.

"Divide and conquer" is an ancient stratagem employed by the colonialists. In the postcolonial period, tyrants have employed it with brutal relish to render the opposition ineffective. Since most developing countries are polyethnic, dictators have played one ethnic group against another to maintain their grip on power. Muammar Qaddafi has been a master at this. The tactic may even be employed along occupational (workers versus employers) or professional (students versus lecturers) lines.

Crackdowns on Street Protests

Every now and then, an event may occur that provokes public outrage and sends people into the streets to protest. Such protests may be:

- against a rigged or stolen election, as occurred in Ethiopia (May 2005), Zimbabwe (March 2007), Kenya (December 2007), and Iran (June 2009).

- against the general state of political repression and lack of human rights, for example,
  — pro-democracy demonstrations in Tiananmen Square in China in 1989
  — buddhist monks' protest against Chinese rule in Tibet in March 2008 and 2011
  — buddhist monks' pro-democracy protests in Myanmar (Burma) in April 2008 and September 2009
  — protests against oppressive rule and marginalization by the Uighurs of China in June 2009.
- against an economic crisis or harsh living conditions, as in Egypt in April 2010, or against a lack of jobs, as in Tunisia in December 2010 when riots eventually toppled the dictator, Ben Ali.
- against a specific government policy, for example, a hike in fuel or food prices.
- against other issues such as police brutality and corruption.

In Latin America, protests and other contentious strategies were common and played an important role during democratization in the 1990s, declining somewhat afterwards. The last decade, however, has witnessed a resurgence of overall protest activity, with varying degrees of intensity and political relevance. In countries such as Argentina, Bolivia, Ecuador, and Peru, "street protests have become a way to vent grievances about social injustices, to achieve certain political objectives, and to express policy demands. In other cases, like Chile and Brazil, protests are more sporadic and far less meaningful in effecting policy change."[41]

Nevertheless, there have been two constants in street protests against despotic regimes. The first has always been the excessive use of force to quell them. Dictators frequently panic and unleash the full fury of their security forces against often unarmed protesters. In Myanmar (Burma), the military junta ferociously crushed a peaceful nationwide uprising in 1988, killing an estimated 3,000 civilians. In Libya, brutal clampdowns on street protesters claimed in excess of 6,000 lives in February 2011 alone.

The second constant has always been attempts to shut down the media and prevent images of the protests and the brutal clampdown from being circulated around the world. Hundreds of thousands of

Iranians poured into the streets to protest the re-election of President Mahmoud Ahmadinejad in a brazenly rigged vote on June 11, 2009. The illegal regime reacted by shutting down independent media outlets and blocking access to the Internet and cell-phone text messaging. Phone lines of opposition figures were tapped, and Internet activity was closely monitored. Opposition leaders were trailed and placed under close surveillance. To effect a news blackout, the government blocked certain websites and services, including Farsi BBC, Facebook, Twitter, and Gmail. Foreign journalists, such as BBC correspondents, were barred from leaving their hotel rooms to report in the streets, and several newspapers were closed down.

These were exactly the same techniques initially employed—but to no avail—by the despotic regimes of Ben Ali of Tunisia and Mubarak of Egypt. In Guinea, troops loyal to Captain Moussa Dadis Camara opened fire on unarmed protesters in September 2009, killing 157 of them. Some female protesters were raped by the soldiers in broad daylight.

EXTERNAL PROPS OF DESPOTIC REGIMES

After securing the support base, capturing key state institutions, and establishing social control, the next priority for a despotic regime is legitimacy. It is important to demonstrate to the rest of the world that the regime is "popular" and is supported by a large section of the people, including the educated class. A smattering of fawning lawyers, doctors, engineers, and professors accords the despotic regime a veneer of respectability and legitimacy. As we saw, this intellectual support may be purchased outright with Mercedes-Benzes or government posts. Indeed, many intellectuals have succumbed to these enticements, and eagerly sold off their principles and integrity to serve the dictates of tyrants.

Foreign recognition or support is a crown jewel and is actively sought. External props generally comprise the activities and pronouncements of foreign governments, institutions, groups, and individuals that confer respectability, legitimacy, or recognition on tyrannical regimes. Typical props are diplomatic recognition, cultural exchanges, expressions of solidarity, economic development assistance, military aid, and economic or military pacts or alliances. In addition, foreign loans from international development agencies such as the World Bank and the

International Monetary Fund (IMF), as well as membership in international organizations such as the United Nations, all confer respectability on a despotic regime.

The despot may use weapons supplied under military assistance programs to suppress the opposition and to strengthen his grip on power. The tanks Hosni Mubarak sent to crush street protesters at Tahrir Square on January 29, 2011, and the F-16 jets that buzzed the crowd had been supplied by the United States. The despot may use development aid to fund projects for his supporters or his tribal region and thereby buy loyalty or political support. He may even steal some of the development aid. Between 1981 and 2010, Egypt received more than $50 billion in US aid. But Mubarak was said to have amassed a £25 billion (or US$40 billion) fortune for his family since grabbing power in 1981.[42] Thus, various external actors, groups, institutions, and factors have unwittingly contributed to the entrenchment of despotism in postcolonial Africa and elsewhere in the developing countries. In some instances this role was indirect, benign, or inadvertent, while in others, support for despotic regimes was more blatant and active. For example, during the Cold War, allies were actively sought by both sides. More recently, the so-called war on terror and the quest for oil and other strategic minerals have all played to the advantage of despots.

Democracy was not on the priority list of either super power during the Cold War. Seduced by the charisma and the verbiage of Third World despots, the West provided them with substantial military and economic aid. But the heavy Western investment in these tyrants, who were often blatantly corrupt and brutally repressive, invariably drew the ire of the people of the Third World. The subsequent overthrow of these dictators often unleashed an avalanche of intense anti-American or anti-Western sentiment. Tensions rose even further when these corrupt ex-leaders almost always managed to escape to the West to enjoy their booty.

The Cold War is over, but there are other wars being waged by the United States or the West that have been hijacked by despots to milk the West of financial and military aid. The war on drugs in Latin America, for example, has aided and abetted some despotic regimes—especially the *caudillos*—in Latin America.

The declaration of the "war on terror" after the September 11, 2001, terrorist attacks in New York and Washington is another example. Immediately after this declaration, all sorts of scoundrels and crackpot despots claimed that they too were fighting against terrorism in order to receive US aid, when they themselves were the real state terrorists. The regimes of Meles Zenawi of Ethiopia, Omar al-Bashir of Sudan, Yoweri Museveni of Uganda, and Robert Mugabe of Zimbabwe made such fatuous claims. Even former president Charles Taylor of Liberia established an anti-terrorist unit to terrorize the people! And the warlords of Mogadishu, Somalia, who had been terrorizing residents of the city, formed themselves into the "Coalition Against Terrorism" and received CIA funding in 2006. The Zenawi regime in Ethiopia has been pocketing over US$1 billion in Western aid in its ostensible efforts to fight terrorism. On March 4, 2011, when Libyan dictator Muammar Qaddafi came under siege by his own people who were seeking freedom, he claimed that he was fighting a war on terrorism and that the terrorists were Al Qaeda elements!

However, it is futile to single out any one particular foreign power for censure. Today's geopolitical landscape is such that any despot can find a foreign patron in the blink of an eye. The United States may embrace a despot who has oil or land to lease for military bases, and who can be an ally in the wars on drugs and on terrorism. Russia will support any despicable despot who is rabidly anti-West and seeks nuclear and missile technology. So too will North Korea. The French will support any lunatic who promotes French culture, seeks admission into *La Grande France*—or greater global French community—and protects French economic interests. And China practices chopsticks mercantilism, willing to embrace any African despot who has bauxite, chromium, and other mineral deposits.

To conclude, the importance of this chapter lies in the fact that knowing the enemy is the first rule of combat: his modus operandi, strengths, and weaknesses. The internal and external props that keep a dictator aloft have been identified. As we shall argue in chapter 7, street demonstrations are not enough. An effective opposition strategy is to sever these props methodically. For example, foreign patrons should be warned that loans given to illegitimate despotic regimes *without the consent of the people* constitute "odious debt" that will not be paid back by the people. Further, unauthorized payments, gifts, or contracts by the illegal regime should be reclaimed, revoked, or returned. For example, in March 2011, Sir Howard Davies, the director of the London School of Economics, resigned after revelations that the institution had been involved in a deal with Qaddafi worth £2.2

million—or about $4 million—to train hundreds of young Libyans to become part of the country's future elite.[43] North American singers Beyonce and Nelly Furtado said they will return money they received for performing at private parties for the Qaddafi family or donate it to charity. And Mrs. Suzanne Mubarak turned over to the state millions in bank accounts in Egypt, as well as a villa, after street protesters ratcheted up demands for her prosecution.

In sum, the modus operandi of dictators is essentially the same. They have "a vision" for their countries, which cannot be questioned, and all must be forced to follow that vision. Those who do not share that vision are unpatriotic traitors who must be dealt with harshly and "re-educated." Instilling fear in the people and, thereby, forcing or cowing them to submit to the will of the dictator is the basic mode of operation—essentially one of control. To achieve that objective, dictators seize and debauch all key state institutions to serve their will. In order of importance, these are the security forces, the civil service, the media, the judiciary, the electoral commission, and the central bank. Dictators are always looking for supporters to legitimize their rule or vision. Such supporters may be sought both externally and internally. However, control is never—and can never be—total. Inevitably, cracks emerge in the system through which people make a break for freedom.

CHAPTER 5

THE DEMISE OF DESPOTIC REGIMES

"Without the guarantee of political system reform, the successes of re-structuring the economic system will be lost and the goal of modernization cannot be realized."

—Wen Jiabao, Prime Minister of China[1]

THE INEVITABLE ECONOMIC COLLAPSE

A DICTATORSHIP IS INHERENTLY UNSTABLE and will eventually collapse under the weight of its own internal contradictions and intrigues, for it violates the natural order of things. Natural law is the body of rules that species must follow in order to live and work in peace and harmony: They must avoid physical harm or damage to another's work and property, they must honor their obligations or contracts with others, and they should compensate those on whom they inflict harm and whose property they damage. When people "live and let live," the natural order of the human world (or natural law) is said to prevail. When people respect that order and the boundaries that define it, they act justly—justice being nothing more than respecting the order of the human world and recognizing in word and action what belongs to another.[2] Clearly, a dictatorship violates natural law, and anything that violates the natural order eventually becomes extinct. The demise of a despotic regime, however, starts sooner when its economy begins to falter.

The State Interventionist Behemoth

All despots, despite being afflicted with intellectual astigmatism, profess to have vision, often defined in terms of protecting the people, improving the lot of the people, accelerating economic development, launching some new revolutionary order, and pursuing lofty ideals, such as justice, equality, and freedom. Despots see the state machinery as the vehicle for achieving their vision, regardless of opposition to it. Thus, the flipside of despotism is the massive state interventionism it engenders. Despots seek total control—economic, social, political, and intellectual—and only the machinery of the state affords them the capacity to attain this. Most find a convenient ally in the ideology of socialism or communism—hence the preponderance of leftist despots. Though history provides examples of despots on the right, such as the fascists of the early and mid-twentieth century, despotism is generally incompatible with capitalism, since it precludes heavy state interventionism.

To establish their populist credentials, despots may promise to make housing, food, and other essential commodities "affordable to the masses" through state subsidies. This objective may be achieved by issuing a whole battery of diktats, edicts, state controls, regulations, and legislation to channel economic activity in a certain direction in consonance with their vision, and to transfer huge resources to the state for purposes of development. To enforce these regulations and diktats necessitates the creation of a large number of government ministries and departments; but state interventionism creates its own set of problems that inhibit or defeat the achievement of the despot's vision.

First, state controls end up benefiting the ruling gang of vampire elites and the whole coterie of sycophants and supporters. For the masses, price controls end up making food more expensive! Second, state interventionism results in a bloated bureaucracy and stifling red tape, which provide rich opportunities for rent-seeking, corruption, and bribery. For example, to secure an ordinary permit to put up a house in Mubarak's Egypt required obtaining permits from no fewer than 30 government agencies with overlapping jurisdictions.[3] It is worse for a permit to build a church, which may be refused outright, as is often the case in many Islamic countries, although mosques can be built in secular countries with relative ease. To set up a business in Nigeria, an entrepreneur had to comply with the 1963 Immigration Act, 1964 Indigenization Guidelines, 1968 Companies Decree, 1972 Nigerian Enterprises Promotion Decree (amended in 1973, 1974, and 1977), as well as other stifling regulations pertaining to what could be imported, who could be hired, and how much could be repatriated abroad.

Frustration in dealing with bureaucracies in the developing world is widespread. Compliance with the multiplicity of regulations is irritating and time consuming. Tempers flare when applicants and potential investors are endlessly shuttled back and forth between government agencies to obtain permits from senior government officials who, more often than not, are absent—on extended lunches with their young mistresses. Frequently, one government department does not know what the others are doing. Processes that should take no more than a few hours may take weeks or even months. The bureaucracy is wracked by appalling inefficiency, waste, graft, and administrative ineptitude.

To get anything done quickly, it might be necessary to pay a bribe. Thus, the byzantine maze of state controls and regulations provides lucrative opportunities for self-enrichment. Revenue collection, passport control, and even government stationery can all be skimmed, diverted, manipulated, or used for illicit gain. Civil servants demand bribes, exploit their positions in government, and manipulate the state's regulatory powers to supplement their meager salaries. Almost every government regulation and nuance of policy can be mined. Since every permit has its price, civil servants invent endless new rules and extort bribes. In fact, every official transaction can provide an avenue to amass wealth, leading to poor service and failed government programs.

In the Farsi language of Iran, the kickback is called *kar chaq kon*. Mahmoud Asgari, the proprietor of two medium-size printing houses in Tehran, complained bitterly: "If I do not pay a 'success fee' for any contract I sign with government organizations, big or small, I will be out of business very quickly."[4] The "success fees" range from 10 to 30 percent of the total value of a contract paid to government officials, which could be as much as US$600 for a job. Petty corruption is tolerated because it has become a way of life and is necessary to secure contracts, business loans, and even jobs.

Corruption now permeates all levels of Venezuelan society, according to Gustavo Coronel, who was a member of the board of directors of Petróleos de Venezuela from 1976 to 1979 and, as president of Agrupación Pro Calidad de Vida, was the Venezuelan representative to Transparency International from 1996 to 2000. Bureaucrats rarely follow existing regulations, and ordinary citizens must pay bribes to accomplish bureaucratic transactions, which are seldom completed. Coronel says that "the dramatic rise in corruption under Chávez is ironic since he came to power largely on an anti-corruption campaign platform."[5]

More perniciously, despots and the ruling clique quickly discover that state controls and instruments are exactly what they need not only to enrich themselves, but also to punish their rivals, silence their critics, and reward their supporters. For example, import licenses may be denied as a means of punishing businesses associated with the opposition. State controls may also be used to parcel out large chunks of the economy to relatives, kinsmen, cronies, or secretive military groups. The Islamic Revolutionary Guard Corps is now believed to control a third of the Iranian economy.[6]

Price Controls

When prices begin to rise because of uncertainty and difficulties in procuring supplies as the result of import controls or weather-related adversities, despots may resort to draconian measures that are unrelated to the underlying causes in order to halt the price increases. These measures are popular not only with despotic regimes but also with democratically elected governments because they are politically expedient. They portray the government as attacking a problem to make some commodity affordable to the masses. But price controls are another set of state measures that actually exacerbate the problem they are intended to solve. They create shortages and black markets and destroy the productive base of the economy by killing the incentive to produce. Assume that the market price of a commodity is $3. If a government forces producers to accept a government-dictated price of $1, they will withdraw their goods or underproduce. The result, with unchanged demand, is a shortage, which the price control was intended to alleviate. To escape the controls imposed by President Hugo Chávez and supplement their income, many Venezuelan farmers sell their crops at "unregulated street markets for a higher price; others, such as dairy producers, are exacerbating a milk shortage by making more goods whose prices aren't regulated, such as cheeses."[7]

Thus, the immediate effect of a price control is the creation of a shortage—a first-generation problem. The shortage, in turn, may create a black market, where the commodity is illegally sold above the control price—a second-generation problem or a secondary unintended consequence. On the black market, hoarding, bribery, profiteering, and shady deals may flourish as the commodity becomes more and more scarce. Measures designed to curb profiteering or hoarding attack the second-generation problems; that is, they attack the symptoms rather than the root cause of the disease, which is the price control itself.

Furthermore, if the official price is $1, but the price on the black market is $3, this creates an incentive for anyone to buy the commodity at the official price and resell it on the black market to reap a huge profit—a practice that was known in Ghana as *kalabule*. Everyone then wants to acquire the commodity at the official price. Political connections can be an advantage. Even government officials themselves engage in this practice, using their office to acquire commodities at official prices and having their wives, relatives, and cronies resell on the black market.

Economists call this kind of activity "rent-seeking" (in Iran, it is called *rantkhari*). In many other cases, the shortages may be contrived. For example, a civil servant may claim that there are no application forms for a passport. However, a bribe of, say, $5 would produce such an application form instantly. In this case, a "shortage" of application forms is manufactured to enable the civil servant to extort a "premium," a "commission," or a "rent" for its "scarcity," as others do in a real black market. However, rent-seeking activities retard economic growth because they do not produce wealth but merely redistribute it. Rent-seekers become rich by extracting "commissions" on contrived shortages.

Contrary to popular misconceptions, price controls do not make commodities "affordable." Rather, they make them more expensive because of the hidden costs involved in searching for the scarce goods ("search costs") and the time wasted standing in line. These hidden-opportunity costs render the commodity much more expensive and can only be eliminated by removing the price controls.

Here is an example of the economic damage one specific price control wreaks. Nigerians believe that, since their country is an oil-producing country, they have the God-given entitlement to cheap gasoline. So the state fixes the price of petrol (gasoline) at $2 a gallon. However, its dilapidated state-owned oil refineries cannot produce enough gasoline to supply the country with gasoline at that price. (Funds allocated for refinery repairs during the Abacha era were embezzled.) So to supply gasoline at that price, Nigeria's government imports about US$4 billion a year of petroleum products to sell at a loss of about US$2 billion a year. But there is more to this economic insanity. Since the price of subsidized petrol is only a third of the price charged in neighboring countries, much Nigerian petrol is smuggled across the border, aggravating the already chronic fuel shortages in Nigeria. Then the same government re-imports, at market rates, what is presumably the same Nigerian fuel back into Nigeria to sell at lower subsidized prices!

A similar situation prevails in Iran, an oil-producing country plagued by chronic fuel shortages. In January 2008, fuel shortages in subzero temperatures in the northern province of Mazandaran led to riots. Similar protests were reported in towns and cities such as Sari and Babol. According to the National Council of Resistance of Iran, crowds "called the leaders of the regime 'a bunch of thieves and murderers' and ridiculed Ahmadinejad by saying, 'instead of fighting the whole world you should resolve our basic requirements.'"[8]

Equally devastating for the Venezuelan economy have been the price controls imposed by President Chávez in 2003 to combat inflation when he froze the price of basic foods, such as rice and meat, after a two-month national strike. Later, he capped phone and electricity rates: after the cost of some products, such as drywall, doubled in 2006, he set prices for 45 construction materials. The results were rampant scarcities of building materials, cars, food and other goods, causing costly delays and pushing Venezuelan inflation to an annual rate of 17 percent in December 2006.[9]

Decay of State Institutions

The despot is not elected, but he needs supporters; he acquires them by dispensing patronage and by appealing to "tribal solidarity" from his kinsmen. He rewards them by assigning them positions in key state institutions and corporations. Tenure of office and promotions are based not on competence and merit, but rather on allegiance to the president, ethnicity, and sycophancy. Very quickly, professionalism and efficiency vanish from institutions such as the civil service, the judiciary, the parliament, and the police. Low productivity, ineptitude, and venality pervade these institutions. The rot is not confined to one area but seeps into all areas of government. Parliament becomes a joke. Police are on the take, and security forces protect the despot and the ruling bandits, not the people. The judiciary is tainted with trials settled by bribes.

Even though the state soaks up scarce resources through heavy taxation, it fails to generate economic growth or deliver basic social services.

The performance of state-owned enterprises (SOEs) in the developing world has been worse than scandalous. In fact, nowhere in the Third World has their performance been superior to that of privately owned businesses for the simple reason that SOEs do not face "market discipline." They are often overstaffed with party functionaries and rack up losses upon losses, which are covered with budgetary subventions, and they are often riddled with gross inefficiency, waste, graft, and incompetence. Yet in Venezuela, Chávez seeks to create more of these state-controlled albatrosses. In August 2010, prosecutors and police raided a stockbroking company after Finance Minister Alí Rodríguez Araque decided to place four commercial banks under state control. "President Hugo Chávez issued a stern warning that he was prepared to nationalize the entire private banking system in the country if that were necessary."[10]

Government-owned utility companies rarely deliver safe, clean drinking water, electricity, and sanitation, let alone market products. People become disgusted and turn away from the state sector because it cannot provide even the most basic services such as education and health care. As they withdraw from the state sector, they take their taxes with them or evade them altogether by bribing tax officials. The government then discovers that, despite steep hikes in excise taxes and import duties, as well as the introduction of vampire taxes (value-added taxes [VAT]), its revenues still cannot cover expenditures. The central bank is then ordered to cover the deficits by printing new currency, fueling inflation, or changing the currency altogether, thereby robbing people of their life's savings. People begin to scoff at the pious utterances of the vampire ruling elites regarding probity, accountability, unity, hard work, and sacrifice as the statements reek of insouciant hypocrisy. As Richard Sandbrook notes,

> Political institutions such as the presidency, the parliament, the party, even the judiciary, lose whatever public esteem they commanded. Bureaucratic institutions also become ineffective and lose their technical rationality. Nepotism and patronage swell the bureaucratic ranks with incompetents and time-servers. Those civil servants who are competent and honest are demoralized by the graft, fraud and theft of public property. Indiscipline and lassitude paralyze the bureaucratic apparatus.[11]

Administrative capability deteriorates. Institutionalized bureaucratic norms and practices are flouted. Simple routine tasks that would normally require a day's work by a civil servant take weeks—if they are ever accomplished. Accounting controls are often nonexistent, and two departments within the same government ministry may not even know what the other one is doing. The capacity to execute plans, to implement reform, or even to manage the budget collapses. The economy suffers in the process. Economic development projects are delayed or are never completed.

Declining Investment

Countries ruled by despots become a wilderness to foreign investors for a variety of reasons: weak currencies (except, notably, in extractive industries, where output is priced in dollars), exchange and price controls, a feeble local private sector, poor infrastructure, small domestic markets, stifling bureaucracy, political instability, uncertain legal systems, and corruption. Crumbling infrastructure, chronic instability, and the despotic government's penchant for terror and violence as well as the forcible seizure of foreign-owned property all deter investors—both domestic and foreign. Economic growth contracts when investment dries up.

In Zimbabwe, President Robert Mugabe, unpopular and desperately trying to cling to power, has unleashed his wrath against all enemies, real or imagined. Scores of independent businessmen were picked up in 2005 on dubious corruption charges, hauled before courts, and then released. Some were alleged to have had talks with the opposition Movement for Democratic Change or to have made donations to the group. Others received anonymous phone calls telling them to back off politics or face unspecified consequences.[12] The clear aim was intimidation: to discourage independent businessmen from supporting the opposition, and to punish those who had. Similar attacks on private businesses have occurred in Venezuela and Iran. But in all cases, as we saw in chapter 1, investors have fled.

Bloomberg News reported that in Venezuela, "foreign investors sold US$778 million more in Venezuelan assets than they bought in the first nine months of 2006, according to the central bank; a decade ago, in the same period, they added US$5.9 billion more than they disposed of."[13] But Chávez shows no sign of relenting:

- October 4, 2010: He signed a decree to expropriate Agroislena C.A., a leading farm-supply business.
- October 10, 2010: He nationalized Industrias Venoco, the country's largest independent auto lubricants company. Chávez accused the company of "over-charging."[14]
- October 25, 2010: Owens-Illinois, an American glass maker, became the two-hundredth business nationalized in 2010. About 400 companies have been nationalized since Chávez became president in 1999. Most companies received no compensation, although the Venezuelan constitution forbids expropriation without a court verdict and fair compensation.[15]

The Surge of Corruption

Political corruption covers a whole range of activities that are illegal and is generally defined as the use of public office or legislated powers by government officials for illicit private gain. It may involve misappropriation of public funds or embezzlement, demand of bribes, and extortion. It exists in *all* societies, but it is important to establish from the outset that it is no more acceptable in traditional than in advanced societies. Senegalese scholar Cheikh Anta Diop reveals that:

> Ghana probably experienced the reign of a corrupt dynasty between the sixth and eighth centuries. Kati tells of an extremely violent revolt of the masses against it. The members of that dynasty were systematically massacred. In order to wipe it out completely, the rebels went so far as to extract fetuses from the wombs of the royal family.[16]

In modern times, however, the incidence of corruption has become far more pervasive and catastrophic under despotic regimes. In fact, nearly all the serious cases of grand theft, injurious plunder, rancid venality, and naked looting on a mass scale in recent history occurred under dictatorships—the Suhartos, the Marcoses, the Mobutus, the Mubaraks, and Nigeria's military bandits. "The entire system in North Korea is fraudulent, and abuses are so systemic that corruption has become an incurable disease," said Andrei Nikolaevich Lankov, Kookmin University professor.[17] "When it comes to corruption and abuses by government officials, North Korea probably ranks first in the world.

Money can buy anything in North Korea," said Choo Myung-hee, a North Korean defector.[18]

There are three reasons for this. First, state interventionism comes with a plethora of controls that create a bewildering labyrinth of hurdles and precipices. To navigate this may require the payment of bribes or commissions that go straight into the pockets of the administering officials. Second, the institutions needed to combat corruption effectively are often packed with the allies and cronies of the despot, rendering them incapable of discharging their functions. Third, the state interventionist and control behemoth breeds corruption. Thus, even where institutions for fighting corruption exist, efforts to combat corruption are not likely to be effective when the beast is in place.

The first step in fighting corruption is to expose it. This is the business of independent and free media. Once corruption has been exposed, it is the function of the attorney general to prosecute government officials alleged to have misused their office for private gain. Third, when a government official is found guilty, an independent judiciary is required to uphold the rule of law and punish that official for all to see. But none of this is likely to occur under a despotic regime.

As we saw in the previous chapter, the media under a despot are seldom free, for the regime controls the flow of information. Therefore, cases of corruption are not likely to be exposed. The auditor general is the one person who is supposed to uncover corruption in government ministries, but his annual reports are duly shelved.[19] Occasionally, an intrepid editor or journalist in the private media may report such cases of corruption, but they are always punished severely with jail terms or even death. Further, the attorney general, who may himself be corrupt, is not likely to prosecute any member of the ruling gang of bandits. Nor is he likely to prosecute relatives of the despot. Kenya's attorney general, Amos Wacko, has not prosecuted a single official bandit in the 20 years he has been in office. Moreover, an independent judiciary is not likely to exist under despotic regimes. The judges are appointed by the despot and may themselves be corrupt. In 2002, over 200 Kenyan judges were sacked for corruption.

With no controls, checks, or means to combat corruption, the despot and the ruling vampire elites loot with impunity. They always escape justice and walk off scot-free. It is no accident that most of the countries at the bottom of Transparency International's annual survey of corruption (Corruption Perception Index [CPI]) are ruled by despotic regimes.

CORRUPTION PERCEPTION INDEX (CPI)

Rank	Country	CPI 2009 Score	Surveys Used	Confidence Range
158	Tajikistan	2.0	8	1.6–2.5
162	Angola	1.9	5	1.8–1.9
162	Congo Brazzaville	1.9	5	1.6–2.1
162	Democratic Republic of the Congo	1.9	5	1.7–2.1
162	Guinea-Bissau	1.9	3	1.8–2.0
162	Kyrgyzstan	1.9	7	1.8–2.1
162	Venezuela	1.9	7	1.8–2.0
168	Burundi	1.8	6	1.6–2.0
168	Equatorial Guinea	1.8	3	1.6–1.9
168	Guinea	1.8	5	1.7–1.8
168	Haiti	1.8	3	1.4–2.3
168	Iran	1.8	3	1.7–1.9
168	Turkmenistan	1.8	4	1.7–1.9
174	Uzbekistan	1.7	6	1.5–1.8
175	Chad	1.6	6	1.5–1.7
176	Iraq	1.5	3	1.2–1.8
176	Sudan	1.5	5	1.4–1.7
178	Myanmar	1.4	3	0.9–1.8
179	Afghanistan	1.3	4	1.0–1.5
180	Somalia	1.1	3	0.9–1.4

Note: Index is computed from responses to a survey by businessmen. Responses are given on scale of 1 to 10; the lower the score, the more corrupt the country is perceived to be.
Source: Transparency International, http://www.transparency.org/policy_research/surveys_indices/cpi/2009/cpi_2009_table

And what the despots and the vampire elites steal is no chump change. Consider:

- "In July 1999, *Forbes* Magazine estimated [the late dictator of Iraq] Saddam Hussein's personal wealth at $6 billion, acquired primarily from oil and smuggling."[20]
- As reported in the *Telegraph* (UK) "Nigeria's past rulers stole or misused £220 billion ($412 billion). That is as much as all the western aid given to Africa in almost four decades. The

looting of Africa's most populous country amounted to a sum equivalent to 300 years of British aid for the continent. Former leader Gen Sani Abacha stole between £1bn and £3bn. The figures were compiled by Nigeria's anti-corruption commission."[21]

- During the years of Hugo Chávez's presidency, corruption has exploded to unprecedented levels. Billions of dollars are being stolen or are otherwise unaccounted for, squandering Venezuelan resources and enriching high-level officials and their cronies. Chávez's government has received between US$175 billion and US$225 billion from oil and new debt. Along with the increase in revenues has come a simultaneous reduction in transparency. For example, "the state-owned oil company ceased publishing its consolidated annual financial statements in 2003, and Chávez has created new state-run financial institutions, whose operations are also opaque, that spend funds at the discretion of the executive."[22]

Africa has seen large-scale plunder of its resources by kleptocrats and despots. The African Union estimates that corruption costs the continent about US$148 billion a year—a figure that far exceeds the paltry US$30 billion Africa receives in foreign aid from all sources. Angola, Cameroon, the Democratic Republic of the Congo, Gabon, Egypt, Kenya, and Nigeria are the worst cases. Sudanese President Omar al-Bashir "has been accused of siphoning off up to US$9 billion of his country's funds and placing it in foreign accounts, according to leaked US diplomatic cables."[23] Evidently capitalist greed was not invented by the West.

Pakistanis dismiss President Asif Ali Zardari as "Mr. Ten Percent," because they believe that he demands and pockets a ten percent commission on all contracts. In defiance of a Supreme Court order, his government refused to ask the Swiss government to reopen a money-laundering case against Zardari that it had earlier dropped. In 2007, President Pervez Musharraf enforced an amnesty that set aside corruption charges against Zardari and other political leaders, but it was ruled unconstitutional by the Supreme Court in 2009.[24] There is an old Pakistani saying: "If you shake the hands of the president, you have got to see if your fingers are still there." The African version says: "If you shake the hand of the president, you have to see if your legs are still there." Africa's kleptocrats do not steal a billion here and there. They cart away the entire treasury—sink, bulbs, and all.

Why most developing countries are poor has little to do with race, religion, or ideology, but much to do with their defective system of governance. The richest people in the United States—for example, Warren Buffett and Bill Gates—made their fortunes in the private sector by actually creating something of value: Berkshire Hathaway and Microsoft. By contrast, in the developing world, the wealthiest are often presidents, ministers, and government officials who looted the public treasury, turning the whole notion of "wealth creation" upside down.

Of course, there were robber barons in America's history: John D. Rockefeller, Andrew Carnegie, Cornelius Vanderbilt, J. P. Morgan, John Jacob Astor, Jay Gould, and James J. Hill. But they invested the loot in America, building railroads, steel mills, banks, and oil companies, and their enterprise drove the American industrial age from 1861 to 1901. By contrast, Africa's kleptocrats stash their loot overseas. According to a March 26, 2010, report by *Global Financial Integrity*, Africa lost US$854 billion in illicit financial outflows from 1970 through 2008; the outflows from Africa may be as high as $1.8 trillion.[25] Then at least once a decade, a cacophonous gaggle of rock and Hollywood stars hold summits and rock concerts to help poor Africa. It is a theater of the absurd with the blind leading the clueless.

Economic Contraction and Collapse

A despotic regime has difficulty attracting foreign investment or spurring domestic investment since the prevailing environment—characterized by oppression, brutality, cruelty, absence of rule of law, corruption, and crumbling infrastructure—deters investors, both foreign and domestic. To fill in the investment gap, the regime is forced to rely more and more on foreign aid if it is not mineral-rich, but foreign aid does not provide the key to self-sustaining growth. Foreign aid simply sustains governments in their pursuit of ruinous political and economic policies. It may even have perverse incentive effects: the more damage a despot does to the economy, the more he qualifies for even greater amounts of aid to alleviate the suffering of his people.

To secure investable resources, the despot may resort to the coercive apparatus of the government. Like the colonial state, the vampire state is extractive. In fact, there is little difference between the two—except the skin color of the operators. Under colonialism, resources and wealth were plundered for the development of metropolitan European countries. Little social and economic development occurred in the colonies themselves. Today, the tiny cabal of ruling vampire elites uses its governing authority to exploit and extract resources from the productive members of society in developing countries. These resources are then spent lavishly on themselves by the elites and siphoned out of the country—a double whammy. As Ronald Robinson asks plaintively, "What incentive does the peasant have to produce more when through taxation the surplus is siphoned off to be spent in conspicuous consumption?"[26]

People become alienated, as the Nigerian scholar Claude Ake notes eloquently:

> Most African regimes have been so alienated and so violently repressive that their citizens see the state as enemies to be evaded, cheated and defeated if possible, but never as partners in development. The leaders have been so engrossed in coping with the hostilities which their misrule and repression has unleashed that they are unable to take much interest in anything else including the pursuit of development.[27]

People lose faith in the ability of the government to provide basic services (housing, health care, water, and electricity) and jobs and to combat corruption. As repressive rule continues with time, the mass of the people begin to regard the state and its organs with fear, suspicion, and cynicism. A growing sense of alienation and disaffection among the larger population sets in, and a huge credibility gap emerges between the people and the leadership. Those who control the state become increasingly insecure, repressive, and less responsive to the wishes of society.

The economy limps along or contracts. The contraction is accelerated by large-scale flight out of the formal economy, as people turn increasingly to clandestine economic transactions in the parallel or informal economy to keep their incomes and assets out of the reach of the vampire state. These are defensive survival mechanisms. The parallel economy is called *magendo* in East Africa and *kalabule* in Ghana, but everywhere its activities are similar. They involve hoarding, exchange of goods above the official price, smuggling, illegal currency deals, bribery, and corruption. With time, larger and larger segments of the economy slip out of the control of the government, which soon finds that its control does not extend beyond a few miles of the capital.

Desperate Measures

As investors flee the country and the wealthy secretly transfer their wealth out of the country, the economy begins to collapse. Jobs are not being created, and unemployed youth become restless. Government revenues begin to shrink because of reduced economic activity and tax evasion. Meanwhile, government expenditures are exploding because of costly subsidies, waste, inefficiency, and corruption. Budget deficits balloon. Desperate, a despotic regime is forced to either drastically cut costs or find additional resources to maintain its support base. But cutbacks in payrolls, benefits, and subsidies could provoke a blowback and ignite civil unrest, as occurred in Mozambique in September 2010. Cuba faced this prospect in September 2010, when it announced it would lay off at least half a million state workers. The plan was part of President Raul Castro's pledge to shed some one million state jobs, a full fifth of the official workforce. To stem civil unrest in Iran, a senior cleric, Ayatollah Ahmad Jannati, warned that Iranians would face economic hardships in 2011 when the government phases out the US$100 billion it pays to keep down the prices of essential goods.

To secure additional resources, a despotic regime might resort to drastic measures. It might print money, which will fuel inflation. It might seize any foreign-owned property that is left in the country. Or it might simply rob people of their life savings through fraudulent currency changes.

Currency Changes

Currency change is the most insidious tactic that a despotic regime in dire need of funds may resort to. It is devilishly designed to steal the people's money. In recent times, this tactic has been employed in Ghana (1982), Nigeria (1984), Zimbabwe (2006), and North Korea (2009). In Zimbabwe, the Mugabe regime repeatedly turned to the printing press to finance its obscene budget deficits, with the result that inflation was raging at the rate of 1,200 percent per year in 2006. A piece of chicken cost over 3 million Zimbabwean dollars. Eventually, Zimbabwe's currency collapsed in February 2009 when the inflation rate hit 6.5 quindecillion novemdecillion percent—65 followed by 107 zeros. The currency was replaced by the US dollar and the South African rand.

On November 30, 2009, chaos erupted in North Korea after the government of Kim Jong Il revalued the country's currency. It drastically reduced the amount of old bills that could be traded for new, which wiped out personal savings. The revaluation and exchange limits triggered panic and anger, especially among market traders who had kept their profits and savings in old North Korean *won*. The revaluation replaced old 1,000-won notes with 10-*won* notes, but strictly limited the amount of old currency that could be exchanged to 100,000 *won*, which at the then black-market rates amounted to $40. "All North Korean currency that individuals possessed in excess of that amount became worthless under the revaluation. Amid widespread protests, the limit was raised to 150,000 *won* in cash and 300,000 *won* in bank savings."[28]

Rising Public Discontent and Resentment

Despots delude themselves into believing that they can fool their people all the time. It is only a matter of time before the people realize that all the long, grandiloquent speeches, revolutionary rhetoric, hoary vituperation, and posturing are just a charade. They do not create jobs, put food on their tables, or put gasoline in their cars. People can see that commodity shortages are rampant, hospitals lack basic essential medicines, roads are pitted with yawning potholes that are big enough to swallow trucks, electricity supply is sporadic, the water tap spits a drop now and then, and jobs are scarce. Even more annoying, people are forbidden to complain about grotesque mismanagement and administrative ineptitude. The despot must be praised all the time; any whiff of criticism is swiftly and brutally squashed. It does not take long for people to realize that they have been duped—again.

With inflation running at 30 percent annually, government services deteriorating, and crime hitting the poor the hardest, Venezuelans are simply fed up with the Chávez regime. Some even joke that they would be safer in Iraq than in Venezuela. According to the *New York Times*, "In Iraq, a country with about the same population as Venezuela, there were 4,644 civilian deaths from violence in 2009, according to Iraq Body Count; in Venezuela that year, the number of murders climbed above 16,000. More than 90 percent of murders go unsolved, without a single arrest."[29]

What incenses people even more is the widespread corruption and ostentatious living of so-called revolutionaries. Said Maria Escalante, a school principal in Barquisimeto, Venezuela, who first embraced the

Chávez "revolution" and later became thoroughly disenchanted with it: "The reality is that the government has deteriorated with so many big corruption scandals. I think what is happening is that President Chavez does not listen to the people."[30]

When the people become tired of rampant corruption, street protests often morph into political campaigns that lead to the ouster of the despot—as in Iran in 1979, the Philippines in 1989, Indonesia in 1998, Tunisia in 2011, and Egypt in 2011. It was corruption and suppression of opposition voices during the shah's rule that caused Iran's constitutional monarchy to collapse—allowing conservative clerics to seize power and establish a hard-line Islamic state.[31] But then the clerics betrayed the ideals of their own Islamic revolution. Such was also the case with Hugo Chávez, who rose to power on a vigorously anti-corruption campaign. Evidently, those who do not learn from history are bound to repeat it.

In Iran, history is being repeated. Dissent has emerged within the inner circle of Ahmadinejad's Islamic Republic in Iran, which was hit with defections after the brutal clampdown on street protests following the fraudulent election Ahmadinejad claimed to have won. "I want the regime to be overthrown," said Farzad Farhangian, a former press attaché in the Iranian Embassy in Brussels, who defected in September 2010.[32] He followed Hossein Alizadeh, the second in command at the Iranian embassy in Norway, where the consul, Mohammed Reza Heydari, had already resigned. All three openly support Iran's democratic opposition, the Green Movement. They have every reason to be angry: The "revolution" had failed and betrayed them. In 1978, before the 1979 revolution, "Iran produced 6 million barrels of oil a day; in 2000, 4.5 million; mostly recently 3.5 million. This will fall further in 2011."[33] The regime blames Western sanctions against its nuclear program, but, more realistically, mismanagement and crumbling production facilities are the main culprits.

Paranoia and Overreaction

Since the tyrant knows he has done evil, he is afraid of his own shadow. He sees conspiracies all around him. Paranoia and overreaction characterize despotic rule. One of the despot's most nettlesome problems is how to guard his claim to the presidency. No potential challenger must be permitted to gain a power base. The people love him, so any show of public disaffection rattles the regime and must be squelched instantly—

lest it spread. The security forces, in particular, are extremely sensitive to any whiff or sign of protest and criticism, and they often react with hysteria when they suddenly find themselves overtaken by events they had not foreseen. Such miscalculation may cost them their jobs—or even their lives. In this atmosphere of intrigue and suspicion, divisions eventually emerge within the ruling circle—divisions that a smart opposition should always foment and exploit. "Rebels" or "reformists" may appear to challenge the existing order or move the ruling party in a new direction. A case in point occurred in Mexico in 1987 when Cuauhtémoc Cárdenas and other politicians from the ruling Partido Revolucionario Institucional (PRI) (Institutional Revolution Party) that had held power for more than 70 years announced the creation of the Corriente Democrática (Democratic Current) within the party to discuss an alternative way of nominating the PRI's candidate for the presidency other than *el dedazo*, by which the incumbent picked his successor by pointing his finger. The Democratic Current nominated Cárdenas as its candidate. Although he did not win in 1988, his efforts, together with worsening crises (Zapatista rebellion and mounting street protests), paved the way for a defeat of PRI at the polls by Vicente Fox in 2000.

Breakaway factions have appeared in ruling parties in many developing countries:

- **Uganda:** In 2001, Dr. Kizza Besigye, once the physician, confidant, and cabinet minister of dictator Yoweri Museveni, broke away to form his own party, the Forum for Democratic Change, to contest the presidential elections in 2001 and 2006. Another cabinet minister, Jaberi Bidandi Ssali, broke ranks to form the People's Progressive Party.
- **Kenya:** In 2002, Raila Odinga, the then secretary general of Kenya's African National Union Party (KANU), which had held power since independence in 1963, resigned and formed the Rainbow Movement, which later teamed up with several other parties to form the National Rainbow Coalition (NARC) that eventually defeated Daniel arap Moi's protégé, Uhuru Kenyatta.
- **Iran:** After the disputed June 2009 election, wide splits occurred within Iran's regime. Though the supreme leader, Grand Ayatollah Ali Khamenei, backed President Ahmadinejad, several clerics did not. Among them were many senior clerics in Qum,

including Grand Ayatollah Nasser Makarem Shirazi, Grand Ayatollah Hosssein Ali Montazeri, who died in December 2009, and former president Akbar Hashemi Rafsanjani. In November 2010, a rift erupted when parliament attempted to impeach the president. Some 74 lawmakers accused the president and his government of "14 counts of violating the law, often by acting without the approval of the legislature."[34]

- **North Korea:** Kim Jong Nam, the eldest son of the leader, Kim Jon Il, told Japanese television that he opposed the generational transfer of power to his younger half-brother, Kim Jong Eun.[35]
- **Russia:** After Moscow mayor Yuri Luzhkov criticized President Dmitri Medvedev in September 2010 for indecisiveness and suggested that his predecessor, Vladimir Putin, now prime minister, should return to the presidency, he was sacked. Luzhkov later announced plans to set up a new political movement to challenge the ruling party.

Such political feuds and infighting can have serious political and economic ramifications. They may spell the beginning of the end of despotic rule and the opening up of the political space. Breakaway factions or leaders have the goods on the despot: an intricate knowledge of how the regime functions and the dastardly deeds and crimes it has committed.[36] Fearful that malcontents might spill the beans, the despot may not seek to crush them.

Political feuding can also cause serious economic problems as it creates uncertainty and deters long-term investment. In November 2010, Russia's central bank raised its forecast capital outflows to US$22 billion for the year, up from its October estimate of US$12 billion. Monthly outflows had risen from US$3 billion in July and August to about US$3 billion a week. Analysts suggested that the ousting of Mayor Yuri Luzhkov in Moscow might have triggered the October acceleration in outflows. Business groups worried that they could get caught in the crossfire if the infighting escalated.[37]

POLITICAL INSTABILITY

A despotic regime is inherently unstable because it is repressive and lacks legitimacy. Its credibility also erodes with time as allegations of corruption, malfeasance, and mismanagement become rampant. The massive bureaucracy it creates to carry out its diktats is plagued by graft and inefficiency and becomes dysfunctional. The threat to such a regime may come from four sources (political parties are not included because the despot can always ban them):

1. Popular protests over economic hardships—lack of jobs, rising prices, non-delivery of basic social services—and perception of corruption
2. Politically marginalized groups that have been excluded from the gravy train
3. Intrigue and jostling within the palace—palace coup
4. The military

As the economy deteriorates with unemployment soaring, prices rising, and commodity shortages becoming rampant, public anger and disappointment may erupt into street protests. There have been many such protests in the developing world over price hikes for food, gasoline, and other basic necessities. Though they may not have any political intent or motivation, these protests can deliver an indictment of the regime, and smart opposition leaders can capitalize on them and transform them into a potent political campaign against the despotic regime, as occurred in Tunisia in December 2010 and Egypt in February 2011.

The despot becomes panicky in the face of street protests. He knows that, if he reacts brutally with excessive force, he risks international condemnation and being seen as "anti-people." Former Tunisian president Zine El-Abidine Ben Ali cracked down hard on street protests at first and then relented—as did Hosni Mubarak of Egypt. On the other hand, if he allows the street protests to continue, they might trigger a palace or military coup against him. Some despots choose to implement some hasty reforms, but to no avail. Half-baked reforms only infuriate the people, who perceive them as a sign of weakness and are emboldened to demand the resignation of the despot, as happened in Tunisia and Egypt.

Even when such public protests do not occur, the perception of corruption can often lead to the downfall of the despot. His orders are ignored or sneered at, even by his own lieutenants, who may now think that his "revolution" is a scam and that they are being taken for fools. "Why work for such a corrupt buffoon, who has built palaces for himself amid massive social misery and suffering?" they might ask. People start sabotaging government operations and helping themselves to government property. The perception of corruption can be damaging to a despotic regime. It brought down the shah of Iran in 1979 and is most frequently cited as the justification for nearly all the military coups that have taken place in the developing world.

Even where corruption is not the issue, the regime's governing style can trigger instability. By definition, a despotic regime is a politically closed system—run by the despot and a small coterie of inner advisers, allies, and henchmen. All channels for political change are blocked or shut down, and elections are a farce because the despot always wins. Thus, it is only a matter of time before some group decides that effecting change through the ballot box or some other peaceful means is all but impossible. They might reckon that, if the despot cannot be persuaded by the force of argument, he might perhaps be persuaded by the argument of force. They may pick up guns and start a guerrilla movement or a rebel insurgency.

Rebel insurgencies are always started by politically excluded groups. They often start in the countryside and make their way toward the seat of power in the capital. There have been a plethora of such rebel insurgencies and guerrilla movements in the developing world in the past decades, such as the *mujahideen* of Afghanistan, who fought against the pro-Soviet backed government in the 1970s, and the Tamil Tigers, who began a violent offensive against the government of Sri Lanka in the 1980s. In Latin America, guerrillas have operated in such countries as Colombia (the Revolutionary Armed Forces of Colombia [FARC]), Mexico (the Zapatistas), Nicaragua (the Sandanistas), and Peru (Shining Path and Tupac Amaru [MRTA]). Africa has had more than 30 rebel insurgencies since 1960.

Rebel insurgencies, however, are not to be recommended as they often degenerate into civil wars. They can rage for years, or even decades, because despots are often incapable of crushing them. In fact, no African despot has been able to put down a rebel insurgency. They wreak wanton destruction, cause utter chaos, and inflict a horrendous human toll. More than 5 million perished in the Democratic Republic of the Congo as a result of civil war and war-related diseases between 1996 and 2004. Sudan's civil wars claimed more than 4 million. Further, civil wars destroy infrastructure and hasten the collapse of the economy and even the entire state, resulting in a failed or collapsed state, as happened in Liberia, Sierra Leone, and Somalia. Rebuilding after a civil war takes billions that the poor countries do not have.

The greatest threat to a despot is more likely to come from within his own military. Military despots often seized power by staging coups, and they fear that other military officers may entertain similar designs. As Samuel Decalo puts it, "Military hierarchies often carry within them the seeds of their own destruction or instability. Most of them have been rocked by internal power struggles, factionalism, decay of cohesion and discipline, personal power gambits, and successful or attempted coups."[38] Richard Sandbrook also emphasizes this point:

> The armed forces are generally the strongman's Achilles heel. To capture and neutralize the army, the ruler has two options. He can transform it into a force led and, perhaps, manned by his followers, or he can build up a personally loyal counter force. But there is a catch. Either route may provoke the officer corps if they perceive a threat to their prestige or professional autonomy.[39]

Tyrants spend an inordinate amount on an elaborate security cum military structure to protect themselves and suppress their people. They create layers upon layers of security—just in case one level fails—and shower security agents with gifts, perks, and amenities. But they don't trust the military completely, so they create a special division force (like Qaddafi's 32nd Presidential Brigade, led by his son), and equip it with better weapons than the ordinary soldiers have, so that the brigade can put down any uprising or coup attempt from the military. Despite the enormous amount they spend on elaborate layers of security, however, in the end, despots are hoist by their own petard.

- In December 2008, Captain Moussa Dadis Camara seized power in a coup after the death of the long-time ruler of Guinea, Lansana Conté. On December 3, 2009, on the first anniversary of his coup, Camara was shot in the head by his former aide-de-camp in an assassination attempt. He survived, and was sent to Burkina Faso, which is also ruled by a military despot, Blaise Compaoré, to recover.[40]
- On August 2, 2005, army officers overthrew President Maaouiya Ould Sid'Ahmed Taya of Mauritania in a bloodless revolt. He was toppled by his former security chief and close

colleague, Colonel Ely Ould Mohamed Vall. "My situation reminds me of the old adage: 'God, save me from my friends, I'll take care of my enemies,'" President Taya told Radio France Internationale from Niger. "I was stunned by the coup d'etat . . . and even more so when I heard who were the authors."[41]

REFORMING A DESPOTIC REGIME

As we have seen above, despotism is untenable and will eventually collapse or be toppled—often violently. Although there is no such thing as an "enlightened despot"—an oxymoron—let us allow that a few of them may see the light and make a feeble attempt to reform their abominable systems. In fact, there are often reform-minded people in the despot's circle who might persuade him to change course; one example is the reformers in the government of former Soviet leader Mikhail Gorbachev. But such reformers can also be sidelined or worse. Nonetheless, a dictatorship is a controlled society. Liberating such a society requires reform in several key areas: economic, political, intellectual, institutional, and constitutional. Economic liberalization requires removal of state controls on the economy, greater reliance on the private sector, and a move toward a market economy. Political reform involves opening up the political space and establishing some form of democratic pluralism and accountability. By intellectual reform is meant permitting freedom of expression, assembly, and movement, as well as freedom of religion. Everyone, including the rat at the top, must obey the same law. It is the *law* that rules, not the whims of the despot. Institutional reform also involves the establishment of a more independent judiciary to uphold the rule of law and instilling professionalism into the civil service and the police, military, and security forces, who are supposed to protect the *people*, not the bandits and killers in power. Constitutional reform requires redefining the roles of the executive and the structure of the state.

A despot may attempt reform grudgingly and haltingly in a process infused with self-doubts. Political reform is out of the question as that would amount to committing political suicide. Intellectual freedom does not come into consideration, for that would expose the deficiencies and failures of the despotic regime. Institutional reform would cut into his exercise of power and undermine his support base. For example, the independent judiciary needed to enforce the rule of law would pose too much of a threat to the despot. Reform of the civil service would cause massive layoffs of redundant party supporters. Thus, the despot might opt for economic reform. But reform in one area alone is not sufficient and might even bring the house down on him.

Piecemeal reform is worse than no reform at all because reform in only one area of the political economy creates stresses in the other areas. It is akin to tuning up the engine of an automobile without repairing the defective brakes. The whole political economy of a dictatorship must be reformed. And in this exercise the *sequence* of reform is critical. This author has always argued that the ideal sequence should start with intellectual freedom, then political reform, constitutional reform, institutional reform, and finally economic liberalization. If a despotic system must be reformed, the people must have the intellectual freedom to determine what sort of political or economic system would be most suitable for them. The freedom that helped bring down the Soviet Union was *glasnost* (openness). Economic liberalization before political reform puts the cart before the horse, and political reform before intellectual freedom puts the wheel before the cart.

Despots seldom level the playing field. They favor economic liberalization only for those businesses allied to themselves. Those who prosper are those with political connections or insider knowledge, such as the oligarchs in Russia. But they seldom keep their wealth in the country. Eventually, however, the day of reckoning arrives when economic prosperity hits the political ceiling. This may be triggered by a fall in copper prices (Chile), a slump in cocoa prices (Ivory Coast), the 1997 Asian financial crisis (Indonesia), the death of a dictator and succession woes (Ivory Coast and the former Yugoslavia), a stolen election (Madagascar and Iran), or social unrest provoked by a lack of jobs and deteriorating living conditions (Tunisia, Egypt, and Yemen). For example, people who have lost money on account of a financial crisis want explanations, and they want those responsible to be held accountable. When prosperity enriches only the ruling vampire elites, leaving the mass of people in abject poverty (crony or vampire capitalism), growing social inequality may provoke resentment and erupt into street protests if the regime hikes prices of food or other essential items.

If the despot is "enlightened" enough to open up the political space and address public grievances, or if he flees, it allows steam to be vented and the economic prosperity to continue. Unfortunately, most despots keep the political lid on, and the pent-up frustration erupts into a revolution ousting the despot and causing all the gains made under economic liberalization to unravel. Such was the case in Indonesia, Ivory Coast, Madagascar, and the former Yugoslavia. It is a real dilemma for despots: If they open up the political space, they will be tossed out in an election. If they refuse, they will be consumed by the flames of the ensuing revolution. It is a no-win situation for the despot.

China currently faces this dilemma. Its economic liberalization program has been widely successful, transforming China into a great economic power. But the program has also produced Rolls Royce communists and vulture capitalists—like the oligarchs in Russia. According to a report released by China's central bank in June 2011, "Thousands of corrupt Chinese government officials have stolen more than $120bn (£74bn) and fled overseas, mainly to the US . . . Between 16,000 and 18,000 officials and employees of state-owned companies left China with the funds from the mid-1990s up until 2008."[42] The officials used offshore bank accounts to smuggle the funds into the United States, Australia, Canada, and Holland.

Already, demands for intellectual and political freedom are getting louder. If the Communist Party adamantly refuses to heed these demands, China may disintegrate like the Soviet Union, with Tibet and the far-western provinces breaking away. And all the gains made under economic liberalization will be dissipated. We discuss in greater detail the issue of reform sequence in chapter 8.

CHAPTER 6

STIRRINGS FOR FREEDOM

"The sentence violates the Chinese constitution and international human rights covenants. It cannot bear moral scrutiny and will not pass the test of history. I believe that my work has been just, and that someday China will be a free and democratic country . . . I have long been aware that when an independent intellectual stands up to an autocratic state, step one toward freedom is often a step into prison. Now I am taking that step; and true freedom is that much nearer."

—Liu Xiaobo, 2010 Nobel Peace Laureate, serving an 11-year prison term for "incitement to subvert state power"[1]

"We have seen this story in the churches of Soweto and the theaters of Prague. We know how it ends. We are able to write today, free of fear and full of hope, because our people won our freedom back. In time, Liu and the Chinese people will win their freedom."

—Vaclav Havel, former president of the Czech Republic, and Desmond M. Tutu, archbishop emeritus of Cape Town, both Nobel Laureates[2]

"Lay down your gun, as I hate this very abnormal shedding of blood. The gun in your hand speaks the language of fire and iron"

—Mohammad Reza Shajarian, Iranian poet in the song "Language of Fire"[3]

THE TRIGGER

AS WE SAW IN THE PREVIOUS CHAPTER, public anger and resentment always simmer under the surface during a dictatorship. The government is dysfunctional, and basic social services such as clean water, electricity, and sanitation cannot be delivered. Commodity shortages are pervasive. The economy limps along or even contracts; it cannot provide jobs for the youth. Corruption is rampant. The few who are rich because of their political connections live ostentatiously. The gap between rich and poor grows wide. The so-called revolution the despot instigated was a hoax. Nobody believes him anymore. People are suffering severe economic hardships: lack of jobs, high cost of living, deteriorating economic conditions. Yet the people living under despotic regimes can't complain; they are expected to heap constant praise on the dictator. It is an affront to their intelligence and an insult to their dignity.

People can take this effrontery and deprecation of their dignity for only so long. Already bubbling under the surface, public anger and discontent may suddenly and spontaneously explode into full-blown rage that spills onto the streets. The trigger may be electoral fraud, but oftentimes it has little to do with politics. A hike in the price of some essential commodity after the withdrawal of subsidies, an increase in taxes, a lack of jobs, or social destitution can ignite civil unrest.

In September 2010 in Maputo, Mozambique, a 30 percent hike in the price of bread and other commodities sparked three days of rioting that claimed the lives of 13 people. More than 400 people were arrested as a result. The government subsequently rescinded the price hike and promised to subsidize the price of bread so as to keep it at its original price. It also pledged to restore subsidies for electricity and water. However, it is a dead-end street for the cash-strapped government, which will soon find itself unable to pay the subsidies.

Iran faced a similar quandary. Unable to afford the US$100 billion annual subsidies on fuel, water, and foods such as wheat, sugar, rice, and milk, Ahmadinejad's regime contemplated cuts. Fearful that such cuts could trigger price increases, causing further economic hardships in a country already afflicted with high inflation and widespread unemployment, top police officials sprang into action and warned of sinister foreign plots. "The enemy is lying in wait to create problems," said Tehran's police chief, Hossein Sajedinia. "We must not give them opportunities to hurt the revolution."[4] This sentiment was echoed by another senior Tehran police commander, Ismail Ahmadi-Moghaddam: "With economic pressure they intend to push the country toward chaos, riots and insecurity, and want to bring about civil disobedience."[5] Those delusional statements spoke volumes about police chiefs who were clueless about who the real enemies were—misguided government measures.

When the Iranian government placed restrictions on currency exchanges in September 2010, it provoked unrest in currency markets. About the same time, at the Tehran bazaar and in other bazaars around the country, a strike was staged by gold traders in reaction to plans to introduce a 3 percent tax on gold transactions. Bazaar merchants feared the tax would skim profits. Back in July, large parts of the Tehran bazaar had gone on strike for 12 days to protest proposed income-tax increases. As the *Wall Street Journal* reported, "A prominent textile merchant was killed when pro-government paramilitaries raided the bazaar demanding that shopkeepers reopen for business."[6]

The Maputo riots and the Tehran strikes did not have an overt political objective but they did inflict severe political damage. They shattered public confidence in the regime's ability to solve economic problems. Further, the riots and strikes were in open defiance of the regime and could encourage other groups—even those with a political agenda—to mount similar challenges. The brutal crackdown resulting in deaths also worked against the regime, eroding its credibility. It even created rifts among the ruling clerics in Iran and Mozambique.

A note of caution is in order, however. By themselves, street protests and riots are not enough to bring down a dictator or effect regime change. They are necessary, but not sufficient: necessary because all avenues for peaceful change have been blocked by the despot, but not sufficient because they do not always succeed. They may serve as the spark, but an accelerant or a catalyst is needed to finish the job. Street protests may be likened to striking a match, but unless the old wooden shed is doused with gasoline—an accelerant—the match won't raze it to the ground. A smart opposition can capitalize on the venting of public anger on the streets by managing and channeling the energy into effecting regime change. But this effort has to be well thought out and carefully managed and calibrated since street protests or strikes are often spontaneous uprisings over economic rather than political issues. Further, protesters may not necessarily ally themselves with a particular opposition political party and may be focused on their own sectarian interests.

Nonetheless, well-coordinated street protests can succeed in bringing down a despotic regime, as occurred in Tunisia on January 14, 2011, and in Egypt on February 11, 2011, but this can happen only with the aid of an auxiliary agent, such as some key state institution or professional body. The following are critical state institutions that can be helpful in bringing about change:

- The civil service
- The military, police, or security forces
- The judiciary
- The media
- The electoral commission

These institutions play vital roles in governance and constitutional rule that most people overlook. Constitutional rule requires institutional checks and balances. The judiciary ensures that the rule of law is followed by all, including the despot, civilians, and the military. Institutional checks mean that one institution can be used to fight another. For example, if the military—whose purpose is the protection of the people—seizes power, as too often occurs in developing countries, it takes another institution or professional body, not an individual person or party, to fight the military regime successfully. This is important because a military junta can "eliminate" an individual who poses a political threat and ban a political party, but it cannot eliminate an institution or professional body such as the civil service, the judiciary, or the media that is essential for the functioning of society.

For each of these institutions to serve its function, it must be *independent*—meaning free from political interference, intimidation, and corruption. If institutions are independent, they can be powerful allies for the opposition or street protesters. Consider the mass street protests in Egypt in January 2011. The tide turned when, on February 1, the military announced on state television that it would not fire on the street demonstrators. The protesters had won over the institution of the military. Furthermore, the street protesters had the media—in particular, Al Jazeera—on their side. By the time the Mubarak regime shut down Al Jazeera, it was too late.

In the initial stages of the Egyptian revolution, the opposition political leaders were in disarray. The largest opposition group, the Muslim Brotherhood, was ambivalent about joining the street protesters. Subsequently, however, the opposition leaders coalesced around Mohamed ElBaradei, the Nobel Laureate who was selected to negotiate with the Mubarak regime. The vital importance of opposition unity cannot be overemphasized.

For mass street protests to succeed, they must be supported not only by opposition political leaders, but also by important professional bodies such as lawyers, doctors, judges, bankers, teachers, and students. A junta or despotic regime cannot ban and shut down the operations of any of these professions. As we shall see shortly, a strike by well-organized professional bodies can oust a despotic regime.

Since 1970, there have been more than 20 popular revolutions in the world; some succeeded in ousting a dictator, others did not. Nearly all the "successful" revolutions received sympathy or aid from some key state institution or some professional body. Below, we provide a list of these "successful" revolutions and analyze why they succeeded. In all cases, the villains were despotic regimes—both military and civilian— and there was increasing public discontent over economic hardship (rising cost of living and unemployment) and deteriorating social conditions (rising crime and non-delivery of basic social services), as well as anger over repression—lack of political freedom and civil liberties.

SUCCESSFUL REVOLUTIONS

These are the successful revolutions that toppled dictators:

1. Professional bodies' strike in Ghana, 1978
2. Professional bodies' strike in Sudan, April 1985
3. People Power Revolution (EDSA I or Yellow Revolution) in the Philippines, February 1986
4. Singing Revolution in Estonia, Latvia, and Lithuania, 1988–1990
5. Velvet Revolution in the Czech Republic, November 1989
6. Africa's village revolutions, 1991–1994
7. Student protests in Indonesia, May 1998
8. The Kume Preko Revolution in Ghana, 1995–2000
9. Rose Revolution in Georgia, November 2003
10. Orange Revolution in Ukraine, November 2004
11. Tulip Revolution in Kyrgyzstan, 2005
12. Black Revolution in Pakistan, March 2007–August 2008
13. The Bouazizi or Jasmine Revolution in Tunisia, January 2011
14. Egyptian revolution, January–February 2011

Three revolutions on this list require further elaboration.

The Kume Preko Revolution in Ghana (1995–2000)

On December 31, 1981, when Fte./Lte. Jerry John Rawlings seized power in a military coup in Ghana, it was the second time he had burst onto the political scene; the first was in June 1979. Back then, he cleaned up, held democratic elections in which he did not participate, and then returned to the military barracks after a mere three months in office. He was tumultuously hailed as a national hero. An adoring public nicknamed him "J.J.—Junior Jesus." But when he returned again in 1981, I was not so sure of his "sainthood."[7] An avowed Marxist revolutionary, Rawlings proceeded to establish the most brutal, the most cruel, the most barbarous, and the most economically ruinous administration in Ghana's history. Even though my own sister, Sherry, was part of his government, I fought that military junta relentlessly, tooth and nail—on principle. Though Rawlings's Provisional National Defense Council (PNDC) bore the hallmarks of a brutal military junta, it earned a unique distinction for the depths of depravity and barbarity into which it sank. Amnesty International estimated that, between 1981 and 1992, over 200 Ghanaians "disappeared." The regime was infamous for "shit bombing"—dumping human excreta in the offices of newspapers critical of Rawlings's policies.

After the collapse of the former Soviet Union in 1991, the Rawlings regime came under intense pressure from both internal and external sources to reform its abominable political system. Rawlings put in place a coconut commission to write a constitution that was to his liking, and he transformed his PNDC into the National Democratic Congress (NDC)—removing the "P" from PNDC. The constitution limited the tenure of the president to two terms, but Rawlings insisted that all those years he had served as president—from 1981 to 1992—did not count because Ghana had not had a constitution then. So he stood for election in 1992 and "won."

We vowed to remove that canker from the Ghanaian political scene. We drew inspiration from the revolutions in Eastern Europe and the winds of change that swept across Africa in the early 1990s, toppling despots in Benin, Cape Verde Islands, and Zambia, among others. The turning point came on December 4, 1994, when police raided the premises of Dr. Charles Wereko-Brobbey and took the broadcasting equipment of Radio Eye. The operators of the "illegal" or pirate radio station, Dr. Wereko-Brobbey and Victor Newmann, decided to present a petition to parliament. They were joined by supporters numbering about 1,000, but the marchers were attacked by government-hired thugs. We cobbled together a team of high-powered lawyers to argue that the closure of Radio Eye was unconstitutional, and we eventually won in court. That victory "forced the government to issue many FM frequencies for other private stations, creating a new era of 'broadcast pluralism.'"[8] It opened the airwaves and paved the way for a proliferation of FM radio stations, which helped toss the regime out of power in the 2000 elections. Note: The broadcasting format the new FM stations adopted was call-in shows, which allowed the people to vent their anger and frustrations. Security officials could not arrest the callers or the hosts of the programs. During this same period, we also waged a ferocious campaign for a free print media. Despite being shit-bombed, the newspapers in Ghana fought gallantly and flourished.

The regime's Achilles heel, however, was the economy. Despite the billions poured into Ghana, economic performance was lackluster. Government expenditures were spiraling out of control owing to the excess spending on security. Hungry for revenue, the regime began taxing anything that moved, imposing user fees on public latrines, hospital visits, and even clean water. The last straw was a value-added tax (VAT) the regime was contemplating imposing in March 1995.

In privately owned newspapers across Ghana, I attacked VAT as a "vampire tax." "Ghanaians are over-taxed," I railed. A group of us, including Dr. Wereko-Brobbey and Victor Newmann, the operators of Radio Eye, mobilized the people to protest the impending tax. The regime was caught off guard and rescinded its decision to introduce VAT—chalk up one victory for the opposition. Emboldened, we organized protest rallies to express our disgust at the regime and demand freedom of expression and political reform.

The first such peaceful demonstration in the streets of Accra, the capital, brought out over 80,000 people on May 12, 1995, and was dubbed "Kume Preko" (You might as well kill me). Indeed, government-hired thugs opened fire on demonstrators, killing four of them. But pro-democracy activists were not deterred. We organized another demonstration at Kumasi, calling it "Sieme Preko" (You might as well bury me). Subsequent street protests followed in other cities; I spoke at a number of them. The momentum was building to a fever pitch. Elections were scheduled for the following year, 1996. Giddy over the success of the Kume Preko demonstrations, we vowed to toss out Rawlings's barbarous military-cum-civilian regime.

We set up a group called Alliance for Change (AFC), composed of 10 individuals. (More details of our strategies are provided in the next chapter.) I set up a correspondent group in the United States called the Committee of Concerned Citizens of Ghana (CCCG) to coordinate with AFC. I set up another group, Ghana Cyberspace Group (GCF), with one Yaw Owusu to mobilize young Ghanaian professionals. Unfortunately, we lost the 1996 elections; the reason had less to do with the evil Rawlings regime than with our own ineffectual strategies and blunders—for example, incessant bickering among the opposition parties. But we did not give up.

We aggressively pushed for the liberation of the airwaves. The country had become extremely polarized, and the first private radio station to emerge following the pioneering battle with Radio Eye was called "PEACE FM." The name was ingeniously deceptive. Who could be against peace at a time of tension? The station played music most of the time, but also had a program to which citizens could call in on their cell phones and vent their grievances and frustrations. Needless to say, that program became extremely popular. Other FM stations appeared—both pro- and anti-government—and their number grew rapidly, making it impossible for the government to control them.

By 2000, Ghana's economy was in a coma. Inflation raged at 60 percent, unemployment hovered around 30 percent, interest rates had reached 50 percent, and the currency had virtually collapsed. Elections were scheduled for December 2000. Rawlings could no longer run, as he had served two terms. His vice president, John Attah-Mills, was to stand on the NDC ticket. His opponent was John A. Kufuor, leader of the New Patriotic Party (NPP) and a personal friend who also served as the opposition alliance presidential candidate. By December 2000, it was clear from all indications that Rawlings's NDC had no intention of relinquishing power and was determined to steal the elections. And even if they lost, they had up their sleeves Plan B, which was to declare a state of emergency and demand a national recount.

Two days before the December 7 elections, explosions rocked Kumasi, the stronghold of the opposition NPP. On election day, government-hired thugs known as "macho men" beat up, intimidated, and prevented opposition supporters from going to the polls. But the FM radio stations kicked in and played a stupendous role in ensuring transparency that had not been seen in an election in recent African history. An army of reporters from local radio stations whizzed around the polling stations asking tough questions of officials and voters, broadcasting every irregularity and peculiarity. Sometimes their broadcasts brought election and security officials scurrying in to head off a potential problem. As *The Economist* put it, "Live radio, it turned out, is a better and cheaper monitor of the honesty of African elections than the local and international observer teams, whose reports will emerge only after the battle has been lost and won."[9] The FM radio stations made it impossible for the NDC to steal the election. Since none of the candidates won more than 50 percent, a run-off was scheduled for December 28. The country was on pins and needles. The NDC regime was getting ready to activate Plan B. Then something happened.

Initial results showed J. A. Kufuor ahead. Without consulting Rawlings, John Attah-Mills called Kufuor to concede defeat and congratulate him: it was too late to activate Plan B. The FM radio stations immediately broadcast the concession speech all over the airwaves. As Thomas Friedman, a columnist for the *New York Times,* pointed out, the four most democratic countries in West Africa today—Benin, Ghana, Mali, and Senegal—all have private, flourishing FM talk radio stations. "Let's stop sending Africa lectures on democracy. Let's instead make all aid, all I.M.F.-World Bank loans, all debt relief conditional on African governments' permitting free FM radio stations. Africans will do the rest," he wrote.[10]

The Bouazizi or Jasmine Revolution in Tunisia (December 17–January 14, 2011)[11]

Tunisia had been ruled by President Zine el-Abidine Ben Ali since 1987. He won all five elections he contested. Though the constitution originally limited the presidency to two terms, he twice amended it in order to stay in office. *The Economist* reported that "His widely loathed wife, Leila Ben Ali, promoted the interests of her Trabelsi clan; the most prominent were her brother, Belhassen Trabelsi, and her son, Muhammad Sakher El Materi, who Ben Ali was grooming to succeed him."[12]

However, lack of jobs and deteriorating social conditions proved to be the regime's downfall. In 2010 only 1 percent of the rural population had access to clean water, and unemployment was 14 percent. When Mohamed Bouazizi, who was trying to earn a living by selling fruits and vegetables, set himself ablaze in the town of Sidi Bouzid on December 17, 2010, after his goods were confiscated by the police, there were outbursts of rage, and demonstrations spread across Tunisia.

The protests reached the capital of Tunis on December 27 with about 1,000 citizens expressing solidarity with the residents of Sidi Bouzid and calling for jobs. That rally, which was called by independent trade union activists, was stopped by security forces, but the protests spread nonetheless. The following day, the Tunisian Federation of Labor Unions held another rally in Gafsa that was also blocked by security forces. At the same time, other groups started to join the protests. About 300 lawyers held a rally near the government's palace in Tunis.

The police broke up a protest in Monastir peacefully, but used force to quell other demonstrations in Sbikha and Chebba. However, the momentum endured, with more protests on December 31 and further demonstrations. The tempo increased, with public gatherings by lawyers in Tunis and other cities rallied by the Tunisian National Lawyers Order. Mokhtar Trifi, president of the Tunisian Human Rights League (LTDH), asserted that lawyers across Tunisia had been "savagely beaten."[13]

The original protests were over jobs, economic malaise, and social despair. However, protesters soon started adding new demands: changes in the government's online censorship, which blocked a lot of media images from being broadcast, and an end to Tunisian authorities' phishing operations which took control of user passwords and thwarted online criticism. Several online activists claimed that their e-mail and Facebook accounts were hacked.[14] More than anything else, though, it was the brutal police crackdown resulting in dozens of deaths that outraged and electrified more people to join the protests. Demonstrators began fighting the police in pitched battles, even torching a police station. Finally, Ben Ali was forced to withdraw the police.

On January 5, Mohamed Bouazizi, who had launched the uprising by setting himself ablaze, died in the hospital, and his funeral in his hometown of Sidi Bouzid became a rallying cry. The next day, the Tunisian Bar Association staged a general strike to protest attacks by security forces on its members. Reports suggested that 95 percent of Tunisia's 8,000 lawyers took part, demanding an end to police brutality against peaceful protesters.[15] The chairman of the national bar association said, "The strike carries a clear message that we do not accept unjustified attacks on lawyers. We want to strongly protest against the

beating of lawyers in the past few days."[16] Teachers also joined the strike
in solidarity. Ben Ali tried to perform the "coconut boogie":

- **One swing forward:** Make concessions and promises of political
  reform, vow not to seek re-election, and offer cash bribes. Ben
  Ali sacked the interior minister, ordered all detainees released,
  promised to create 300,000 jobs, raised salaries for the army,
  and denied that he was planning to install his son-in-law as his
  successor.
- **Three swings back:** Lash out at street demonstrators, accuse
  them of being extremists, mercenaries, and agents of the CIA,
  Mossad, and even Al Qaeda (as Qaddafi would claim); brutally
  clamp down with tanks, jet fighters (as Mubarak would do), and
  live ammunition; and arrest opposition leaders and scores of
  protesters.
- **A jerk to the left:** Pound on a table and jab the air with a
  clenched fist, vowing to die a martyr—showing defiance
  (Qaddafi).
- **Then a tumble:** Make a hard landing on a frozen Swiss bank
  account. (Switzerland froze the accounts of Ben Ali, Mubarak,
  and Qaddafi.)

Ben Ali was laughed off, however, and the protests continued to
spread across the country despite a curfew and brutal crackdown that
left over 50 people dead. A distraught Ben Ali tried to mollify the protesters with a promise of fresh elections to replace him in six months.
No deal. Divisions had already appeared within his own administration
and the security forces. There were signs that the army and the military
sympathized with the protesters. Reuters reported that, "Witnesses in
at least two towns said that police had vanished, while opposition activists had said senior army chiefs were refusing to fire on protesters."[17]

On January 14, Ben Ali imposed a state of emergency and sacked
his government amid violent clashes between protesters and security
forces. Gatherings of more than three people were banned, and he again
promised fresh legislative elections within six months in an attempt to
quell mass unrest. However, it was too late. That night, the army seized
control of Tunisia's main airport and closed the country's airspace.
Though members of his extended family were reportedly arrested, Ben
Ali managed to flee the country. It was reported that he first headed to

France but after being denied entry, changed course to Jeddah, Saudi Arabia.[18] Prime Minister Mohamed Ghannouchi took over briefly as acting president. Ben Ali's official resignation was announced on January 15 on Tunisian state TV, and Ghannouchi handed over power to parliamentary speaker Fouad Mebazaa.

The Bouazizi Revolution, which claimed over 70 lives, had an electrifying effect all over Africa and the Arab world. It inspired street protests against aging autocrats in Algeria, Egypt, Jordan, Sudan, Syria, and Yemen. When it is all over, Arabs should build a giant statue for Mohammed Bouazizi. For far too long, Arab despots have used Islam to repress their people; Bouazizi's action freed them from Arab despotism.

The Egyptian Revolution
(January 25–February 11, 2011)

In Egypt, President Mubarak made the mistake of declaring January 25, 2011, "police day." A celebration of the police who had been brutalizing and terrorizing the people? It was too much to countenance. Drawing inspiration from the ouster of Ben Ali in neighboring Tunisia, a group of young pro-democracy activists—called the Revolutionary Youth Movement—decided to replicate the accomplishments of the Tunisian experiment, and they made Mubarak's "police day" their "day of rage." The established opposition parties in Egypt had been feckless, divided, and constantly feuding, but these new plotters and organizers were from the youth wings of the opposition movements. The following account of their strategy is culled from the February 11 edition of the *Wall Street Journal*.

The protests were begun by a group of about a dozen young people, including representatives from six youth movements connected to opposition political parties, groups advocating labor rights, and the Muslim Brotherhood. "They met daily for two weeks in the cramped living room of the mother of Ziad al-Alimi, a leading youth organizer for Mr. El Baradei's campaign group."[19] They chose 20 protest sites that were usually associated with mosques and were located in densely populated neighborhoods. The idea was that such a large number of scattered sites in different parts of the city would strain security forces and draw larger numbers of people. The group called publicly for protests at those sites but did not make public the twenty-first site they had chosen. There were other organizers as well, including Wael Ghonim, the Google executive. However, the Revolutionary Youth Movement seems to have masterminded the uprising at Tahrir Square.

Three days before the protest, the youth plotters slept away from home, fearing that the police might pick them up in the middle of the night. They also stopped using their cell phones, fearing that they might be monitored, and used phones belonging to relatives and friends instead. Small teams scouted out the secret twenty-first site: the Badaq al-Dakrour neighborhood's Hayiss Sweet Shop. It was in a working-class slum area; the organizers were depending on the participation of ordinary Egyptians, who had no access to the Internet, to make the protest a success. "On January 25, security forces predictably deployed by the thousands at each of the announced demonstration sites."[20] Then four field commanders of the youth group converged on the twenty-first site and mobilized the people to march unchecked by police to Tahrir Square (Liberation Square). The occupation of Liberation Square was a huge victory for the revolution.

A visibly disturbed Mubarak sent his police goons to beat up, tear-gas, and douse the protesters with water cannons. They did not budge. Then he sent in the military: a column of tanks. But, as in the Philippines in 1986, the protesters formed a human chain to block them. Mubarak next sent F-16 fighter jets to buzz the crowd. It did not work. Things began to turn in favor of the protesters when the army chief announced that the Egyptian military would not fire on its citizens. This announcement emboldened the protesters, who carried some of the soldiers high on their shoulders. A desperate Mubarak tried some of his old tricks. He suddenly withdrew the police from the streets and organized thugs on horses and camels to beat up and shoot the demonstrators. Some of the captured thugs were found to be carrying police ID cards. When he shut down the Internet, young Egyptians found alternative ways of communicating.

On January 28, 2011, Mubarak sacked his government and formed a new one. He hastily announced new political reforms, pledged not to seek re-election in September 2011, and denied allegations that he was grooming his son, Gamal, to succeed him. (Ah, the coconut boogie again.) He indicated to Egyptians that he would like to finish his constitutional term and said that if he left, there would be chaos because the Muslim Brotherhood would take over. But his rants were greeted with the chants, "Leave, Leave, Leave!" and "Mubarak, Your Plane Is Ready."

On January 29, 2011, Mubarak appointed a vice president for the first time in 30 years. Threats were made against the street protesters, but yet more people came to Tahrir Square. When it became apparent that the Mubarak regime was playing for time, I sent a message to pro-democracy activists via Twitter, Facebook, and e-mail telling them to ratchet up the pressure by taking control of state television (as in the 2005 Tulip Revolution in Kyrgyzstan); the airport (as in Kyrgyzstan in 2005 and in Bangkok on November 27, 2008); and parliament (as in Hungary in 1956 and Indonesia in 1998). On February 9, protesters pulled a feint: They announced plans to seize state television, which was across Tahrir Square. When security forces deployed heavily to guard it, protesters changed tack and marched to the entrance of the parliament building.

On February 10, in a highly anticipated speech, Mubarak announced that he would not step down and would remain in office until September, when his term would end. The crowd was enraged and vowed to show up at the square in even greater numbers. The military, ever attuned to the demands of the protesters, pushed Mubarak aside; on February 11, he announced that he was stepping down and handing over power to a Supreme Military Council. Tahrir Square exploded in one giant jubilation and celebration. In all, over 300 lives were lost in the violent upheaval.[21]

WHY SOME REVOLUTIONS SUCCEED

A careful study of the courses of these revolutions and this author's own experience reveal that, though the nature and circumstances surrounding despotic regimes may be different, nine main factors or principles can be isolated:

1. The trigger
2. The instigating group
3. The receptivity of the authoritarian regime to democratic change
4. The nature of the despotic regime—military junta or civilian
5. Auxiliary and helpful factors
6. The nature of the opposition strategy
7. The time factor
8. The cultural connection
9. Demonstration effects

The successful revolutions usually began as massive street protests by the youth—often university students—that caught both the government and the established opposition political elite by surprise. The trigger was often steep hikes in taxes or in the prices of basic necessities (Ghana, Poland in 1988, Sudan) or some crude attempt by a despot to perpetuate himself in office, either through a fraudulent election, manipulation of the constitution, or some bald-faced attempt to impose a new political order in which the military dominated: think of Ignatius Kutu Acheampong of Ghana, Gaafar Mohamed el-Nimeiri of Sudan, Ferdinand Marcos of the Philippines, Eduard Shevardnadze of Georgia, Viktor Yanukovych of Ukraine, Pervez Musharraf of Pakistan, and Askar Akayev of Kyrgyzstan.

The receptivity of the authoritarian regime to democratic change also influenced the character and course of the revolution. Where the regime was willing to accept change, the revolutions tended to be nonviolent, peaceful, and of short duration. Such was the case with the former Soviet republics, which formed the Commonwealth of Independent States (CIS), and the color revolutions (with the exceptions of Romania and Yugoslavia, which were more violent and protracted). The former Soviet republics broke away peacefully from the former Soviet Union because the communist apparatchiks had already accepted the need for reform. In 1985, Mikhail Gorbachev had introduced *glasnost* and *perestroika* (restructuring), which resulted in the Singing and Velvet Revolutions. Similarly, Africa's village revolutions were successful and peaceful because the ruling elites had accepted the need to reform their ramshackle political systems, even though there were few street protests.[22] However, where the autocratic regime was recalcitrant or unwilling to accept reform, revolutions turned confrontational and bloody, and street protests were brutally crushed: East Germany (1953), Hungary (1956), Czechoslovakia (1968), China (Tiananmen Square, 1989), Romania (1989), Ghana (1995), Georgia (2003), Ukraine (2004), Kyrgyzstan (2005), Ethiopia (2005), Lebanon (2005), Pakistan (2008), and Zimbabwe (2008) are examples.

Equally important was the nature of the despotic regime. The military variety tends to be more ruthless than its civilian counterpart. This distinction is important because the strategies required to fight a military junta are different from those needed for a civilian regime. Recall that it takes an institution to fight another institution; for example, the civil service, the judiciary, and the media:

- Civil servants went on strike in Ghana in 1978 and 1979 and in Benin in 1989, helping topple military dictators.
- The judiciary went on strike in Pakistan from March 2007 to August 2008, ending Musharraf's military dictatorship.
- The media in the form of FM radio stations became active in Ghana in 2000.

The most potent weapon against any military junta is a civil service strike. Shut down the civil service and any military regime will collapse. There are not enough soldiers to replace the civil servants. A civil service strike paralyzes the government and, as in Ghana and Sudan, can lead to palace coups. But new military rulers then come under intense pressure to return the country to civilian, democratic rule, as happened in Ghana (1979), Niger (1996), Nigeria (1998), Ivory Coast (2000), and Guinea (2009).

Even then, auxiliary factors can be critical when the ruling regime is adamantly resistant to change. Among these helpful factors are the following:

- **Unity of Opposition Forces**
  No single individual, group, or political party can fight an entrenched dictator alone. An alliance of opposition forces is needed to unite against a common enemy. This cannot be emphasized enough. Further, the opposition must be broad-based—not confined to the urban areas or restricted to certain professional, religious, sectarian, or tribal groups. And the message must be very clear: *FREEDOM*. It is not a cause to be monopolized by a sectarian group. In Poland, for example, Solidarity was broad-based with 9 million members. Such was also the case in the successful revolutions discussed above.
- **The Aid of an Auxiliary Institution**
  In the 1980s the Roman Catholic Church played an instrumental role in Poland, thanks to the influence of Pope John Paul II, and in the Philippines, when Cardinal Archbishop of Manila Jaime Sin urged the people to go to the defense of the rebel officers and they responded.

  The media, especially independent bloggers, was crucial in the color revolutions (Czechoslovakia, Georgia, and Ukraine).

In the Philippines the role played by Radio Veritas and Radyo Bandido was widely acclaimed. We have already noted the role played by the FM radio stations in Ghana. In the Philippines, President Francisco Nemenzo stated that, "Without Radio Veritas, it would have been difficult, if not impossible, to mobilize millions of people in a matter of hours." Similarly, an account of the event said that, "Radio Veritas, in fact, was our umbilical cord to whatever else was going on."[23]

The judiciary played its independent and professional role in Georgia in 2003 when the supreme court annulled the first run-off election and ordered a second one that, under intense scrutiny, became more transparent. In Pakistan the judiciary led the frontal assault on Musharraf's military dictatorship in 2007.

Support of professional bodies is crucial. Lawyers, trade unionists, teachers, and others went on strike to support street demonstrators in Ghana (1978), Sudan (1985), and Tunisia (2011). Even bankers joined the protests in Ghana.

- **A Rift among the Ruling Elite**
  The emergence of "rebels" or "reformers" often helped the opposition forces. Noteworthy are Mikhail Gorbachev in the Soviet Union (1985), Cuauhtémoc Cárdenas in Mexico (1987), Goosie Tandoh in Ghana (1996), Abdusallam Abubakr in Nigeria (1998), Viktor Yushchenko in Ukraine (2004), and the National Democratic Party (NDP) in Egypt (2011).

- **A Split in the Security Forces**
  The game was usually over for a despot when his own security forces were split: Philippines (1986), Romania (1989), Nigeria (1998), Georgia (2003), Guinea (2009), and Tunisia (2011). Within the Philippine military and the police, disillusioned junior officers silently conveyed their grievances. "This led to the formation of the Reform the Armed Forces Movement (RAM), Soldier of the Filipino People (SFP), and Young Officers Union (YOU). RAM which was led by graduates of the Philippine Military Academy Class of '71, Lt. Col. Gringo Honasan, Lt. Col. Victor Batac, and Lt. Col. Eduardo Kapunan, found an ally and mentor in the Defense Secretary Juan Ponce Enrile."[24] In Tunisia, senior army chiefs refused to fire on protesters.

- **Neutralized Security Forces**
  In Georgia, the security forces were either neutralized
  or charmed with roses (hence the Rose Revolution). In
  Kyrgyzstan, the security forces were overwhelmed by the
  presence of huge crowds of people, leading large numbers
  of police officers to switch sides. In Tunisia, the military
  sympathized with the street protesters. In Egypt, the riot
  police were outwitted by the youth movement, and the crowd
  at Tahrir Square managed to charm the soldiers, who had been
  sent in a column of tanks to crush them.

The nature of the opposition's tactics also plays a huge role in success or failure. In Egypt, even though they were not initially united, opposition forces executed some brilliant tactical maneuvers and were strategic in their planning. They took over government buildings, police stations, state television, and airports.

Few people have the stomach for an extended protest that entails an extraordinary amount of sacrifice in terms of effort, time, and lost income. Enthusiasm to demonstrate in the streets quickly fades or wanes with the passage of time, which is the opposition forces' worst enemy. The Romanian Revolution lasted 7 days; the Rose Revolution 21 days; the Orange Revolution 34 days; the Tulip Revolution 6 days; the Jasmine Revolution 28 days; and the revolution in Egypt 18 days.

As we shall discuss in the next chapter, the demand for democracy needs to be framed in a way that does not feed into the despot's paranoia. This call must be couched in a cultural medium so as to look "indigenous" or "home grown" and establish a cultural connection. For example,

- In Iran, Mohammad Reza Shajarian used Persian poetry
  to protest the barbaric clampdown on street demonstrators
  following the fraudulent election in June 2009.
- In Africa, the sovereign national conferences gave Africa's
  village revolutions an authentically indigenous character.
  They were modeled after Africa's own cultural and political
  institution—the village meeting. If it takes a village to raise a
  child, so too must it take a village to resolve a political crisis.
  Framed this way, it was impossible for Africa's autocrats to
  dismiss the calls for reform as "Western imperialist plots."

Finally, large-scale demonstrations can have profound effects. Events in Poland and Tunisia inspired pro-democracy activists in neighboring countries.

Yet, evidently, it is not enough to organize mass street protests. In themselves, they are necessary but not sufficient to effect regime change. Many additional factors are necessary.

WHY THE OTHER REVOLUTIONS FAILED

Next, we examine the following unsuccessful or stalled revolutions:

1. Tiananmen Square (China), April 1989
2. Mass Protests in Ethiopia, November 2005
3. Venezuelan Protest, November 2007
4. Monks Protests in Burma, September 2007
5. The Orange Revolution in Kenya, January 2008
6. Street Protests in Zimbabwe, March 2008
7. The Green Revolution in Iran, June 2009
8. The Libyan Revolution, March 2011

This part has been difficult to write but it must be written. In these revolutions, protesters exhibited extraordinary courage and bravery in confronting hideously repressive regimes. They were brutally beaten, tortured, and thrown into jail with severe injuries. Hundreds paid the ultimate price for challenging authoritarian rule. It would be callous and cruel to imply that their sacrifices were in vain. The purpose of this section is not to rub salt in the wounds of those courageous souls. Far from it. Rather, it is intended to be cathartic—a critical appraisal of mistakes made and suggestions for avoiding their repetition and further loss of life next time around. We discuss some of these failed revolutions more critically below.

Tiananmen Square (China), April 1989

This picture will forever remain indelibly etched in human memory. It depicts a lone student protester standing in front of a column of tanks to halt their advance on fellow students. He and his colleagues showed great courage and imagination but they stood little chance. The Tiananmen Square revolution did not succeed for the following reasons:

- The communist regime was not willing to change.
- There was an overwhelming presence of armed security forces that had not been neutralized or split.
- There were no other auxiliary agents at work to aid the students—no free media, independent judiciary, etc.
- The protests were not broad-based; it looked like a "student thing." Though the students enjoyed much public sympathy and support, there were no other civil society groups—such as lawyers and trade union groups—willing to join them.

Mass Protests in Ethiopia, November 2005

The protests erupted after fraudulent elections in May 2005. It took over five months for the results to be declared, provoking the unrest. But the attempt to unseat the despotic regime of Meles Zenawi was unsuccessful for the same reasons that the Tiananmen Square revolt failed.

- The Zenawi regime was not willing to change.
- There was an overwhelming presence of armed security forces that had not been neutralized or split.
- There were no other auxiliary agents at work to aid the students—no free media, independent judiciary, etc. Ethiopia, a country of 80 million people, has only one radio station, and it is controlled by the government.

Protests in Myanmar (Burma), September 2007

In September 2007, Buddhist monks, nuns, and civilians led protest marches against the military junta. Marching peacefully through Rangoon, up to 100,000 people joined monks demanding better living conditions for the people and national reconciliation. The protests were sparked by the government's decision to double the price of fuel in August 2007, a serious hardship in this impoverished nation. The "monks called for the entire country to join them in their campaign to overthrow the government, and the marches spread to at least 25 towns and cities, including Mandalay, Sittwe, and Pakokku."[25]

According to the BBC, when columns of monks, one reportedly stretching for more than one kilometer (0.6 miles), entered the city center, thousands of bystanders cheered and applauded their arrival. Civilians who joined in, some of them weeping, pinned scraps of monks' robes to their clothing. These civilians included officials from the opposition National League for Democracy (NLD) party, led by Aung San Suu Kyi, who had won the Nobel Peace Prize in 1991 and had spent most of the years from 1989 under house arrest. Two well-known actors, comedian Zargana and film star Kyaw Thu, encouraged the Rangoon marchers by going to the golden Shwedagon Pagoda to offer them food and water.[26]

The organization that emerged to lead the protests, the Alliance of All Burmese Buddhist Monks, vowed to continue marches until it had "wiped the military dictatorship from the land."[27] For nearly ten days, the military junta tolerated the monks' protest, but in the end they cracked down hard. Sadly, the protest did not succeed because the military junta was unwilling to accede to reform. Further, the monks were not joined by students, workers, or soldiers. They had no sympathizers in the military. Rather than attempting to go to the home of Aung San Suu Kyi, they should have occupied government buildings and shut down the civil service. Again, it takes an institution to fight a military dictatorship, and the monks did not have an auxiliary institution on their side.

The Green Revolution in Iran, June 2009

The trigger was the fraudulent election Mahmoud Ahmadinejad claimed to have won in June 2009. The election fraud sparked mass street protests that, at one point, exceeded one million demonstrators. But the protests were brutally put down by Basij militiamen on motorcycles. Subsequently, members of opposition parties were jailed, their newspapers and websites were shut down, and opposition rallies were prohibited. Phones were monitored and Internet use disrupted. Some followers of the opposition were beaten and raped, while some died in custody. Estimates of the deaths exceeded one hundred. Ahmadinejad's political rivals, Mir-Hossein Mousavi and Mehdi Karrubi, were not spared in the crackdown. Karrubi was attacked, his car was shot at, and his son was beaten while in temporary detention. Mousavi's nephew was killed. While all this was fodder for revolutionary change, it did not happen.

Perhaps it is necessary to revisit the 1979 Islamic Revolution and the reasons for its success. Among these reasons were the following factors:

- The Shah fled Iran in January 1979, signifying that the battle was already lost and that the opposition had won.
- Security forces were overwhelmed by the sheer number of protesters.
- The opposition was unified: "Khomeini worked to unite the opposition behind him (with the exception of the unwanted 'atheistic Marxists'), focusing on the socio-economic problems of the Shah's regime (corruption and unequal income and development), while avoiding specifics among the general public that might divide the factions—particularly his plan for clerical rule which he believed most Iranians had become prejudiced against as a result of propaganda campaign by Western imperialists."[28]

By contrast, the Green Revolution of 2009 lacked some of these factors. First, the regime had not succumbed and was not willing to accept political reform. Second, the extensive security apparatus, in particular the Basij militia, had not been neutralized or overwhelmed. The militiamen could charge into the street protesters on their motorbikes at will and beat them with impunity. The opposition made no effort whatsoever to protect the street demonstrators. In the Filipino People Power Revolution, the people protected the rebel army officers—just as in the monks' protest in Burma in September 2007 when people formed human barriers on each side of the road to protect the monks and nuns, and walked hand-in-hand with the monks, forming a chain. There was no such protection in the Iranian Green Revolution. At the minimum, the opposition could have:

- blocked access to the routes the protesters were going to use with large trucks and buses.
- encouraged the demonstrators to carry quarts of oil to squirt on the pavement in front of approaching Basij militiamen on motorbikes and then let gravity take care of them.
- had a tightknit row of trucks both in front of and behind the protesters and a convoy of buses alongside the protesters to seal off side streets as they advanced.

Furthermore, the protests lacked strategic planning. Protesters should have seized control of the airport, state television, or parliament. Recall that on March 20, 2005, during the Tulip Revolution, protesters in Kyrgyzstan seized Osh airport and on March 24 took over state television. In Thailand, the Yellow Shirts seized Bangkok airport on November 27, 2008. Other groups of protesters have taken control of parliament, for example, in Hungary in 1956 and in Russia in 1991. Indonesian students occupied parliament on May 12, 1998.

There were many other serious missteps by the Iranian opposition leaders. First, they were unable to capitalize on divisions among the ruling clerics and the hardliners. Ahmadinejad was attacked by members of the parliament, by the judiciary, and even by Supreme Leader Ayatollah Khamenei himself. Despite supporting Ahmadinejad after the 2009 election, Khamenei has frequently challenged the president on topics such as leadership style, policies, and appointments. Ahmadinejad's chief rival, Ali Akbar Rafsanjani, a former president and the head of the influential clerical council, the Assembly of Experts, warned that Iran could become a "dictatorship" if it continued on its current course.[29]

Second, there were divisions within Iran's opposition itself. There were about ten opposition groups with little coordination among them. Even more confusing, there were three groups in the opposition camp with differing ideologies and goals. The first group—Khatami, Mousavi, and Karrubi—sought not regime change but change within the regime. They claimed that Ahmadinejad had abandoned "the true teachings" of Ayatollah Ruhollah Khomeini, who founded the Islamic Republic in 1979. The second group consisted of Khomeinist former officials such as former Deputy Premier Behzad Nabavi and former Foreign Minister Ibrahim Yazdi, who sought to promote the "Turkish model," which would normalize ties with the West while building an Islamic system with the military as ultimate arbiter. The third group sought regime change. Among them were former Deputy Interior Minister Mostafa Tajzadeh, former Majlis member Mohsen Armin, and clerics such as Grand Ayatollahs Hassan Sanei and Asadollah Bayat-Zanjani.

Third, the opposition was not broad-based. It was perceived to be elitist, middle-class, and urban-based. The inability of Mousavi and Karrubi to galvanize support outside the urban middle class and among less educated voters prevented them from expanding the movement.

Fourth, the opposition message was not clear, and was often contradictory. Mousavi once called the Ahmadinejad regime "illegal" and demanded a vote count. Then he reversed himself. Most unfortunate were the oppositions' condemnations of the UN sanctions imposed on account of Iran's nuclear program. Condemning the sanctions put the opposition leaders on the same side as Ahmadinejad. They should have avoided the issue or remained noncommittal, saying only that Iran's nuclear program would be thoroughly reviewed under their leadership. In condemning the sanctions, the opposition leaders lost much international support since nuclear nonproliferation is an issue of concern to all nations, rich and poor—not just to the United States.

Fifth, Facebook and Twitter were a poor choice of means of communicating with opposition supporters. They are too "open," and the government was able to shut them down, which it did. Audio cassette tapes (Ayatollah Khomenei used them in 1979) and DVDs would have been better. Better yet would have been a pirate radio station in Iraq or a neighboring country.

Finally, the time factor worked against the opposition. If, after months of street protests, nothing is accomplished, enthusiasm starts to wane, and it becomes increasingly difficult to rekindle it and galvanize the demonstrators. In the 1979 revolution, strikes began in August 1978 and by February 1979 the monarchy had collapsed—a period of six months.

All was not lost however. If the Green Revolution in Iran did not succeed in June 2009, another will succeed because the current Islamic Republic is a travesty of justice. The spirit of the 1979 revolution that toppled the Shah of Iran has been betrayed. The corrupt monarchical regime of Mohammad Reza Pahlavi was replaced by a corrupt cabal of clerics who are desperately clinging to power through brutal force. History will repeat itself.

The Libyan revolution, which gained momentum in the initial stages, did not succeed on its own because Muammar Qaddafi's security forces were not effectively neutralized; it took an outside intervention with a no-fly zone and air strikes to make a difference. Rebel forces seized Qaddafi's compound on August 24, 2011 after he fled.

SUMMARY AND POSTSCRIPT

There is always low-level anger and resistance to despotic regimes that can explode onto the streets at any time. The trigger can be electoral fraud or an ordinary pocketbook issue such as steep hikes in the price of fuel and basic necessities. Such protests can morph into a demand for democratic change. By themselves, mass street protests are not enough to effect regime change. If the regime is willing to accept political reform, change can be brought about peacefully. This gives truth to the aphorism that dictators unwilling to make peaceful change make violent revolutions inevitable. However, if the regime is stubbornly resistant to reform, the success of revolutionary change will depend upon several factors. Among the important factors is the nature of the regime—military or civilian—as each requires a different strategy. Since the military is an institution, it takes another institution—say, the civil service or the judiciary—to fight a military junta. Other important factors are the help of auxiliary institutions (the media, the church, professional bodies, etc.), the opposition strategy, and the time factor. Time is of the essence, and mass street protests have only a small window of opportunity to achieve their goal. If the street protests drag on for too long, people start losing interest and enthusiasm. In the next chapter, we shall discuss effective opposition strategies; but first a sobering postscript is necessary.

The ideals and gains of a revolution can be betrayed and reversed, which has happened in too many countries. Africa's struggle in the 1960s was a revolutionary phenomenon that overthrew an alien and oppressive colonial rule. But true freedom and prosperity never came to much of Africa. Incoming nationalist leaders retained the old repressive and authoritarian colonial structures and continued with the oppression and exploitation of the African people. Thus, independence came in name only: one set of masters (white colonialists) was replaced by another set (black neocolonialists).

Exactly the same phenomenon occurred in the post-Soviet republics. The collapse of the Soviet Union did not bring much freedom to the post-communist republics, collectively known as the Commonwealth of Independent States (CIS)—hence the color revolutions. But even more disconcerting, the color revolutions did not bring much freedom either—only new faces to run the old Soviet-style nomenclature. In Georgia, Ukraine, and Kyrgyzstan the color or flower revolutions wilted. We will delve into this more in chapter 8.

CHAPTER 7

THE STRATEGY

"We've done a lousy job in government. While Zanu-PF have used the last 21 months to refocus and reinvent themselves, we've lost our identity. Zanu-PF are as brutal and corrupt as before, but much richer. They've got an almost total grip on the Marange diamonds [in the east of the country] and still control the media and security forces. They're much better organized than we are. The polls may still show us in the lead, but almost half the electorate refuse to say how they will vote. There's likely to be massive apathy among MDC supporters. If we went to the polls now, I think we could lose. We've got to start fighting."

—A senior official of the Movement for Democratic
Change (MDC) in Zimbabwe.[1]

OPPOSITION WEAKNESSES

THIS PART OF THE BOOK HAS BEEN DIFFICULT to write because, as we noted earlier, it would be callous and even cruel to suggest that freedom fighters who have been jailed and tortured for their courageous struggle for freedom should have done things differently and, thus, by inference, deserved the punishment or fate they suffered. However, this is not the intention. As we saw in the previous chapter, not all revolutions succeed. Failed revolutions not only cost lives and resources but also set back the march to freedom.

For every force in nature there is a counterforce.[2] A force dominates because a counterforce is either nonexistent or weak. Democracy has suffered a steady decline for the fifth year in a row because the counterforce or the resistance—both domestic and international—has been weak or crumbling. With such weak resistance, tyrants triumph, dominate, and become smug. In too many places, the opposition is hopelessly fragmented, disorganized, and prone to squabbling. The opposition's message of freedom has also become contaminated with religion, ideology, tribalism, secession, and other sectarian issues. (We take up the case of international opposition in chapter 9.) African and Middle Eastern autocrats are masters at outsmarting their quarrelsome opponents and quashing protests. For those of us in the struggle, for corrective steps to be taken critical self-appraisal and review of strategies are necessary. There have been far too many cases where the opposition has blundered and squandered golden opportunities, allowing tyranny to become more entrenched. Here are a few examples.

Ethiopia: There were 92 opposition parties—most of them ethnically based—challenging the despotic regime of Meles Zenawi in the May 2010 election.

Syria: According to *The Economist,* Syrian anger is not only directed at President Bashar Assad and his regime but also at the opposition. Half a year into the uprising that had resulted in over 2,200 dead, Syrian opposition groups have been unable to unite. Conferences upon conferences and statements after statements have not produced a united front. On August 29, a new national council was formed and published a list of 94 members, but many immediately distanced themselves from it (some subsequently agreed to be included).[3]

Uzbekistan: Since 1989, the country has been ruled by President Islam A. Karimov, a former Communist Party boss, who crushes and silences the political opposition. When a presidential election was held in Uzbekistan in 2007, his three opponents each publicly endorsed him! In the 2009 parliamentary elections, all four parties in the race staunchly supported Karimov.

Too often, those who set out to liberate their countries from tyranny end up selling out, fighting among themselves, and sowing confusion and carnage. Some opposition leaders are themselves closet dictators, exhibiting the same tyrannical tendencies they so loudly denounce in the despots they hope to replace. Too often in the past, many such "liberators" transformed themselves—in less than a year—into another bunch of vile despots or "crocodile liberators" far worse than the dictators they replaced.

The opposition movement itself needs to be reformed. In too many countries, the leadership of the established political opposition is wooden, senile, and out of touch with domestic realities. Some have preached the same message for decades without getting any traction. Others have spent decades in exile. Very few can be said to be techno-savvy. Many are not even capable of surfing the Internet and sending text messages and e-mails to the youth. When the established opposition becomes moribund, a third force emerges that shoves it aside. This third force may take the form of a rebel insurgency, in which rebel leaders take "to the bush" after losing faith in the ability of the opposition to effect political change. Or it may take the form of a youth movement to sweep the opposition leaders away, as occurred in Tunisia, Egypt, and elsewhere in the Arab world in January 2011. When the Muslim Brotherhood in Egypt chanted, "Islam is the solution," a youth at the Cairo demonstrations held a placard that read, "Tunisia is the solution." As Sudanese commentator Magdi El Gizouli noted, the January 30, 2011, protesters were "equally frustrated by the inadequacies of the oppositional political parties, a concern that found its expression in the slogan *'shabab la ahzab'* (youth, no [political] parties)."[4]

OPPOSITION UNITY OR ALLIANCE OF DEMOCRATIC FORCES

As we saw in the previous chapter, two key ingredients in a successful nonviolent revolution are the receptivity of the regime to change and opposition unity. No single individual or group by itself can effect political change. It takes a united opposition or an alliance of democratic forces. At any moment in time, resistance to despotic rule comes from several sources—political parties, professional groups, student groups, church groups, business groups, trade union workers, and ordinary citizens—both inside and outside the country. But too often they operate separately or independently. Some advocate democracy, others intellectual freedom, and still others religious freedom. However, their activities are not coordinated. There is no concerted effort, no road map.

The primary focus of all opposition groups should be to remove the despotic regime from power and establish a level political playing field. The despot will never establish a level political or economic playing field. Thus, when a transition process is being drawn up, all energies should be on halting or changing that process. All other issues (such as who should be president, what type of ideology the country should follow, a political platform, whether the country should have a new currency or a new flag) are irrelevant and secondary. These issues are divisive, and nothing delights a tyrant more than a divided opposition.

If the despotic regime is drawing up rules for a transition to democracy, all energies must be focused on ensuring that the rules are indeed fair and just and that the political field is level. An independent electoral commission is imperative for a free and fair election, and all energies must be channeled to ensure that the commission is indeed independent.

This was not the case in Belarus in the December 19, 2010, presidential elections. Long-term dictator Alexander Lukashenko won handily because his government controlled the media, the intelligence agency (called the KGB), security, and police forces. In addition, the head of the Electoral Commission, Lidiya Ermoshina, was in the pocket of Lukashenko. Worse, the opposition was split between nine opposition candidates challenging Lukashenko.[5] They did not stand a chance.

Elders' Council

A great deal of coordination and calculation are required on the part of the opposition in crafting strategies to remove a tyrant through the ballot box. Accordingly, there is an obvious need for some group—say, an elders' council—to coordinate the activities of all opposition groups to achieve focus and impact. In too many countries, opposition and dissident activities are disparate. Democracy activists and dissidents operate separately on an ad hoc basis. There is a need to join forces and prioritize causes. An elders' council is able to make this determination based upon the needs of the situation. Here are examples of such "councils" in the past:

- The Gathering in Sudan in 1985
- The Danube Circle in Hungary in 1988
- The Civic Forum in Czechoslovakia in 1989, led by Václav Havel. It included Prague-based members of the Charter 77 dissident movement.

- Public Against Violence in Slovakia in 1989

The Alliance for Change (AFC), founded in Ghana in 1995, of which this author was a part, comprised ten individuals. Among them were a lawyer, a university professor, a newspaper editor, a radio journalist, an activist, and a female member of parliament. There was no opposition leader in the group. We all signed a covenant:

- All in the group must eschew political ambition
- No one may use any of the group to advance their own personal, political, or sectarian interest
- All must hold the interest of Ghana supreme above all others.

It was necessary to draw up this covenant to allay any suspicions opposition leaders might have had about our group. In fact, in 1995, I held a press conference in Accra, disavowing any political ambition and any interest in the presidency of Ghana or any other African country or any interest in a diplomatic or ministerial appointment.

We decided that the ballot box was to be our main focus and the means to remove the Rawlings dictatorship from power. As such, we channeled all our energies into three areas:

- Opposition alliance, which was required for victory at the polls
- The electoral process: a clean voters' register, the registration of opposition supporters, public rallies, transparent ballot boxes, and voting free of intimidation and violence
- The media—in particular, FM radio stations—to get our message out.

Any such coordinating group must be composed of eminent persons who are capable of commanding respect from all parties and have no axes to grind and no political ambition. They should be able to reach out to all parties—political leaders, civil society group leaders, the media, the youth, and so forth. Their foremost priority should be to forge an alliance of all democratic forces and opposition parties to ensure focus, as well as to ensure that democratic forces are not working at cross purposes.

Political events in Bangladesh, Czechoslovakia, Nicaragua, Poland, and other countries outside Africa have demonstrated eloquently that one person alone seldom succeeds in the battle to remove a tyrant; nor does one political group or organization. It takes a coalition of forces, groups, or organizations. This implies that coordination of pro-democracy activities is mandatory.

In Nicaragua, a coalition of 14 opposition parties called the National Opposition Union (UNO), including ideological mortal enemies (communists and capitalists), succeeded in ousting the Marxist dictatorship of Daniel Ortega in March 1990. The opposition coalition sensibly put forward only one candidate, Violeta Barrios de Chamorro. Had they put forward six or even three candidates, Ortega would have won easily since the opposition vote would have been split.

No matter how despised a tyrant, he always has some support base. There have been too many cases in which despots have "won" elections because the opposition vote was split:

- Kenya: In the December 1997 elections, the opposition parties numbered 26, and they fielded 13 presidential candidates to challenge the incumbent despot, Daniel arap Moi, who won.
- Zambia: In the December 27, 2001, presidential elections, the candidate of the ruling party (MMD), Levy Mwanawasa, won with just 29 percent of the vote. There were 10 opposition candidates.
- Ethiopia: In the May 2010 elections, 92 opposition parties challenged the despotic regime of Meles Zenawi.
- Belarus: In the December 2010 elections, there were nine opposition candidates.

To defeat a tyrant electorally, a coalition of opposition parties must field only one presidential candidate. If a coalition president is chosen, he or she should be restricted to only one term of office. If an interim president is chosen to oversee the transition process, he should be debarred from running in the coming presidential elections.

RULES OF COMBAT

Once a coalition of democratic forces has been cobbled together, the second imperative is to lay down the rules of combat. The first rule is to know the enemy—the type of dictator (civilian or military), how he operates, his strengths and his weakness. Then the opposition devises effective counterstrategies and a means of defeating him. Chapter 4 provided a detailed look at the modus operandi of despotic regimes: they take over and subvert key state institutions (the civil service, the judiciary, the media, the army, etc.) to serve their interest. Obviously, there is a need to wrest control of at least one or two key state institutions from their grip. This is especially important when dealing with military regimes, since it takes an institution to fight a military institution. Furthermore, one does not fight an enemy on the turf on which he is strongest, but where he is weakest.

A military regime thinks tactically. It sets an objective, identifies obstacles that stand in its way, and sets out to obliterate them methodically. Soldiers are not trained to reason with their enemies; they shoot first and ask questions later. They are poor at governance, as that entails compromise and bargaining with a panoply of competing groups. They are also terrible at economic management, believing that economic growth and efficiency are achieved by barking orders, which is why the economy is the first casualty of military rule. Street protests can be effective against a military regime if they exploit its numeric weakness. Thus the opposition s-t-r-e-t-c-h-e-s the military geographically with simultaneous strikes or protests across the country. Tunisian and Egyptian protesters employed this tactic and s-t-r-e-t-c-h-e-d security forces by holding simultaneous protests in several cities and towns.

A civil service strike is similarly effective against any military regime because there are not enough soldiers to replace the striking civil servants. Another Achilles heel of a military regime is the military itself. There are always soldiers with grievances or rebel soldiers within its ranks.

Thus, a smart opposition strategy would be to:

1. Look for some grievances such as the shutdown of a radio station or a newspaper or price increases.
2. Organize simultaneous cross-country strikes or protests.
3. Seek to shut down the civil service.
4. Recruit some other key state institution such as the media or the judiciary.
5. Look for rebel soldiers within the military.
6. Be prepared to change strategies quickly as conditions change.

A despotic civilian regime requires a different set of strategies to fight. It may also think tactically. It sets an objective, identifies obstacles that stand in its way, and sets out to woo, co-opt, or bribe anyone contributing to those obstacles. A civilian despot is more concerned about his image and popularity than is his military counterpart and is therefore extremely sensitive to negative press. Whereas a military regime bans political parties outright, a civilian despot may allow some token opposition parties to exist to give the regime a veneer of democratic legitimacy—as, for example, in Rwanda and Ethiopia. Nonetheless, a civilian regime, like its military counterpart, maintains itself in power by seizing control of key state institutions. Parliament, in particular, is a rubber stamp, dominated by the despot's party, and can repeal constitutional term limits or vote into law any whim of the despot.

An opportunity for reform presents itself when there is a split within the ruling regime. A split within the military in a civilian regime can also be helpful. A smart opposition looks for these splits and forges a strategy accordingly. It may even foment such splits with cultural and patriotic arguments or appeals—not abstract or theoretical ones. Further, the opposition must also be strategic in its planning. After days of street protests, Iranian or Libyan protesters could have seized control of such strategic sites as the airport, state television, or parliament.

The second rule of combat is to avoid collateral damage or civilian casualties. In many of Africa's civil wars, villagers were not only caught in the crossfire but were actually targeted. Strategies must be surgical, impinging only on the regime and its supporters.

INDUCEMENTS TO THE DESPOT

To break down a despot's resistance to change, it may be necessary to reach out and offer some inducements, but this must be done discreetly. On October 14, 1993, Lieutenant-General Raoul Cédras left Haiti for Panama on a US military aircraft with his family and fellow coup leader Brigadier Philippe Biamby. As the *Washington Times* reported, "In exchange for their agreement to leave Haiti peacefully, the U.S. government agreed to grant them access to their money, which had been frozen in U.S. bank accounts. It was estimated that those accounts held about $79 million."[6]

Such "safe passages" or "buyouts" have been tried in Africa. In the 1990s, Nigeria's pro-democracy forces once considered taking a $1 billion loan to buy out or provide the military vagabonds a "safe passage out of the country."[7] This loan would have been added to Nigeria's foreign debt of $35 billion in 1994.

The idea was also floated to deal with several African crises. A buyout could have prevented the implosion of Somalia and Rwanda. According to Wikileaks, Secretary-General Kofi Annan of the United Nations offered Robert Mugabe a lucrative retirement package in an overseas haven if he would stand down as Zimbabwe's president. The extraordinary offer was allegedly made in 2000 at the millennium summit of world leaders in New York.[8] Mugabe's wife, Grace, however, turned down the offer.

The buy-out should not be ruled out as a means of dealing with the dictatorships in Myanmar (Burma), Chad, Sudan, or even Venezuela. However, the buy-out must be offered from a position of strength, not from a weak opposition group, and preferably by an eminent outsider. And if a military junta is being bought out, it must dismantle the entire oppressive military structure.

Alternatively, assurances that there will be no witch-hunts or reprisals taken against the despot and his officials may be considered. Such assurances, however, cannot be given unilaterally by a single opposition leader, but should be the outcome of a sovereign national conference or a stakeholders' conference so that it looks like a collective decision. For example, South Africa's Truth and Reconciliation Commission came out of its Convention for a Democratic South Africa (CODESA) in 1991. Whites who were guilty of apartheid crimes against blacks were forgiven when they confessed and apologized to their victims.

AGGRESSIVE PUSH FOR FREEDOM OF EXPRESSION AND FREE MEDIA

We have belabored the fact that freedom of expression was not invented by the West but has existed in many traditional societies for centuries. It is guaranteed by Article 19 of the UN Universal Declaration of Human Rights of 1948, by Article 9 of the Africa or Banjul Charter of Human and People's Rights, and by the constitutions of many developing countries, including China, Iran, and Zimbabwe. However, freedom of expression is the most important of *all* the human rights—even the so-called developmental rights such as freedom from hunger and disease. How does a starving or sick person communicate his condition if he does not have freedom of expression?

The corollary of free speech is a free media. It is the most powerful weapon against *all* dictatorships. This fact can be recognized by deduction. A dictatorship likes to hide its failures, keeping the people and the world in the dark about its crimes. Free media expose their lies, failures, and incompetence and thereby embarrass them. The exposures also undermine public confidence in their regimes and shatter their credibility. Notice that the media are among the first institutions that a despot grabs and gags. It is no accident that nearly all the grotesque cases of human rights abuses, massive looting of state treasuries, destruction, and state collapse occur under dictatorships in which a free media does not exist to expose the scourge. Get the media out of the hands of corrupt and incompetent dictators. But how? How we did it in Ghana has been related in chapter 6.

The Battle Plan

A good battle plan will include the following elements: creating a strong message, disbanding the military, confronting despots with their own constitutions, circumventing restrictions on freedoms of expression, carefully choosing the opposition media, setting up an opposition militia, and severing the props of the despotic regime.

The Message

The message of freedom must be carefully crafted in such a way that it does not play into the hands of a paranoid despot. Avoid using terms such as "universal values"—paranoid Chinese officials interpret that as a codename for "Western values." For similar reasons, such words as "liberty," "capitalism," or even "democracy" should be avoided. Instead, use equivalents as "freedom," "market economy," and "political choice or freedom." Second, the message of freedom must be clean and unadulterated. It must never be allowed to be contaminated or polluted by religious zealotry, ideology, ethnocentrism, or elitism. For far too long and far too often, the cause of freedom has been hijacked by certain groups to advance their own sectarian agenda. The message of freedom should never be allowed to be mixed up with religion, ethnocentrism, or ideology. The international community cannot defend the human rights of a group whose ideology and beliefs are intolerant of other people's human rights. Moreover, the message "Islam Is the Solution!" is not appropriate to preach in Africa, nor are the messages "Christianity Is the Solution" or "Marxism Is the Solution." Religion is not an issue that will unite Africans. Indeed, when Egyptians poured out into the streets to demand that Mubarak step down in January 2011, the demonstrators chanted, "Tunisia Is the Solution." In fact, organizers of the street protests in Egypt on January 28, 2011, "called on people to come out in force, stressing that *the religion of the protesters was not relevant.*"[9]

The message must be culturally anchored and relevant so that it does not appear to be "borrowed." Using elements of the country's own cultural history or constitution is helpful. For example, Filipino protesters sang "Bayan Ko" (My Homeland), which became a patriotic anthem of the opposition in 1983. The "Song of Estonia" undergirded the Singing Revolution in Estonia, Latvia, and Lithuania in the late 1980s. ("Beautiful Jasmine Flower" is a Chinese folk song that was the theme tune of Beijing's 2008 Olympics. But after Tunisia's Jasmine Revolution, Chinese Communist officials were so jittery that they scrubbed the song off Internet search engines.) African writers can rail against modern-day despotism by drawing upon their own rich cultural history and traditional institutions—telling how despotic tendencies were checked, how bad chiefs and kings were removed from office (examples should be given), and relating stories of indigenous revolutions such as the Yoruba *kirikiri* and the *itwika* of the Gikuyu, mentioned in chapter 3. The despot's name need not be mentioned but the inference is that his rule is "un-African" and therefore illegitimate. This author has employed this tactic frequently.

Second, the message must be purposeful and have an objective. A message that simply insults the president or says "Mugabe Must Go" won't achieve much. A purposeful message is one that

- Portrays the regime as alien or illegitimate,
- Portrays the regime as criminal, breaking its own laws,
- Seeks to weaken the regime's resistance to reform, or
- Creates divisions within the regime or the security forces.

The message should never be about what type of religion, ideology, or president would be best for the country.

Disband the Military

Military rule has been the most invidious and treacherous form of dictatorship. The military is a colonial institution, introduced to suppress the natives' aspirations for freedom. It is an alien institution as most of the natives of the developing world had no standing armies in their traditional systems. In postcolonial Africa, the military has become an insidious scourge on the continent: butchering people, destroying states, and violating human rights. Recall that *all* the failed states in Africa were ruined by military generals. Enough.

On December 1, 1948, President José Figueres Ferrer of Costa Rica abolished the military of Costa Rica after victory in the civil war in that year. In a ceremony in the Cuartel Bellavista, Figueres broke a wall with a mallet, symbolizing the end of Costa Rica's military spirit. In 1949, the military was abolished in Article 12 of the Costa Rican Constitution, and the budget previously dedicated to the military was allocated to security, education, and culture. In 1986, President Oscar Arias Sánchez declared December 1 the Día de la Abolición del Ejército (Military Abolition Day).

Unlike its neighbors, Costa Rica has not endured a civil war since 1948. The country maintains small forces for law enforcement and foreign peacekeeping but has no permanent standing army.

However, instead of leaving disbandment to a presidential decision, there is a better way—a referendum. Ask the people to vote on just three choices:

1. Maintain the military as is,
2. Cut the military in half, or
3. Disband the military altogether.

If the military has served the people well, they will vote to retain it, won't they? So who is afraid of a referendum on the military? Print this message on a tract and distribute it widely in a country ruled by a military junta. To forestall or discourage any future coup leaders, the people need to be prepared. Recall that it takes an institution to fight the military. Accordingly, steps should be taken to deprive a future military junta of the following institutions:

- **The civil service:** Civil servants are required to serve *civilian, not military* governments. Therefore, no civil servant shall serve a military dictatorship; this should be inserted into the civil service code. Any civil servant who violates this code risks losing his or her job.
- **The judiciary:** No judge may swear into office a military coup leader. This should also be enshrined in the bar's code. Any judge who violates this injunction will be decertified.

- **The media:** No media outlet may accomodate, tolerate, or entertain a military despot. Remember that a free media is the most effective antidote against *all* dictatorship.
- **Academia:** No university professor or teacher may support or serve a military dictatorship. Professors who do not understand such elementary concepts as freedom and democracy have no business in a place of higher learning.

And the military itself should enforce its own Military Code, which debars soldiers from political adventurism or intervening in politics or face court-martial.

Hit Them with Their Own Constitutions

Despotic regimes often peddle world-class constitutions that guarantee individual rights, freedom of expression, property rights, and so forth. But they are just for show and are rarely enforced. Consider the following:

China's Constitution

Article 35. Citizens of the People's Republic of China enjoy freedom of speech, of the press, of assembly, of association, of procession and of demonstration.

Article 36. Citizens of the People's Republic of China enjoy freedom of religious belief.

Article 41. Citizens of the People's Republic of China have the right to criticize and make suggestions to any state organ or functionary.[10]

On October 1, 2010, about two dozen Chinese Communist Party elders signed a letter blasting the government's clampdown on free expression. They noted that *freedom of speech and the press are enshrined in China's constitution.* The elders noted that the mismatch between those lofty ideals and the restrictions crudely enforced in practice amounts to a "false democracy" that has become a scandalous mark on the history of world democracy.

Iran's Constitution

With due attention to the essential character of this great movement, the Constitution guarantees the rejection of all forms of intellectual and social tyranny and economic monopoly, and aims at entrusting the destinies of the people to the people themselves in order to break completely with the system of oppression.

(This is in accordance with the Koranic verse, "He removes from them their burdens and the fetters that were upon them" [7:157]).[11]

Zimbabwe's Constitution
Chapter III
The declaration of Rights
13. Protection of right to personal liberty.
20. Protection of freedom of expression.
21. Protection of freedom of assembly and association.
22. Protection of freedom of movement.[12]

All three constitutions guarantee freedom of expression but not the corollary, free media. Many despotic regimes have similar constitutions, so set up a pirate radio station. If the despot shuts it down, get a team of high-powered lawyers to take the case to court. We did it with Radio Eye in Ghana and we *won*, freeing up the airwaves and leading to media pluralism that eventually helped toppled the Rawlings dictatorship.

The African Charter of Human and Peoples' Rights (Banjul Charter) The African (Banjul) Charter on Human and Peoples' Rights was promulgated in Banjul, Gambia, in 1979, adopted on June 27, 1981, and entered into force on October 21, 1986.[13] The charter recognizes many fundamental and widely recognized civil and political rights, including the right to freedom from discrimination (Articles 2 and 18), equality (Article 3), the right to due process concerning arrest and detention (Article 6), the right to a fair trial (Articles 7 and 25), freedom of religion (Article 8), freedom of expression (Article 9), freedom of association (Article 10), freedom of assembly (Article 11), freedom of movement (Article 12), freedom of political participation (Article 13), and the right to property (Article 14). By June 15, 2009, 53 countries had ratified the charter. It was not written by Western imperialists or Martian invaders.

When signatories don't respect their own constitutions and charters, take them to court to force them to do so. This strategy is being employed elsewhere:

- On October 23, 2010, nearly 2,000 people gathered in central Moscow to demand not only the resignation of Prime Minister

Vladimir Putin, but also political reform and freedom of assembly. The Russian opposition protests on the thirty-first day of each month are a nod to the Article 31 of the Russian Constitution, which guarantees the right of assembly.

- On October 15, 2010, hundreds of Tibetan schoolteachers signed and sent a petition to the government of Qinghai Province in western China, demanding that schools preserve the use of the Tibetan language in instruction. The petition demanded that the government abide by the Chinese Constitution, including Article 4: "All ethnic groups have the freedom to use and develop their own spoken and written languages and to preserve or reform their own folkways and customs."[14]

Circumvent Restrictions on Freedom of Expression

Activists should always be looking for some event or strategy that allows them to allude to freedom of expression or allows them to express their views freely without fear. For example:

Celebrate Human Rights Day   October 21 is Africa's Human Rights Day. It is a day when *all* journalists, professors, and writers should seek to publicize Africa's charter. Print it in the newspapers. Article 9 guarantees freedom of expression. It is also a day when African lawyers should file briefs of human rights violations at the African Court on Human and Peoples' Rights in Banjul, Gambia.

Adopt Another Country   One safe strategy this author adopted in fighting the barbarous military regime of Fte./Lte. Jerry Rawlings of Ghana in the 1980s and 1990 was to adopt another African country ruled by a military dictator. There were many at that time: General Samuel Doe of Liberia, General Gnassingbé Eyadéma of Togo, General Sani Abacha of Nigeria, General Mobutu Sese Seko of Zaire, among others. I would target General Abacha—my favorite—and write a scathing commentary. In all those vitriolic critiques, I always included an "African solution" to the problem I was discussing. Then I would have the piece published in both Ghana and Nigeria with the byline: "The author, a native of Ghana, is a Distinguished Economist at American University and president of the Free Africa Foundation, both in Washington, DC, USA."

I am not a Nigerian and had no family members in Nigeria so there was little the Abacha regime could do to me. Further, the articles never mentioned Rawlings by name, but every Ghanaian who read them could see that the Rawlings regime was also committing exactly the same atrocities and iniquities. It might be helpful to apply a similar technique. The following countries may be paired:

Africa
Algeria/Libya
Ethiopia/Eritrea
Burkina Faso/Gambia, Chad/ Sudan—military
Uganda/Rwanda
Mozambique/Tanzania
Equatorial Guinea/Zimbabwe

Asia
Burma/Cambodia/Vietnam
China/North Korea

Eastern Europe
Belarus/Russia

Central Asian Republics
Kazakhstan/Tajikistan
Turkmenistan/Uzbekistan

Middle East
Iran/Syria

Latin America
Cuba/Venezuela

For example, an Ethiopian may adopt Eritrea; a Russian, Belarus and vice versa. Better yet, find a friend in the adopted country, write commentaries on your countries, and swap them, using your name on his and his on yours. Pen names can also be used for similar effects.

Sue Them Elsewhere   The streets are not the only places to fight dictators; they should also be fought in the courts, on the airwaves, and in the economic sphere. Most constitutions guarantee the right to private property, so why should the state seize a private business? Diaspora groups can take action against dictators and their henchmen in foreign countries.

US courts now allow foreign victims of atrocities to sue the perpetrators under the Torture Victim Protection Act and the Alien Tort Claims Act. Ethiopian exiles in the United States have been taking Mengistu's henchmen who fled there to court to claim damages. And perpetrators of Rwandan genocide who fled the country are still being hunted and brought to justice in foreign courts.

On December 17, 2010, the Nigeria-based Court of Justice of the Economic Community of West African States (ECOWAS) ordered the Gambian government to pay Musa Saidykhan damages of US$200,000. Saidykhan was editor in chief of the now-banned private bi-weekly *The Independent*. During a brutal government crackdown in the wake of an alleged coup attempt, he was detained for 22 days without charge by the Gambian National Intelligence Agency (NIA). He said he was tortured during his detention. His lawsuit was filed by the Ghana-based press freedom group Media Foundation of West Africa. In June 2008, the ECOWAS court also ordered The Gambia to release and compensate reporter Chief Ebrima Manneh, who disappeared after his July 2006 arrest by NIA agents.[15]

Use Ridicule: Proverbs, Poetry, Folk Songs A common way of breaking the resistance of despots to reform is through ridicule, which can be accomplished through proverbs, poetry, and folk songs.

Consider the following African proverbs:

- "A snake cannot outrun its head" (the Vais of Sierra Leone). It suggests that some final authority or judge exists. This is used when dealing with pretentious, boastful, and incorrigible braggarts. "Who born dog before monkey" (Cameroon) may also achieve the same effect, but with the suggestion that such braggadocio has been encountered before.
- "He who conceals his disease cannot expect to be cured" (Ethiopia). This might be an appropriate axiom for those despots who seek to hide corruption, human rights violations, starvation, and political repression by imposing censorship and restrictions on freedom of expression and the media.
- "Children of the same mother do not always agree" (Nigeria). So why should citizens of the same country always agree? And what is the point of arresting someone who disagrees with the president?

Mohammad Reza Shajarian, Iran's most famous protest singer, uses poetry to subtly criticize the government.[16] He ends every concert with "Morghe Sahar"—Bird of Dawning. At the end of the song, the bird is asked to sing so that the night of oppression can come to an end and the day of liberation can begin. Another of Shajarian's revolutionary songs is "Language of Fire," which begins, "Lay down your gun, as I hate this very abnormal shedding of blood. The gun in your hand speaks the language of fire and iron." The authorities can't stop him because his songs do not denounce the government—he's just singing the classical poetry of which many Iranians are so proud.

Poetry has also become a revolutionary medium in the bar of the Fardoss Tower Hotel in Damascus, Syria. Bayt al-Qasid, or the House of Poetry, becomes a space for free expression on Monday nights in a country where such spaces are rare. Lukman Derky, the operator, says, "The night is about *freedom*." That may explain why it has survived in full view of a government that has little stomach for dissent.[17]

When Liu Xiaobo, serving an 11-year prison term for subverting state power, was awarded the 2010 Nobel Peace Prize, the Chinese Communist government placed his wife, Liu Xia, under house arrest and forbade anyone to travel to Oslo to receive the medal and the $1.5 million award. The Nobel Committee invited the violinist Lynn Chang, a Chinese American who teaches at the Boston Conservatory, to play at the award ceremony on December 10, 2010. He chose two Chinese folk songs. The first was "Jasmine Flowers," which was composed in the 1700s but has become extremely popular in China. The other piece was a more recent folk song called "Colorful Clouds Chasing the Moon," which uses the metaphor of clouds chasing the moon for someone who is missing their loved one.[18]

Choose the Media

A free media is vital for pro-democracy activity and therefore the establishment of one should be of the highest priority. Various media can be used to transmit the message of freedom: poetry, music, folk songs, proverbs, radio, newspaper, television, recordings (audio cassette and DVD), books, tracts, and the Internet (blogs, Facebook, Twitter). It is important to keep in mind that a despotic regime can always block or shut down a critical media outlet and that the remaining ones are often state controlled. However, rebel radio stations can be set up in a neighboring country, at a secret underground location on land, or on a ship moored offshore. Frequencies can be changed to thwart jamming. Tracts, books, and newspapers can be printed outside the country and smuggled in. Nonetheless, the choice of medium must be determined by the content of the message.

General information that discredits the regime (brutal killings, human rights violations, etc.) can be placed on any medium, as can criticisms of policies and of the direction of the government. Messages intended for supporters need to be protected and must be a bit more discreet as they can be intercepted. Messages detailing electoral or opposition strategy should *never* be texted, published, or posted on Facebook or Twitter. Discreet messages can be sent via cassette audio tapes, DVDs, or fax.

- North Korea's information blockade is crumbling as "DVDs of TV shows and CDs of music from free and prosperous South Korea are smuggled into the country."[19]
- In Zimbabwe, NGOs have been distributing "shortwave radio sets to rural residents to enable them to receive alternative radio programs broadcast from abroad. Studio 7, Radio VOP (Voice of the People), and Shortwave Radio Africa—broadcast from Washington, South Africa, and London, respectively—have about 1 million listeners."[20]

Set Up an Opposition Militia

If the regime operates a militia, such as the Basij in Iran, the Janjaweed in Sudan, the Green Bombers in Zimbabwe, and the Black Mambas in Uganda, opposition forces should also seriously consider setting up their own militias—"Black Cobras," for example. If the regime abducts an opposition leader, the opposition must be prepared to retaliate.

Sever the Props of the Despotic Regime

A despot thinks tactically. He sets out a goal, identifies an obstacle (opposition), and sets out to destroy it. He may infiltrate the opposition parties, planting moles in them, and seek to destroy them from within. Obviously, such moles need to be tracked down and squashed. Or the despot may seek to punish supporters of the opposition. As noted earlier, a despotic regime may be considered to be like a table. One does not climb on to the top of the table to battle the despot there. A smart strategy is to identify the props of the regime and sever them methodically, one at a time, thus isolating the regime, both externally and internally.

External Props External supports for a despotic regime come in a variety of forms: diplomatic recognition, foreign aid, and foreign loans from international agencies, among others. Paul Biya, the dictator of Cameroon who has been in power for almost 29 years, has received a long series of loans—known as "Poverty Reduction Growth Facilities"—from the IMF. Biya's security forces killed 100 demonstrators in 2008 who were protesting food price increases and a constitutional amendment that would extend Biya's rule to 2018. According to Amnesty International, many of the victims were "apparently shot in the head at point-blank range." Economist William Easterly notes that, "Other long-serving aid-receiving autocrats are Idris Deby, Chad, 1990-present ($6 billion in aid), Lansana Conté, Guinea, 1984–2008 ($11 billion), Paul Kagame, Rwanda, 1994-present ($10 billion), and Uganda, Yoweri Museveni, 1986-present ($31 billion), Hun Sen, Cambodia, 1985-present ($10 billion). The autocrats of Kazakhstan, Tajikistan, and Uzbekistan have been in power since the break-up of the Soviet Union in 1991, and each has received $3 billion."[21]

The West has known for decades that it was being duped. It has also known of the billions of aid money being siphoned into Swiss banks by the kleptocrats. Patricia Adams of Probe International, a Toronto-based environmental group, charged that, "in most cases, Western governments knew that substantial portions of their loans, up to 30 percent, says the World Bank, went directly into the pockets of corrupt officials for their personal use."[22]

"Every franc we give impoverished Africa, comes back to France or is smuggled into Switzerland and even Japan" wrote the Paris daily *Le Monde* in March 1990. As the *Wall Street Journal* reported in the case of Indonesia on July 14, 1998, "World Bank officials knew corruption in bank-funded projects was common, but never commissioned any broad reports tracking how much was lost to it—in part, some bank officials said, because they feared having to confront the [Suharto] government."[23]

Those who knowingly dish out loans to criminal, illegal despotic governments should be prepared to take the risk of loss, default, and repudiation. They are at liberty to throw away their money, but they should not expect their victims to pay for their folly. Loans to illegitimate governments constitute illegitimate debt that is not repayable under international law. Any foreign government, institution, or agency—Western, Eastern, Third World, or even African—that extends credit to a military or civilian dictatorship should do so at its own risk. This was the message the main opposition parties in Bangladesh conveyed to donor nations in 1990 when they warned that aid given during the rule of President Hussain Mohammad Ershad would not be paid back. Two weeks later, Ershad's military government collapsed when donors withheld funds.

In November 1991, I conveyed the same message in my testimony before a US House of Representatives committee:

> In the field of international law, a loan to an illegitimate government constitutes illegitimate debt to its people. After 1992, any foreign loan or credit to a military dictatorship or a one-party state in Africa, without authorization of their people, will not be paid back. If foreign governments and agencies wish to throw away their money in Africa, they are at liberty to do so. But they should not expect Africans to pay for that indiscretion.[24]

In February 1993, I repeated this testimony before the US House Foreign Relations Committee and urged that US aid to Africa should be restricted to the 17 countries that were "democratic"—a number that has fallen progressively to 15. My testimony had some effect. In November 1993, the Clinton administration overhauled the US foreign assistance program. Burundi, Guinea, Sierra Leone, Togo, and Zaire were among the African countries declared ineligible to receive US aid because they were not democratic. In addition, "US aid would be cut off to any nation where an elected government was overthrown in a military coup."[25]

It may be considered a small victory, but one individual alone cannot do it; it takes a collective effort. The international law that both this author and Bangladeshi opposition parties tried to apply is called the "odious debt principle"; it is an international legal instrument. Pat Adams argues in her book *Odious Debts* that the "Third World's debts were accumulated without public knowledge and consent, with little benefit to the people. Having paid once with their environment as the loans financed destructive development projects—among them hydro dams flooding rainforests and irrigation schemes destroying farmland—the Third World populace finds odious the proposition that it pays one more."[26]

The United States applied the odious debt doctrine in 1898 when it captured Cuba from Spain and refused to repay Cuba's debts to Spain. Costa Rica applied the doctrine in 1923 when it refused to repay the debt incurred by the former dictator, Federico Tinoco.[27] The principle was also resurrected in South Africa, where billions of dollars had been borrowed by former apartheid regimes to oppress the black majority. The Alternative Information and Development Center (AIDC), a nongovernmental organization based in Cape Town, said South Africans should not shoulder the burden and be penalized for the debts of a system that oppressed them. In June 1997, AIDC launched a campaign against this odious debt. In 1999, the Latin American and Caribbean Jubilee 2000 Coalition described the foreign debt of member nations as "illegitimate because in large measure, it was contracted by dictatorships, governments not elected by the people, as well as by governments which were formally democratic but corrupt. Most of the money was not used to benefit the people who are now being required to pay it back."[28] Activists want legitimate debts to be repaid and illegitimate debts repudiated.

Nobel Laureate, former chief economist of the World Bank, and former chairman of the Council of Economic Advisers Joseph Stiglitz made a persuasive case for the repudiation of much of Iraq's odious debt, which exceeded $60 billion. He wrote:

> Iraq needs a fresh start, and the only real way to give it one would be to free the country from what some call its 'odious debts'—debts incurred by a regime without political legitimacy, from creditors who should have known better, with the monies often spent to oppress the very people who are then asked to repay the debts. Most of Iraq's current debt was incurred by a ruthless and corrupt government long recognized as such.[29]

Again, one person alone can't do this. Opposition forces or a council of grand elders need to take up the initiative. An expert on international law should be employed to craft a legal notice to be placed in newspapers (both local and foreign) with copies to the World Bank, the IMF, the Hague (Permanent Court of International Justice), International Court for Debt Settlement, the London Club and the Paris Club (which are groups of creditor nations), and regional organizations such as the African Union (AU), the Organization of American States (OAS), and the Association of Southeast Asian Nations (ASEAN).[30]

Perhaps the threat of repudiating or renegotiating odious debts would force the World Bank, the IMF, and other foreign creditors to be more careful and discerning in lending money to corrupt and illegitimate despots.

Internal Supports   Despots also survive to wreak mayhem on their people on account of the supports they receive in their own countries. Therefore, severing the external props or stanching the flow of loans and arms from them alone is not sufficient. The internal props also need to be identified and removed. Recall from chapter 4 that a despot's modus operandi is to seize control of key state institutions and subvert them to serve his own interests, not those of the nation or the people. These institutions are the military or security forces, the civil service, the judiciary, the mass media, the trade unions, and academia, among others.

De-politicizing these institutions and instilling professionalism in them is one way of wresting control from a dictator's hands. Independent trade unions, an independent judiciary, the removal of legislative controls on the economy, and a free press can also help sever some of the internal supports that have nourished tyrannical regimes. Each of these institutions has a professional code of conduct: the military code, the civil service code, the bar code, the academic code, etc. For example, the military code bars soldiers from intervening in politics on pain of court-martial. Enforce it. Ask and write about the military's function in society: It is to defend the territorial integrity of the country and to protect the people. If the military won't reform itself, disband it or call for a referendum on the military.

The role of the judiciary is to serve justice and uphold the rule of law. Judges who miscarry justice should be removed from the bench. Insert in the bar code a statement that no judge or justice of the peace shall swear into office any military coup leader. A judge who violates this injunction should be decertified. A similar injunction should be placed in the academic code. University professors who serve under military brutes in government should be disqualified from teaching at places of higher learning.

Most important, all these institutions must practice professional solidarity. If one editor or judge is grabbed, all must go to his aid. When military dictator Pervez Musharraf sacked Chief Justice Iftikhar Muhammad Chaudhry and dissolved the Supreme Court in November 2007, the entire judiciary, bar association presidents across the country, and all leading lawyers and human rights activists rose to the defense of the embattled judges, resulting in a revolution that ousted Musharraf. But when Venezuelan military dictator Hugo Chávez tossed Judge María Lourdes Afiuni into jail for issuing a ruling in December 2009 he did not like, the judiciary and bar association did not go to her defense. Shame on Venezuela's judiciary! Shame on the bar association! Inter-professional solidarity needs to be practiced as well: if a monk or a student is grabbed, professors, editors, and judges must rise to his or her defense.

Then there are the intellectual prostitutes and collaborators, many of whom are highly educated and hold PhDs. A multitude of them have sold off their consciences, their integrity, and their principles to serve the dictates of barbarous regimes. As prostitutes, they have partaken of the plunder, misrule, and repression of their people. They need to be identified, warned, and punished.

ENSURING ELECTORAL VICTORY

To win an election, an opposition party must know the electoral rules and processes. There are many aspects of the electoral process that are designed to ensure that the process is fair, free, and transparent. "Fairness" requires that all parties have equal access to resources and airwaves and the opportunity to deliver their messages. "Free" means that anybody who desires to participate in the election process can do so without fear, intimidation, or obstruction. "Transparency" requires that the entire process be free from fraud—that the voter's register is clean, ballot boxes are not stuffed, votes are not counted in secret, and so forth. An electoral commission should be set up to oversee this process. It should be obvious that such a commission must be independent. Independence requires that opposition appointees or nominees be represented on the commission and that the commissioner be approved by the opposition parties. In short, the following rules must be agreed to *before* an election:

- Opposition supporters must be allowed to register to vote.
- The electoral register shall be up-to-date and clean and contain no ghost entries, names of dead people, fictitious names, etc.
- The electoral commissioner shall be independent.

- Political parties shall have equal access to the state media and be free to campaign.
- Ballot papers shall arrive at the polling stations on time.
- There shall be no heavy security forces or militiamen at the polling stations.
- There shall be no campaigning at the polling stations.
- No legal voter shall be prevented from voting.
- Ballot boxes shall be transparent to ensure that they are not stuffed before voting.
- Ballot counting shall be done at each polling station in the presence of representatives of all political parties.
- The results shall be sent to the central tally station and posted at each polling station.
- Overall national results shall be announced within a reasonable amount of time.
- An independent and impartial court shall exist to adjudicate electoral disputes.

All opposition party leaders must be asked by the media whether or not they agree to the rules. If they object to the rules, then they should not take part in the elections, as participation implies acceptance. There is no point in taking part in an election and then later claiming that the rules were unfair.

It must be remembered that it takes an alliance or a coalition of opposition parties to oust an entrenched despot from power; no single individual or party can do it. If an alliance is put together, the alliance presidential candidate should not be the leader of any of the constituent parties and, if he wins the election, must be made to serve only one term in office. If the rules are unfair and the playing fields not level, *all* opposition parties must boycott the elections. A situation in which some decide to participate while others choose to boycott must be avoided. Uncertainty helps the despot and impedes the cause for freedom.

At least six months before an election, certain targets should be identified and "softened." If he is going to steal an election, the despot needs to have the electoral commissioner in his pocket. If he is going to crush street protests, he needs the police and/or the army chief to put them down. Thus, the key officers the despot needs are, in order of importance, the electoral commissioner, the police chief, the army chief, the chief justice, the minister of (dis)information, and the head of the civil service. The opposition alliance should demand that each of these officers be replaced before an election. Amass 10,000 protesters to occupy the electoral commission and demand that the commissioner be replaced because his impartiality is in doubt.[31] Next, work on the police chief, and so on. These actions may not by themselves win the support of auxiliary institutions, but they will put these institutions on notice that their activities are being watched and thus prompt them to act more professionally.

It is clear that action is required on many fronts to defeat a despot; one individual or party alone cannot do this. There is a need for a body, which I have called the elders' council, to coordinate all these activities and to ensure that opposition parties do not work at cross purposes. It is always important for the opposition to be imaginative. What has been enunciated here are general principles; specific strategies must be crafted to fit different situations in different countries.

CHAPTER 8

REVERSALS IN REVOLUTIONS— *AND HOW TO AVOID THEM*

"If China is to advance in harmony with other countries and become a key partner in upholding the values of the world community, it must first grant freedom of expression to all its citizens."

—Thorbjørn Jagland, chairman of the Norwegian Nobel Committee, explaining why the 2010 Nobel Peace Prize was awarded to Chinese dissident Liu Xiaobo, who is serving an 11-year jail sentence[1]

THE ROAD TO FREEDOM AND PROSPERITY is a long journey. It took the United States at least a century and a half, from colonization to the Declaration of Independence. Toppling a despot does not necessarily mean the end of tyranny. In many African countries, a colonial autocrat was replaced by a neocolonial despot, which sparked a second liberation movement, led by military soldiers and rebel movements, in the 1960s and 1970s. But the so-called military saviors and rebel leaders turned out to be far worse than the despots they had ousted—a frequent occurrence in the 1980s and into the twenty-first century. Again, as Africans like to say: "We struggle very hard to remove one cockroach from power and the next rat comes to do the same thing. Haba! (Darn!)"

As we have seen, the cause of Iran's 1979 revolution was betrayed and even reversed, and the color or flower revolutions in eastern Europe have wilted. In some countries, retrograde authoritarianism has emerged and some autocrats have made a full comeback. In other cases, liberators transformed themselves into incompetent autocrats, dealing in corrupt politics, criminality, and even drug trafficking.

A revolution often contains the seeds of its own destruction. Too often, after a despot has been toppled, revolutionaries begin feuding among themselves—devouring each other—and in many cases allowing the ousted despot to claw his way back to power. A few examples:

Benin: Africa's first "village revolution" (sovereign national conference) stripped Marxist dictator Mathieu Kérékou of power and held elections. Nicephore Soglo was sworn in as president in April 1991. But in 1996 Soglo lost the presidency to Kérékou, the "Chameleon," who held it for another ten years.

Congo-Brazzaville, or Republic of the Congo: In February 1991, a national conference dismantled the 12-year-old government of Marxist General Denis Sassou-Nguesso. With the help of France and Angola, the civilian government of Pascal Lissouba was overthrown in October 1997, and Sassou-Ngueso was sworn in as president. He was "re-elected" in 2002 and 2009 for additional seven-year terms.

Indonesia: After popular student-led street protests, the Suharto regime collapsed in 1998, but it still casts a dark shadow over Jakarta. Golkar, Suharto's own party, is very much in control and up to its old shenanigans. Reform is in retreat. Golkar stalwarts are now contemplating declaring Suharto a "national hero."

Pakistan: Pakistan's military dictator Pervez Musharraf was forced to resign after the Black Revolution of 2007. On September 9, 2008, Asif Ali Zardari, husband of the slain former prime minister Benazir Bhutto, was sworn in as president. But Zardari has since been a stunning disappointment, dogged by corruption and other scandals. In October 2010, Musharraf announced the launch of a new political party, the All Pakistan Muslim League (APML), to take part in the general elections in 2013.

The Philippines: Corazon (Cory) Aquino, the charismatic widow of the assassinated opposition leader Benigno Aquino, led the People Power or EDSA Revolution that drove dictator Ferdinand Marcos from office in 1986. During her turbulent six-year rule, her failure to chasten the revolutionary forces she had unleashed at EDSA led to the EDSA II Revolution (January 2001) and the EDSA III (April 2001), which are often described as "mob rule."

EDSA is an acronym derived from Epifanio de los Santos Avenue, the major thoroughfare connecting the five cities in Metro Manila—Pasay, Makati, Mandaluyong, Quezon City, and Caloocan—where street protesters massed.[2]

Kyrgyzstan: In March 2005, Kurmanbek Bakiyev rode the crest of the Tulip Revolution to oust the country's dictator, President Askar Akayev. But Bakiyev turned into another dictator and was chased out of office in April 2010.

Georgia: Georgia's transition from a former Soviet republic occurred with the Rose Revolution of November 2003, in which Mikheil Saakashvili and his allies ousted Eduard Shevardnadze. However, when Saakashvili faced the possibility of losing power in November 2007, he sent riot police to crack down on a demonstration and vandalize a television station.[3] Several of his former allies turned against him.

Russia: The introduction of *glasnost* and *perestroika* by Mikhail Gorbachev in 1985 and the subsequent collapse of the former Soviet Union in 1991 did not bring democracy to Russia. It enjoyed a brief fillip under Boris Yeltsin in the 1990s. However, the ascendancy of Vladimir Putin, a former KGB officer, in 1999 saw a retreat of democracy and the rise of retrograde authoritarianism, which has transformed Russia into a "mafia state." Gorbachev, who once supported Putin, turned against him. In an interview with the *New York Times,* he said that Putin's leadership had "undermined Russia's fledgling democracy by stifling the opposition forces." Gorbachev even called Putin's governing party, United Russia, "a bad copy of the Soviet Communist Party."[4] He said that party officials were concerned entirely with clinging to power and did not want Russians to take part in civic life. In February 2011, he said he was "ashamed" of the way Russia is run today and warned that "the Kremlin could face an Egypt-style uprising." He denounced Russia's ruling class as "rich and dissolute" and lambasted the Kremlin for "eroding the free media and elections" that he introduced in the 1980s.[5]

Ukraine: In late 2004, Viktor Yushchenko and Yulia Timoshenko led the popular Orange Revolution against a rigged presidential election. Yushchenko duly beat Viktor Yanukovych in a new election and took office in January 2005, serving until 2010. Timoshenko, who had served as prime minister from December 2007 to

March 2010, also ran for president in 2010, but Yanukovych was declared the winner, making a full return to power after having been ousted in the Orange Revolution six years earlier.

Nicaragua: In July 1979, Daniel Ortega, a leader in the Sandinista National Liberation Front (SNLF), led a popular rebellion that resulted in the overthrow and exile of dictator Anastasio Somoza Debayle. In the 1990 presidential election, Ortega was defeated by a 14-party anti-Sandinista alliance led by Violeta Barrios de Chamorro, but he won the 2006 presidential election and returned to power.

WHAT WENT WRONG?

Given how often revolutions turn sour, some might say: "Why bother? Let the dictators stay. The devil you know is better than the devil you don't know." Are some states perpetually doomed to invidious cycles of revolutions and reversals? What goes wrong *after* a revolutionary change?

Inexperience, Impatience, and Charged Emotions

It is frequently argued that revolutionary heroes and cadres, having spent years or decades "in the bush," often lack experience in governing and are ill-prepared when power is suddenly thrust upon them. There is some merit in this argument, as there is a vast difference between the skills needed to fight tyrannical regimes and the forces of colonialism on the one hand and those needed to run a government efficiently and develop an economy successfully on the other. Battling the forces of colonialism and tyranny requires agitation, strikes, boycotts, highly charged emotional rhetoric, and unrelenting activism to call world attention to arrant injustices. To govern or run an economy, skills such as institutional knowledge, administrative skills, patience, diligence, and a willingness to compromise are needed.

Many of Africa's liberation heroes in the 1960s lacked the necessary administrative skills and should have retired after winning independence. But they stayed on and, in country after country, drove their economies into a sump. The case of Kwame Nkrumah of Ghana, who won independence for Ghana in 1957, was perhaps the most sorrowful. Nkrumah did not retire after his victory, and he enjoyed much influence in Africa. He proceeded to establish a one-party socialist state and outlawed opposition parties. Tragically for Africa, one country after another followed in his footsteps: Guinea, Mali, Congo-Brazzaville (Republic of the Congo), Tanzania, Zambia, and a host of others. Predictably, in each country, tyranny followed, economies were ruined, and the nationalists were ousted by the military. But the soldiers who ousted them were even worse.

If we fast forward to the 1990s, a case can be made that Lech Walesa of Poland and the leaders of the color or flower revolutions should have retired after the cataclysmic events. But then it would have been a tall order, as these leaders basked in public adulation after ousting tyrannical regimes.

A Changed Political Dynamic and Culture

A successful revolution becomes indelibly etched in memory. The dictator is on the run amid public jubilation. Passions are running high and expectations that the revolution will produce immediate benefits, results, or change in people's lives are at stratospheric levels. Such expectations are impossible to satisfy.

Quite often, the country is broke because the dictator and his henchmen looted the treasury. In addition, the country is saddled with a mountain of foreign debt. Resources must be found, but the public is in no mood for tax increases or belt tightening. It wants improved social services—long denied them by the ousted dictator—and it wants them *now!* If the people's demands and expectations are not met—and quickly—they will resort to the same tactics (street protests) used to oust the dictator. Witness Egypt and Tunisia.

Early Mistakes

Mistakes are bound to be made in the initial stages after the despot has been ousted. With passions running high, decisions must be taken quickly and on the fly. Gorbachev acknowledged that, "Our main mistake was acting too late to reform the Communist Party. The party had initiated *perestroika,* but it soon became a hindrance to our moving forward. The party's top bureaucracy organized the attempted coup in August 1991, which scuttled the reforms."[6] This view is corroborated by the former Soviet dissident Andrei Sakharov, who claimed that democratic reform in Russia stalled because "the reformers didn't try hard enough to institutionalize post-communist changes. All the *no-menklatura* [the ruling elite of the Soviet Union] remained in power."[7] Fast forward to 2011 and the Tunisians found themselves about to repeat this mistake.

After the ouster of dictator Zine el-Abedine Ben Ali on January 14, an interim government was cobbled together that consisted of many of the old guard. Ben Ali's RCD party was not reformed. Most of the powerful *nomenklatura* were retained—the governor of the central bank, the finance minister, the chief justice, the interior minister, and the defense minister, among others. Tunisians rebelled again. There were massive street protests against the make-up of the interim government. Four opposition ministers resigned. Judges went on street protests, demanding that the entire bench be cleaned up. Even the police joined the demonstrators, demanding that the interim government be disbanded. The chant on January 20 was, "We got rid of the dictator, not the dictatorship."

Understanding that profound statement helps explain why things go so wrong in the aftermath of a revolution. Think of a dictatorship as a state vehicle that has been hijacked by a political party, the military, or a single individual. It has been retooled to advance or achieve the vision of the dictator. Tunisia, *The Economist* noted, has a "constitution tailored to bolster Mr. Ben Ali, a sitting parliament packed by the RCD [his party] and institutions such as the police and courts deeply compromised."[8] Getting rid of Ben Ali and leaving the Ali-mobile in place solves nothing.

A simple vehicle is an amalgamation of systems: ignition system, fuel system, electrical system, cooling system, transmission system, suspension system, brake system, as well as other systems. Each system is designed for a specific purpose and must be in good working condition for the vehicle to operate efficiently. When a system breaks down, it must be repaired promptly. Parts designed for one system cannot be used to repair another. Oil, a lubricant, cannot be used as a coolant in the radiator. Periodic maintenance and repair are imperative for the optimal operating efficiency of each system.

However, there are more than 1,000 ways this simple vehicle can be modified and tuned to alter its performance. A bigger or smaller engine size can be installed. Tires, headlights, brakes, transmissions, windows, and so on can be changed. In fact, one can modify and model a vehicle in such a way as to make a "personal statement."

A society operates like a vehicle. Institutions are to society what systems are to a vehicle. Society has such institutions and systems as the military, the police, the political system, the economic system, the educational system, the judicial system, the banking system, the civil service, and the media. Each institution has a specific function to fulfill and should not be crossmatched with different functions.

There are also more than 1,000 ways a simple society can be modified and tuned. A dictatorship is simply a state-mobile that has been hijacked and modified to achieve a certain level of performance by a political party, a religious group, the military, or an individual to achieve a certain objective or vision. This state-mobile has the imprint of the dictator all over it to make a "personal statement."

Getting rid of a Ben Ali or Chávez is only a first step. The Chávez- or Ali-mobile must also be repaired, overhauled, or disassembled. If the vehicle is kaput, just changing the driver won't solve the problem. Arguing over who would be the best driver is even more pointless. The dictatorship must be disassembled. That was the meaning of the Tunisian slogan, "We got rid of the dictator, but not the dictatorship."

Getting rid of the dictatorship is akin to repairing the broken-down vehicle. Its systems have to be repaired—not haphazardly but in sequence. For example, there is no point in installing a new carburetor to improve engine performance when the spark plugs are fouled up, the radiator leaks, and the tires are flat. In a less technical metaphor, it is like putting the cart before the horse. Since the Chávez or Ben Ali state-mobile must be fixed or reformed, it is important to get the *sequence* right. For a dictatorship, the reforms required in many areas may be categorized as the following:

- Intellectual reform: freedom of expression, of the media, of thought
- Political reform: formation of opposition parties, free and fair elections, freedom of assembly
- Constitutional reform: limiting the powers of the executive
- Institutional reform: establishing an independent judiciary, independent media, an independent electoral commission, an independent central bank, an efficient civil service, and neutral and professional armed and security forces
- Economic reform: private enterprise and a market-oriented economy.

The sequence of reform is crucial. The repairs have to be made in an orderly manner. In many countries, this did not happen, which led to reversals of revolutions. The disassembly was fitful, disorganized, out of order or sequence, and readily abandoned. One particular problem area was institutional reform:

- In Russia, the *nomenklatura* remained in power and eventually put their own, Putin, back in power.
- In the Philippines, the military institution was not cleaned up, allowing Marcos loyalists to stage several unsuccessful coups.
- In Indonesia, the Golkar party was not disbanded.

The ideal sequence of reform should start with the intellectual, then the political, constitutional, institutional, and economic. Pushing economic reform before other types of reform is like installing a new carburetor when the spark plugs are fouled up or putting the cart before the horse. Second, as we shall see below, Western-style multiparty democracy can be unsuitable for many developing countries, and it has produced a slew of fake democracies, vampire states, and coconut republics.

THE SEQUENCE

Intellectual Freedom

The necessity for intellectual freedom is derived from the fact that the case for reform must be made by the people themselves. *Reform must come from within.* Internally initiated reform is far more sustainable and enduring than that dictated from the outside by, for example, the World Bank. For the people to come up with their own reform initiatives, they must have the freedom to express their views about the economy and the affairs of the state. Gorbachev started with *glasnost* (openness); Africa needs to start with *blacknost*. If the people are dissatisfied with the affairs of the state, they should be able to say so, throw the rats out of office, and devise a political system that suits their needs and aspirations. With a newly elected political leadership and team in place, the flawed constitution, dysfunctional institutions, and broken economic system can be fixed.

Intellectual freedom is also required for market processes and activity. An efficient market economy requires a free flow of information, a guarantee of property rights, and the rule of law to enforce contracts.

A free flow of information not only enables economic actors in a free market to make sound investment decisions but also facilitates sound economic management. The latter is hardly possible in a viciously repressive environment in which freedom of expression is not tolerated and editors are frequently harassed by a state that doesn't obey its own laws. A free and private press is an effective antidote for corruption and economic mismanagement. Property rights ensure that the government cannot arbitrarily seize what one has toiled to create. The rule of law ensures that if a contract is signed with the government, it can be enforced. To ensure a free flow of information, respect for property rights, and the rule of law requires an independent and free media and an independent judiciary, which hardly exist in many African countries.

Yet, for decades, up until 1990, Western donors, international aid agencies, and multilateral development shied away from advocating for intellectual freedom and political systems, concentrating solely on the economic sphere. They argued that their charters prohibited them from delving into politics. Further, if the developing countries could get their economies right and prosper, a middle class would be created that would agitate for its political rights and, hence, democratic pluralism. This was the track followed by the Western countries themselves and also by the Asian Tigers.

Those who stress the linkage between intellectual freedom and development are from the developing world. Let those who are being helped in the developing countries speak for themselves. Let those who are being oppressed, whose wealth is being looted, whose human rights are being abused, speak for themselves instead of telling them what is good for them.

For far too long, the "we-know-best" mentality has ruled the debate. Remember Ayittey's Law: real reform begins with intellectual freedom. A free media is the corollary of intellectual freedom and the most effective weapon against *all* dictatorships, period.

Political Reform

After the dictator has been chased out of town, the political institutions in the country have to be cleaned up. The ban on political parties has to be lifted and the political space liberalized. The dictator's party, which caused so much economic ruin and social misery, will have to be disbanded. The political structure itself may have to be reformed.

Significant reform can be achieved more readily under a new leader, with political reform and a re-invigorated civil society that enjoys freedom of expression, freedom of assembly, and freedom of movement. But to determine what type of political system or leader is suitable for them, or what type of constitution would be suitable, the people need freedom of expression and a free media. Reform must also come from within. Hence, it is necessary to start with intellectual freedom. Recall that the self-immolation of Mohamed Bouazizi, which started the upheavals in Tunisia and North Africa, was an extreme and ultimate form of freedom of expression.

Constitutional Reform

A new constitution will obviously be needed once political reform has occurred and the rat has been thrown out of office. The new constitution will have to clip the powers of the presidency, the executive, and establish some checks and balances between the legislature and the judiciary. In addition, it will have to restructure the state—from a unitary state to a federal or confederal state in which there is much greater decentralization of power and devolution of authority.

A constitution is a set of laws—usually details a written document—that details and limits a political entity's powers and functions. These rules together make up, i.e., "constitute," what the entity is.[9] The constitution is probably the most serious defect in the state system of a dictatorship because the despot often has his imprints all over it. However, after a revolution, only *partial reform* of the constitution is attempted: reducing the powers of the head of state, his term in office, imposing term limits, enshrining the independence of the legislative, and so on. But this partial reform exercise itself can be debauched. The 1987 Freedom Constitution of the Philippines crafted after the 1986 People's Revolution is 59 pages long with 23,016 words,[10] a constitution that long defeats its purpose of simplicity.

Perhaps it is easier to determine what should *not* be in a constitution:

- It should not be more than 15 pages, maximum.
- It should not be too specific about what is expected of the president.
- It should not define what an "emergency situation" is and what sort of actions the president should take in such an event.

- It should not list and define all basic rights, such as the right to a fair trial or to decent housing.

Duties, rights, and obligations evolve and change with time. For example, *freedom of expression* can be exercised in many ways: through art, music, speech, dance, and so on. A constitution can only guarantee this freedom without necessarily specifying exactly *how* that freedom is exercised. Owing to technological advances, new forms of expression—such as Facebook and Twitter—are constantly emerging.

A constitution should be regarded as a *social contract* between the rulers and the governed—in effect, the people give power to the rulers to perform certain duties and functions. Should the rulers fail to fulfill the obligations of the contract, a breach occurs, and the people can hold the rulers accountable by withdrawing that power through impeachment or the ballot box. In this sense, the people are "sovereign" and their interests supersede those of the rulers. The constitution guarantees the *freedom* of the people. The *more* power given to the state, the *less* freedom the people have. The ultimate purpose of a constitution, then, is to limit the powers of the state (government), not to shower the head of state with more powers, as is the case with constitutions in most developing countries.

The US Constitution is among the shortest. The preamble contains only 52 words, followed by 7 short articles, 10 amendments called the Bill of Rights, added in 1791, and 17 additional amendments, ratified between 1795 and 1992. About 20 percent of the US Constitution stipulates things the federal and state governments *shall not do*. Only 10 percent grants positive powers, but the bulk of it—about 70 percent—seeks to bring the United States and its government under the rule of law. The US Constitution does not even mention "democracy." The Framers believed that the purpose of government was to secure and protect citizens' rights. Thus, the Bill of Rights establishes the rights of the people against infringement by the state or by government. The only claim citizens have on the state is to a trial by jury. The rest of the citizens' rights are protections against infringement by the state. The Framers were also skeptical of "democracy," as they believed it could result in an elected tyranny, or tyranny of the majority, that could infringe upon citizens' rights.[11]

It is not being argued here that developing countries should copy the US Constitution. Every constitution has a cultural and historical imprint because it is drafted in cognizance of the country's own culture and history. The most lugubrious constitution ever crafted was Ghana's 1972 constitution, which was trumpeted as "a blend of the US and French Constitutions." The Framers did not realize that the two constitutions conflict with each other. While in the French Constitution the state guarantees certain rights to its citizens, the US Constitution assumes that its citizens are, in the words of the Declaration of Independence, already "endowed by their Creator with certain unalienable rights" that must be protected against the state. Among these rights are "life, liberty, and the pursuit of happiness" (to quote the Declaration of Independence again).

A developing country may craft a constitution that adopts different founding principles such as justice, equality or fairness, and freedom. For example, a non-discriminatory, proactive equality constitution may consider:

1. All religions equal,
2. All ethnic groups equal,
3. All ideologies equal,
4. All genders equal,
5. All political parties equal,
6. All professions equal,
7. All age groups equal, and
8. All economic classes equal.

A pro-equality state would protect the rights of all these groups and ensure that there is no overt discrimination or persecution of any. Thus, no one can hijack the state to promote the interests of one particular group, class, ideology, or religion.

More importantly, a constitution should specify the structure of the state or the nature of the political entity. It may be recalled from chapter 2 that, politically, a large polity can be organized along three main lines:

1. A unitary system of government, in which decision-making is centralized and all decisions are taken in the capital city—the European model.
2. A federal system of government, in which the constituent states have some powers but the center retains greater powers—the American and Canadian model.

3. A confederate system of government, in which the center is weak and the constituent states have more power than the center—the Swiss model and that of some ancient empires.

Nearly all the developing countries, with diverse ethnic make-up, operate by the unitary system, which was bequeathed to them by the European colonial masters. However, this model is not suitable for them. Tack on a Western-style multiparty democracy, and the result is a dangerous system that is despot-producing and perpetuating and group dominating, as I argued in chapter 2.

In concentrating power and decision-making at the center, the unitary system transforms the state into a pot of gold. This sets the stage for various groups—tribal, religious, political, and professional—to compete to capture power. We noted in chapter 3 that, once captured, this centralized power is used to settle old scores, loot the treasury, squash any opposition, and perpetuate the executive in office. The rights of minority groups will always be trampled in a unitary state system, and groups whose rights have been abused, or who have been excluded from the gravy train or the spoils of power, will either seek to capture power for themselves by starting a rebel insurgency, resulting in a civil war, or will break away (secede).

Now throw in Western-style, multiparty, "winner-takes-all-and-eats-all" democracy, and the rat at the top will *never* lose an election. He will fix the rules of the game and secure 90 percent of the vote *all the time.* The combination of the unitary state and Western-style democracy has made the presidency so lucrative a business enterprise that it has been seized as "family property." Despots loot, grow senile, and then start to groom their sons, their wives, their half-brothers, their uncles—even their cats, dogs, and goats—to succeed them. Several African heads of state are said to be grooming their sons to take over after them: Paul Biya of Cameroon, Idris Deby of Chad, Abdoulaye Wade of Senegal, and Yoweri Museveni of Uganda.

Change the constitutional *term* limit to *stay* limit. One stay at the State House and neither you nor any member of your extended family—nor your pets and goats—can run again for the presidency or vice presidency *permanently.* A re-election for a consecutive second term counts as one stay! That is, no more House of Assad in Syria, Kirchner in Argentina, or Putin in Russia. One stay and that's it—*permanently.*

The number of years a political party holds office should also be limited by the constitution to two decades (or 20 years). The Communist Party has held power for more than 90 years in China and 50 years in Cuba and the CCM for more than 50 years in Tanzania. In Mexico, the PRI held power for more than 70 years.

Minority Groups

The unitary system forces people of different ethnicities and religions into a dangerous unitary straitjacket. A constitution for a developing country must explicitly recognize and seek to protect minority rights against infringement, not just from the government but from other groups as well. Too often we have seen pogroms—Tutsis being slaughtered in Rwanda, blacks being enslaved in Sudan—religions being desecrated—churches being bombed and razed—and cultural heritage being destroyed. This lack of protection has led many minority groups to seek autonomy over their own affairs and to protect their culture or to rebel. The Western form of majority rule does not afford them protection because—unlike systems based upon consensus in which all minority positions are taken into account—the majority rule format allows minority positions to be ignored. But it is a grave mistake to ignore minority rights. In Africa, it takes only a small group of rebels to wreak mayhem.

Western liberal democracy—together with a unitary system of government—is a dangerous model that should not be exported to the developing world, where ethnic rivalries and passions are potent. The combination produces:

1. One-man, one-vote, one-time. Those who win the first time will put in place mechanisms and measures to ensure that they will "win" all subsequent elections. In Afghanistan, Hamid Karzai and his extended family will dominate Afghan politics for decades to come. In Iraq, it will be Ayad Allawi and Nouri al-Maliki.

2. Domination of one ethnic/religious group by another. Nigeria is experimenting with rotation of the presidency between the Muslim north and the Christian south. Southern Sudan voted in a January 10, 2011, referendum to break away from the Muslim north.

3. An illiberal democracy.[12]

4. Results the West may not like, as in Algeria, when the Islamic Salvation Front (FIS) won the parliamentary elections in

1991; in the Palestinian Authority, when Hamas won the parliamentary elections in 2006; or in Afghanistan, when Hamid Karzai blatantly stole the November 2009 election.

In the traditional polities that encompassed different tribes, strong centralized rule was the exception. Confederacies and indirect rule, which gave other groups extensive local autonomy, were the norm. To be sure, kinship cannot be used as a foundation for a modern political state, but there are certain time-tested principles that are still applicable today: decentralization of power, checks and balances, rule of law, confederacies or federations, to mention a few. The modern unitary state systems established in many developing countries lack these features.

Fortunately, action is being taken in some developing countries. In April 2010, Pakistan passed the Eighteenth Amendment to its constitution to "achieve longstanding demands for greater provincial autonomy, and rename the North-West Frontier Province 'Khyber-Pakhtoonkhwa,' in recognition of the ethnic Pashtuns (or Pakhtoons) who make up the majority of the population there."[13] On August 4, 2010, Kenyans voted for a new constitution that will devolve power to the county governments. The counties will be allocated a certain amount in resources, which they will be free to spend as they see fit.

Though these limited attempts at decentralization of power should be applauded, it must be remembered that the unitary system of government is still in place in both Pakistan and Kenya.

The Constitutional Convention

After a despot has been toppled, much work remains to be done, but passions still run hot. To undertake reform methodically, it is probably best to have an interim, caretaker, or transitional administration for a five-year period to allow passions to cool and cooler heads to prevail. Such an interim administration should be composed of technocrats who will serve only one term, with no possibility of standing for election. This enables reforms to be pursued without bias or jostling for political advantage.

Next, constitutional reform needs to be tackled by a constitutional convention. It should have delegates not only from political parties and civil society groups but also from ethnic and religious minority groups to hammer out a new political dispensation as well as a new constitutional configuration toward greater regional autonomy. A good constitution begins by assuming that the state is a "predatory monster" and the head of state is a bandit or crook—not a "messiah" to be worshipped. Recall the Igbo word *ezebuilo*, which means "a king is an enemy." Thus, the constitution serves to protect the people from the king.

The constitutional convention will also have to wrestle with the issue of democracy. It is not just about free and fair elections. Decisions must be made as to whether the Western form (multiparty majority vote), the indigenous form (based on consensus), or a hybrid form will be more suitable.

The Western form:

- Entails campaigning, advertising, influence-peddling, political rallies, and so on. This can be extraordinarily expensive and uniquely favors the corrupt incumbent regime with access— both legal and illicit—to state resources.
- Absorbs resources that a poor country could devote to development.
- Always, always results in allegations of fraud, violent protests, arrests, needless deaths, and chaos.
- Seldom results in changes of regime, as noted above. Dictators do not lose elections, period. In fact, in all of the 2010 multiparty elections in a host of countries (Belarus, Burkina Faso, Burma, Egypt, Ethiopia, Rwanda, Sudan, Tanzania, and Venezuela), not a single despot lost power.
- Can result in a stalemate in which no candidate wins 50 percent of the vote, necessitating an expensive runoff. It may also happen that, in the parliamentary system, a party may not win enough seats to form a government, necessitating a coalition government. The Italian political experience is one of coalition governments that barely hold together for two years in office.

In a decentralized system geared toward consensus, the Muslim Brotherhood would pose less of a threat of the theocracy feared by the West. The Brotherhood's position could not dominate in a consensus model. The circle of negotiation would be wider as well. But in the present unitary state system and Western-style multiparty democracy, a win by the Brotherhood would mean lights out. The issue is not so much who should or should not monopolize power: no one should be able to monopolize power. The real issue is a systemic flaw that allows power to be monopolized. The Western system is a godsend to *anyone* who seeks to monopolize power.

It should be clear that no single individual or party can deliberate on all these issues: the transition period and the nature and sequence of reforms. They must be addressed by a representative body. Consider this alternative: allow members of various political parties and groups to choose their leaders for a national assembly. Then select the president or head of state from these group leaders—a two-stage election process that cuts down on the waste of resources and on fraud.

Loya Jirga in Afghanistan   An example of such an institution is Afghanistan's traditional forum for decision-making, called the *loya jirga*, of which there are two types. The first is called by the people themselves at a time of national crisis to deliberate and decide upon matters of war and peace, the election of an *amir* or king, and the restoration of national sovereignty and national independence. The second type is used when the circumstances and rules of the game compel the ruler or leader to consult people with regard to urgent and important matters, like enactment of fundamental law, ratification and endorsement of treaties reached with outside powers, and defense of territorial integrity and national sovereignty.[14] The *loya jirga* has been part and parcel of Afghanistan's political heritage for centuries:

- **1707:** Mirwais Khan Hotak held three *jirgas* to help the people liberate the western part of Afghanistan from the ruthless Saffavid ruler, Gurgin.
- **1747:** Held at Sher-i-Surkh near Kandahar City, the *jirga* chose Ahmad Khan, later Ahmed Shah Abdali, as king.
- **February 1977:** Mohammad Daoud Khan convened a *jirga* to legitimize his rule, pass a new constitution, elect a new president, get approval for launching his national revolutionary party, and ratify some laws and agreements reached with other countries.[15]

In late 2001, a *loya jirga* was convened under the aegis of the United Nations in the German city of Bonn to map out Afghanistan's future. There were 2,000 delegates, and the chairman was Ismail Qasim Yar. On June 13, 2002, they elected Hamid Karzai as president of the incoming interim government of 18 months; he received 83 percent of the votes cast.

At that Bonn *loya jirga*, the voters had a choice—a list of candidates to choose from. But there was no expensive campaigning or advertising, no vote buying, no allegations of fraud, no violence, no intimidation, and no deaths. The traditional *loya jirga* could not only have served as a constitutional convention but could also have been refined and improved to serve as the basis of a modern government for Afghanistan.

South Africa's 1991 Convention for a Democratic South Africa (CODESA), which was used to dismantle apartheid, could also have served the purpose of providing a foundation for a durable multi-racial form of democratic government. Its 228 delegates were drawn from about 25 political parties and various anti-apartheid groups. The de Klerk government made no effort to control the composition of CODESA. CODESA strove to reach a "working consensus" on an interim constitution and set a date for the March 1994 elections. It established the composition of an interim or transitional government that would rule until the elections were held. More important, CODESA was sovereign. Its decisions were binding on all participants, including the de Klerk government.

Institutional Reform

Institutional reform is another key reform that is often botched after a despot has been ousted. It is attempted piecemeal, haphazardly, and then readily abandoned. Remember that the despot seized control of all key institutions, packed them with his allies, and subverted them to serve his "vision." In fact, most of the problems of developing countries originate from the absence of the following six key institutions:

1. A free and independent media
2. An independent judiciary
3. An independent electoral commission
4. An independent central bank
5. A neutral and professional armed security force
6. An efficient and professional civil service.

The first five institutions are required for a functioning democracy, and all six are critical in ensuring good governance, which the United Nations defines as the process of decision-making and the process by which decisions are implemented (or not implemented).

It has 8 major characteristics: It is participatory, consensus oriented, accountable, transparent, responsive, effective and efficient, equitable and inclusive and follows the rule of law. It assures that corruption is minimized, the views of minorities are taken into account and that the voices of the most vulnerable in society are heard in decision-making. It is also responsive to the present and future needs of society.[16]

Getting It Wrong in Tunisia and Egypt

When the above sequence was not followed, reversals of revolutions have occurred in Africa and elsewhere. In many cases, the transition to democracy was hasty. Further, various types of reform were undertaken haphazardly and out of sequence. This scenario is being played out now in Tunisia and Egypt. Recall that after the ouster of dictator Zine el-Abedine Ben Ali on January 14, 2011, an interim government was set up that consisted of many of the old guard (Ben Ali officials) in top key positions. Although a few changes were made, most of the powerful Ali *nomenklatura* remained. Street protests and resignations by four opposition ministers did not change things. The interim administration was headed by Mohamed Ghannouchi, formerly Ben Ali's prime minister, and tasked with organizing free and fair elections in six to nine months. This setup raised several red flags:

1. Ghannouchi, a Ben Ali stalwart, was not credible; he was forced to resign.
2. A much broader-based group, say a Grand Majlis, was needed to deliberate on constitutional reform and political dispensation for the country. A stakeholders' conference was needed to solicit input from the youth, women, trade unionists, lawyers, and so on. The interim administration, made up of Ben Ali allies, was a poor choice.
3. The six- to nine-month transition period was too short. A new constitution needed to be drafted and put to referendum. Electoral rules needed to be rewritten because they gave Ben Ali's RCD party an entrenched advantage. The RCD had to be disbanded. But doing so without giving sufficient time for other parties to form (six months is too short) would give the established Islamist party, Ennahida, an unfair advantage.

Recall the Tunisian chant, "We got rid of the dictator, not the dictatorship." Getting rid of the dictatorship in Tunisia means disassembling the institutional framework that bolstered Ali's autocratic rule.

Six to nine months is too short a time to accomplish that. The constitution, the judiciary, the police, and other key state institutions all have to be reformed and "dewormed."

In Egypt, a similar scenario emerged. After Hosni Mubarak was ousted, former U.N. official and Nobel Laureate Mohammed ElBaradei suggested a "one-year transition" to free elections. However, before elections take place, he said that Egypt would need a new constitution, to be drawn up by a provisional council that would include members of the military and opposition.[17] Note the sequence in Egypt: street protests (freedom of expression); Mubarak ousted (political change); a one-year transition period for constitutional reform. Again, the one-year transition period suggested by ElBaradei is too short. It may be noted that it took South Africa three years (1991–1994) to organize elections and the United States 13 years from the day of independence (1776) to the day the Constitution was finally ratified (1789).

However, in Egypt, the question was rendered moot by the intervention of the military.

The Supreme Council of the Armed Forces that eased Mubarak aside announced on February 13, 2011, a six-month transition period and then free and fair elections. That transition period was later extended. The same red flags that popped up in Tunisia, popped up in Egypt as well:

1. The Supreme Military Council was the wrong body to craft a new road map for governing Egypt by fiat, without input from political opposition and other groups. This raises questions about how deeply the military understands the democratic process and the demands of modern politics. In many cases in the past where the military has managed a transition to democratic rule, it was a disaster.
2. A much broader-based group, say a Grand Majlis, was needed. The military might have earned the trust of Egyptians by not firing on the street demonstrators, but the military was full of Mubarak henchmen.
3. As in Tunisia, the six- to nine-month transition period was too short. Mubarak's NDP party had to be disbanded and sufficient time given for other parties to form, or else the short time table would give undue advantage to the NDP and the Muslim Brotherhood, the most effectively organized opposition party.

On July 8, 2011, there was a massive demonstration at Tahrir Square—this time against the Supreme Military Council for its slow pace of reform.

Reform in the aftermath of a revolution is a process that must be carefully thought out and executed. The rush to free and fair elections within six months will endanger the gains of the revolution—and even possibly reverse them—in both Tunisia and Egypt.

Economic Reform

Economic reform generally seeks to move an economy from one that is state-controlled to one that is market-driven and relies on the private sector. It entails cutting down the statist interventionist behemoth, removing state controls (price controls and import and export controls), easing restrictions on exchange rates, selling off unprofitable state-owned enterprises, and opening up the economy to foreign investment and free trade, among others. The general idea is to move to a market economy, which is far more productive than a state-controlled economy. China's may be an exception, but it is not sustainable, as we shall see below.

However, a country does not suddenly move from a state-controlled economy to a market economy in one fell swoop. As noted above, a market economy requires a free flow of information, the rule of law, and a regulatory and constitutional framework in order to operate. Just as one does not establish democracy by suddenly holding elections, neither does one establish a market economy by suddenly removing price and currency controls, withdrawing state subsidies, liberalizing trade within a country, and privatizing publicly owned assets on a large scale. Such was the character of Jeffrey Sachs's shock therapy for Poland, the Czech Republic, and Russia in the post-communist era in the early 1990s. Needless to say, it was an abysmal failure. The institutional reforms and legal framework needed to make economic liberalization succeed had not been undertaken.

The most spectacular failure of shock therapy occurred in Russia, where eight individuals, known as the oligarchs, used insider information and their political connections to gobble up state assets at rock-bottom prices, became instant billionaires, and transferred their wealth into offshore accounts.[18] Unlike America's robber barons, the Russian oligarchs—just like Africa's kleptocrats—produced no new wealth and siphoned their profits out of the country. Their activities led Russia to ban offshore accounts in 1994, but it was too late to save the Russian economy and the ruble. Both collapsed in August 1995.

There has been much controversy regarding the shock therapy. It has been argued that it would have worked if it had been implemented gradually, as has been done in China. But this is idle persiflage; the more important issue is the *sequence* in which economic liberalization follows.

To be sure, economic liberalization unleashed impressive rates of economic growth in Africa, Asia (Asian Tigers), and South America. China's impressive and dizzying rates of economic growth are the result of the program of economic reforms called "Socialism with Chinese Characteristics" that were started in December 1978 by reformists within the Communist Party of China (CPC) led by Deng Xiaoping. The goal of the reform was to transform China's impoverished planned economy into a market economy that will generate strong economic growth and increase the well-being of Chinese citizens. The reforms have been spectacularly successful, enabling China to replace Japan as the world's second largest economy in 2010.

However, economic liberalization pushed by a dictator creates problems and becomes less sustainable when introduced out of sequence. Premature economic liberalization leads to imperfect capitalism—crony, oligarchic, or vampire capitalism—because the despot never levels the economic playing field, which favors his cronies and relatives. For example, "Over his 23 years in power, Mr. Ben Ali and his relatives amassed a fortune in banks, telecommunications firms, real-estate companies and other businesses, giving them control over as much as one-third of Tunisia's $44 billion economy, according to anticorruption group Transparency International."[19] They used their political power to squeeze out business rivals and secure lucrative business deals for themselves. It is akin to what economists call "imperfect competition."[20] Alternatively, economic liberalization under authoritarianism does not necessarily ensure economic freedom.

All successful economic liberalization under dictatorships eventually hits a political ceiling, however. This stage is often reached or triggered by a crisis: falling copper prices in the case of Chile, falling cocoa prices in the case of Ivory Coast, the Asian financial crisis in the case of Indonesia, among others. Investors or people who lost money during these crises demanded explanations or accountability. Furthermore, the theory was that, with greater prosperity, people would demand a greater say in how their countries were governed. But in many developing countries, the prosperity enriches only the ruling vampire elites (crony capitalism), leaving the mass of people in poverty. This produces resentment and sparks rioting over increases in food and fuel prices. When the leadership is "enlightened" enough to flee or to open up the political space and address the grievances of the people, economic prosperity continues. Yet, in Africa, the leadership often refuses to open up the political space, leading to an implosion: Ivory Coast, Madagascar, Zaire, Zimbabwe, among others. These countries followed the "Washington consensus" of economic liberalization, free trade, and unrestricted capital flows. Ivory Coast, once described as an "economic miracle," now lies in ruins. In Egypt, "Many of the country's diverse power groups—including the military now running the country, the Muslim Brotherhood, and the young and mostly secular leaders of the Tahrir Square protests—are united by a desire to roll back the economic liberalization and hold its beneficiaries accountable."[21] China finds itself in a similar quandary.

THE SPECIAL CASE OF CHINA

"England did away with censorship in 1695," reads one scathing passage. "France abolished its censorship system in 1881 . . . Our present system of censorship leaves news and book publishing in our country 315 years behind England and 129 years behind France . . . Even the premier of our country does not have freedom of speech or of the press."
—From an October 1, 2010, Open Letter by
23 Communist Party Elders.[22]

China is a country whose reform program is out of sequence. Its economy has been humming at a dizzying growth rate of at least 11 percent, despite the 2008 global financial crisis. Unlike socialist economies such as those in Cuba, Iran, or Venezuela, China's economy is based on an authoritarian state capitalism that delivers rapid growth but stifles political dissent in the name of social stability. It is enriching those with Communist Party connections, but as the Chinese become wealthier, they will demand greater freedom to spend their money and also a greater say in the decision-making process. The first stirring of this freedom occurred in June 1989 at Tiananmen Square.

Those protests were sparked by the death of a pro-democracy, anti-corruption official, Hu Yaobang, whom protesters wanted to mourn.

By the eve of Hu's funeral, 100,000 people had gathered at Tiananmen Square. The Communist authorities brutally crushed the protests, resulting in the deaths of hundreds of civilian protesters. Inevitably, there will be another "Tiananmen Square," and if the Communist authorities resist granting political freedom, China's economic miracle will evaporate and the country could fragment into pieces—just like the former Soviet Union and Indonesia. Indeed, ousted Chinese Prime Minister Zhao Ziyang made nearly the same statement in June 1989 following the brutal crackdown in Tiananmen Square:

> For years, I've been a bold activist in economic reform but cautious in the area of political reform; I used to call myself 'a reformer in economics and a conservative in politics.' But my thinking has changed in recent years. I now feel that political reform has to be a priority, if it is not made a priority, then not only will economic problems get harder to handle, but all sorts of social and political problems will only get worse.[23]

Since then, there has been increasing talk about political reform. As the *New York Times* reported, "Some officials have been calling for an overhaul of the country's political system, saying it is dominated by powerful interest groups that are shutting out innovation and hurting the Chinese people."[24] But the rising tension caused by the growing inequality of wealth and the demolition of people's homes is creating anxiety.

This is akin to the Russian scenario, where those closest to the source of power had an unfair advantage or insider knowledge and used that advantage to amass great wealth. The *Christian Science Monitor* noted that "As many as 10,000 corrupt Chinese officials have fled the country over the past decade, taking as much as $100 billion of public funds with them, according to an estimate by Li Chengyan, head of Peking University's Anticorruption Research Institute."[25] This power set-up will worsen China's inequality unless there is institutional and political reform. In fact, in August 2010, speaking in Shenzhen, the Chinese city that pioneered many economic changes, Prime Minister Wen Jiabao echoed these arguments in a speech carried by the party's flagship *People's Daily*. "Without the guarantee of political system reform, the successes of restructuring the economic system will be lost and the goal of modernization cannot be realized," Wen said.[26]

Premier Wen's speech was quite blunt: China has to resolve the issue of excessive concentration of unrestrained power and create conditions for the people to criticize and supervise the government. *Global Times* quoted a Communist Party academic as "saying that the slow pace of political reform in China was the root cause of growing social conflict."[27] Ironically, even Prime Minister Wen's statements were censored and blocked from publication in the state-owned media by the powerful Propaganda Department.

It may be recalled that Gorbachev faced similar opposition from Communist hardliners to *glasnost* and *perestroika.* The same reactionary forces are at work in China. When Liu Xiaobo was awarded the 2010 Nobel Prize, Communist hardliners reacted in exactly the same way the Soviets did when the nuclear physicist Andrei Sakharov was awarded the 1975 Nobel Prize for Peace. Like Liu, Sakharov professed democratic values that his Communist rulers dismissed as Western mores being forced on the rest of the world. One of Sakharov's most famous writings is the 1968 essay "Progress, Coexistence, and Intellectual Freedom," which circulated widely in *samizdat* form and was considered an existential threat by Soviet leaders. Said journalist Gal Beckerman: "After Sakharov won the prize, the government-controlled newspaper *Literaturnaya Gazeta* denounced the Nobel committee for acting 'blasphemously'—the same language used by the Chinese 35 years later. The newspaper also accused Sakharov of supporting Nazi and fascist causes, and it compared him to a laboratory rat manipulated by anti-Soviet forces in the West. A trade union newspaper, *Trud,* called the award 'political pornography' and Sakharov a 'Judas' whose prize was his '30 pieces of silver.'"[28] Liu, for his part, is currently imprisoned for signing Charter 08, a manifesto demanding political reform and civil liberties.

Nobel Laureates Václav Havel, former president of the Czech Republic, and Desmond M. Tutu, archbishop emeritus of Cape Town, wrote in an op-ed article in the *Washington Post:*

> The Chinese government can continue to fight a losing battle, against the forces of democracy and freedom that its own premier recently called 'irresistible.' Or it can stand on the side of justice, free Liu Xiaobo and immediately end the house arrest imposed on his wife.[29]

A dictatorship, however, is impervious to reason, and it is unlikely that Communist hardliners in China would allow such political reform or freedom. On October 26, 2010, on its front page, *People's Daily* rejected calls for speedier political reform. It argued that changes in China's political system should not mimic Western democracies, but "consolidate the party's leadership so that the party will command the overall situation." The article went on to say that, "The idea that China's political reform is seriously lagging behind its remarkable economic development is not only contrary to the law of objectivity but also to the objective facts . . . In promoting political reform, we shouldn't copy the Western political system model; shouldn't engage in something like multiparty coalition government or separation of powers among the executive, legislative and judicial branches. We should stick to our own way."[30] The opinion article seemed to be an oblique but stiff rebuff of demands for political reform by Premier Wen, Chinese liberal intellectuals, and Communist Party elders.

The debate over political versus economic reform is, in this author's view, misplaced. We have always emphasized starting with intellectual reform, but the Communists in China are terrified of a free media. Thus, the internal resistance to political reform is inevitably setting China on the course of violent revolutionary change and possible disintegration as Tibet and the far western region of Xinjiang could break away.

As scholar Liu Junning noted:

> Real success for China in the 21st century will depend not on the Communist Party itself, but on the establishment of the rule of law, limited government, and further economic liberalization that opens China's market to the world. Fundamental to this is the right to speak freely. China will truly prosper only when individuals such as Liu Xiaobo, Ai Weiwei and the many other Chinese patriots who speak for reform are safe in the knowledge that they can do so without a late-night knock on the door from the government.[31]

This quote reinforces the critical importance and necessity of intellectual freedom—the first step in our ideal sequence of reform, or Ayittey's Law. The current sequence in China is completely out of whack: economic liberalization or reform before any consideration of political, much less intellectual, reform.

CHAPTER 9

INTERNATIONAL IMPOTENCE
AND HINDRANCE

"After the West won the Cold War, democracy flourished in the world as never before. No more. The tide of political and human freedom hasn't merely slowed but in recent years has turned in the other direction."

—Editorial, *Wall Street Journal*[1]

"After enjoying a good run in the 1980s and 1990s, democracy has been playing defense lately. Dictators have grown wise to people power. China, Russia, Iran and Cuba have been more successful exporting and extolling their systems than democracies have been in promoting theirs."

—Fred Hiatt in the *Washington Post*[2]

DESPOTS HAVE PROLIFERATED SINCE THE DEMISE of the former Soviet Union and the end of the Cold War. As Freedom House noted in its 2011 report, global freedom has declined steadily for five years in a row as despots refine their tactics and learn new tricks to beat back the democratic challenge. In chapter 7, we argued that despots have triumphed because the counterforce—the opposition, both local and international—has been weak or crumbling. Domestic opposition groups are often fragmented, lack focus, and bicker constantly. In this chapter, we hand down the same indictment against the international resistance groups. They are a carbon copy of their domestic counterparts: fragmented, divided, lacking focus, and prone to squabbling. Their choice of tactics is akin to that of the Keystone Cops. The West, or the international community, is impotent—in fact, more of a hindrance—in checking this growing menace of despotism.[3] It can't even put lightly armed Somali pirates out of business, let alone well-fortified despots such as Bashar al-Assad. Barely three days after the United Nations authorized a no-fly zone over Libya on March 18, 2011, sparring erupted over who should lead the coalition effort:

> Italian Foreign Minister, Franco Frattini . . . called for command of operations enforcing the no-fly zone to be passed on to NATO, suggesting the use of Italy's seven military bases by coalition forces lacked proper coordination. U.K. Prime Minister David Cameron also said NATO should lead operations. But France, which just rejoined NATO's command structure in 2009 after three decades, indicated that it doesn't want NATO to play a central role.[4]

HOW THE WEST GOT IT WRONG

The moral and intellectual bankruptcy of Western policies were on full display during the upheavals in North Africa. The West was caught completely flat-footed—totally unprepared, a deer in the glare of oncoming headlights. Shards of Western punditry and sophistry littered the streets of Tunis and Cairo. The so-called Western experts went into hiding; all the analyses and all the predictions they had made were now a pile of rubbish. Fox News couldn't even place Egypt on the map on February 28, 2011. (It placed it in the Persian Gulf area.) The United States looked especially pathetic, having squandered its role as the leader of the free world. It dithered over the Tunisian and Egyptian upheavals. Statements by President Barack Obama on the Egyptian crisis made matters worse. Brilliant eloquence on "change" did not jibe with his speech in Cairo in 2009, which was generally regarded as a sop to Arab autocrats. At one point, Hosni Mubarak said Obama did not understand Egyptian culture—as if Mubarak understood Egyptian demands that he step down and that his plane was ready. The United States looked impotent in the face of the monstrous slaughter of Libya's people by Qaddafi's forces. President Obama demanded that Qaddafi step down. When he didn't, the United States looked incapable of backing up its demand, resulting in considerable loss of prestige and clout. As Libyan freedom fighters were being slaughtered, the West debated to death. Eventually, France and the United Kingdom led an aggressive effort to secure from the United Nation a no-fly zone over Libya to protect its people. But it was a little too late for full redemption. If in Libya, then why not in Yemen or Bahrain to protect their people too? The West now has little or no credibility in advancing the cause of liberty in Africa and the Middle East. Sixty years of engagement policy focused on "stability" have been a disaster. The youth in North Africa accomplished within two months what trillions in treasure and blood and sweat could not accomplish in decades.

In the fight for freedom, you either lead, follow, or get the hell out of the way. The West agonized over whom to side with: the pro-democracy activists or its so-called allies. Since Ben Ali was a staunch Western ally in the war against terrorism, Tunisian pro-democracy demonstrators got no help from the West—zilch. In fact, too often in the past, the West initially found itself on the wrong side of many popular revolutions:

- The People Power Revolution (EDSA I or Yellow Revolution) in the Philippines, February 1986
- The village revolutions in Benin, Cape Verde, Zambia, Malawi, and elsewhere, 1990–1994
- The student protests in Indonesia, May 1998
- Ghana's revolution, 1994–2000
- The Tulip Revolution in Kyrgyzstan, 2005
- Mass protests in Ethiopia, November 2005
- The monks' protests in (Myanmar) Burma, September 2007
- The Orange Democratic Movement (ODM) in Kenya, January 2008
- The Black Revolution in Pakistan, March 2007–August 2008
- The Green Revolution in Iran, June 2009
- The Second Tulip Revolution in Kyrgyzstan, April 2010.

Yet, each time a despot is toppled, the West suddenly emerges to claim some credit and make glorious self-congratulatory statements. The most obscene were claims of credit for the Bouazizi or Jasmine Revolution by Wikileaks and Twitter—as if Bouazizi had had a Twitter account. To be sure, the Internet and social media networks facilitated dissemination, but they did not start the revolutions.

The West can't even define a dictator. He is not one if:

- His country has oil or other strategic minerals.
- He has no nuclear ambition.

- He is willing to allow his country to be used as a military base to supply troops in Afghanistan and Iraq.
- He is willing to cooperate on the war on drugs and the war on terrorism.
- He shaves his beard four times a week.

A dictator is a dictator is a dictator. And there is no such thing as a "good" dictator. The only good dictator is a dead one—not whether or not he has oil, is anti-communist, and has no nuclear ambition.

To be sure, there will be never-ending debates about how the West got it so wrong. For starters, the West has long abandoned the push for democracy and human rights. When the Soviet Union collapsed in 1989, jubilation and euphoria rang throughout the Western world. Champagne glasses clicked. Books were written trumpeting the "end of history" and the triumph of "Western liberal democracy." Francis Fukuyama, for example, wrote glowingly:

> What we may be witnessing is not just the end of the Cold War, or the passing of a particular period of post-war history, but the end of history as such: that is, the end point of mankind's ideological evolution and the universalization of Western liberal democracy as the final form of human government.[5]

But what has occurred since then is *not* "universalization" but the *bastardization* of Western liberal democracy. Fareed Zakaria, who coined the term "illiberal democracy," defines liberal democracy as "a political system marked not only by free and fair elections, but also by the rule of law, a separation of powers, and the protection of basic liberties of speech, assembly, religion, and property . . . This may also be referred to as constitutional liberalism—liberal because it emphasizes individual liberty and constitutional because it is rooted in the rule of law—which seeks to protect citizens from the coercive powers of the state. Thus, constitutional liberalism together with free elections is an unalienable part of liberal democracies."[6] Thus, Western liberal democracy requires "free and fair" elections and the rule of law. But, as we argued in chapter 4, free and fair elections are a fiction. Save the pontification because no dictator is going to lose an election. In all of 2010, not a single incumbent despot lost or was willing to lose an election in Belarus, Burma, Burundi, Egypt, Ethiopia, Ivory Coast, Sudan, or Rwanda. Elections were held but not the kind of elections that produce regime or democratic change. The result is an "illiberal democracy." Zakaria writes:

> From Peru to the Philippines, we see the rise of a disturbing phenomenon: illiberal democracy. It has been difficult to recognize because for the last century in the West, democracy—free and fair elections—has gone hand in hand with constitutional liberalism—the rule of law and basic human rights. But in the rest of the world, these two concepts are coming apart. Democracy without constitutional liberalism is producing centralized regimes, the erosion of liberty, ethnic competition, conflict, and war. The international community and the United States must end their obsession with balloting and promote the gradual liberalization of societies.[7]

The West was blindsided by this new phenomenon. The defect in the Western outlook was to equate dictatorship with communism. It then programmed itself to fight only communism. After defeating communism, it assumed it had vanquished dictatorship for good—hence "the end of history." We now know better. As it turned out, the West defeated an *ideological* dictatorship but in the process aided and abetted the evolution of another type—*systemic dictatorship*—dictatorships that emerge from faulty institutions and systems. Any political system that concentrates power in the hands of one person will degenerate into a dictatorship. The culprit is the *system*—not ideology or culture.

The West was blindsided again by the upheavals in North Africa. For decades, it chose "stability" and partnership with odious autocrats in order to pursue its national interests. It may be called "rapprochement," but the 2011 report from Human Rights Watch was scathing: "Democracies around the world are ignoring abuses by repressive regimes and opting for improved relations rather than condemning rights violations and curtailing aid," the report said.[8] "'Dialogue' and 'cooperation' with repressive governments is too often an excuse for doing nothing about human rights," said Kenneth Roth, the group's executive director. He criticized European Commission President José Manuel Barroso for meeting in Brussels on January 17, 2011, with Islam Karimov, the autocratic president of energy-rich Uzbekistan. "For him to be received warmly by Mr. Barroso is in a sense a culmination of this gradual capitulation," Roth said. He called Karimov a "ruthless leader" and said Uzbekistan's human rights record remains "abysmal," with crackdowns on the opposition and the media and persecution of religious believers. "The European Union has epitomized this failure, this tendency to fall for subterfuge used by these governments to avoid serious pressure," Roth added.[9]

The most serious impediment to the advancement of democracy has been the conflict with Western interests. *All* Western countries subordinate the lofty goal of democracy to their national security interests. Democratization efforts are often abandoned when they clash with these interests. The argument here is not that the West should abandon its interests—all countries pursue their own national interests—but that it should be honest about the fact that promoting democracy is not its primary goal.

In fact, it can be argued that these Western interests—ranging from economic, geopolitical, environmental, and a whole range of other interests—are so numerous that it is impossible to align them with democracy. The free flow of oil, strategic minerals, global free trade, nuclear nonproliferation and disarmament, alliances during the Cold War, and the current wars on drugs and terrorism all stand in the way. As a result, Western policies on democracy often suffer from double-speak, inconsistencies, missteps, and the occasional downright betrayal. The uncertain and halfhearted attempts have produced a harvest of coconut republics and illiberal democracies across the developing world.

Terrorism is certainly a real threat, but the fears of jihadists taking over now appear to have been overblown—pardon the pun. Arab street protesters in early 2011 were not burning American flags or waving photos of Osama bin Laden. The irony is that the US allies in this war against terrorism are the same ones who, with their misgovernance and crony capitalism, created the very conditions of social misery and inequality that bred terrorism! Here are some pertinent features of the Bouazizi revolution that Western experts fail to understand:

1. It was a youth revolution. The youth in Tunisia and Egypt showed eloquently that they were not shackled by the Qur'an. When Mohamed Ghannouchi, the leader of the Islamist movement Ennahda, returned to Tunis after 22 years in exile, about 1,000 supporters went to the airport to welcome him. But among the crowd was another group that carried the sign: "Welcome but no Islamicism, no theocracy, no Sharia, and no stupidity."[10]

2. The youth were not going to stand idly by and watch some Islamist movement hijack their revolution. Said a 34-year-old Egyptian, Hussein Suliman Hussein: "We have one concept that we live by: not Hassan Nasrallah [leader of the political and militant Shiite group Hezbollah], not Khamenei [Iran's Supreme leader], not America. The Egyptian people are in the streets for themselves."[11] Even the Muslim Brotherhood in Egypt distanced itself from Iran and Hezbollah, saying it "regards the revolution as the Egyptian people's revolution, not an Islamic revolution."[12]

3. The youth revolution was not ideological. Both pro- and anti-Western leaders came under siege: Algeria, Tunisia, Egypt, Jordan, and Yemen as well as Libya, Sudan, and Syria.

4. The street protests were expressions of intellectual freedom. Real change begins with intellectual freedom. The self-immolation of Mohamed Bouazizi was the ultimate and extreme form of freedom of expression.

5. The revolution was cross-sectional. In Tunisia, the students were joined by trade unionists, lawyers, and teachers. Even judges and police joined demonstrations. In Egypt, leaders of the protesters appealed to people to join regardless of their religion.

It became apparent that after siding with autocrats for decades, the West has little idea about the aspirations of the people in North Africa and the Arab world. It misled them.

Misleading the Developing Countries

Democracy was not on the radar screen during the Cold War. Instead, the West pushed the developing countries toward economic liberalization. Back then, drawing upon Western economic history, it was argued that the Industrial Revolution in eighteenth-century Europe occurred well before Europe had achieved full democratic pluralism. As people got richer, they started to demand and agitate for their political rights; thus, economic liberalization would unleash forces for democratic change from within. Economic liberalization will indeed engender prosperity, but as we stressed in the previous chapter, to-day's dictators *never* establish a level playing field—economically or politically. Economic liberalization alone will only enrich the ruling vampire elites or those favored by the despot, leaving the masses in abject poverty. A huge chunk of the Tunisian economy was controlled by the four daughters of Ben Ali and the many relatives of his second wife, Leila Trabelsi. Their "tentacles penetrated deep into Tunisia's financial system, extracting sweetheart loans from once-respectable banks."[13] This is an all too familiar story in Algeria, Egypt, and elsewhere in the Arab World, as well as Africa. Growing social inequality, lack of jobs, and deteriorating economic conditions will fuel resentment and public anger.

The Ghost of David Lloyd George

Yet, this line of reasoning—economic liberalization—shaped much of US policy toward Africa in the 1980s and China in the 1990s. For China, the assumption was that the more the United States traded with the Communist dictatorship, the nearer the United States would bring the day of a democratic redemption of the hapless Chinese people. American journalist and political commentator David Brooks noted that, "The theory puts a lot of faith in the power of capitalism to transform tyrannies into democracies. History offers some examples in which the market has sweetened manners, but there are also plenty of instances where the economically minded have overestimated the civilizing power of trade."[14] A bumper crop of similar assumptions can be found in US policy toward Africa. According to Arnold Beichman, senior research fellow at the Hoover Institution,

> The founder of that delusional "linkage" policy was British Prime Minister Lloyd George who formulated the principles of a policy that was to become standard for the West toward the Soviet Union: "to smother Bolshevism with generosity," as the authors of "Utopia in Power" have written. In 1922, Lloyd George said, "I believe we can save her by trade. Commerce has a sobering influence ... Trade, in my opinion, will bring an end to the ferocity, the rapine and the crudity of Bolshevism more surely than any other method."[15]

Of course, trade did not bring an end to Bolshevism, but the ghost of Lloyd George continued to wander around the corridors of the World Bank, the IMF, and the US government for decades. Africa's experience suggests that economic reform under dictatorships is generally not sustainable. An econometric study by Yi Feng concluded that "political institutions affect economic growth significantly and it is crucial to identify the political determinants of economic performance so that appropriate political environments can be created to facilitate growth."[16] He added that economic difficulties may create problems for new democracies, but a reversal of the democratization process is usually even more damaging because authoritarianism has been shown to lead to lower rather than higher growth.[17]

Even in Asia, where the success of the Asian Tigers was roundly celebrated and showcased by the World Bank as proof that economic development can occur under authoritarian regimes, that view is now thoroughly discredited. In an interview, South Korea's former president, Kim Dae Jung, said:

> Many of the leaders of Asian society have been saying that military dictatorship was the way and democracy was not good for their nations. They concentrated only on economic development and building a government around a strong leader who controls economic policy. I believe that the fundamental cause of the financial crisis, including here in Korea, is because of placing economic development ahead of democracy.[18]

Indeed, many of the African countries the World Bank restructured into "economic success stories" did finally hit the political ceiling and began to unravel: Cameroon, The Gambia, Ivory Coast, Kenya, Madagascar, Malawi, Nigeria, Tanzania, Zaire, and Zimbabwe. In 1989, Ivory Coast was declared a success story, but its fortunes began to sink after 1990, with the decline in world commodity prices, and even further with political turmoil after the 1991 elections. It imploded in 2002 and reeled from crisis to crisis. A November 2010 presidential election produced a five-month stalemate, with the incumbent, Laurent Gbagbo, refusing to concede defeat, which nearly plunged the country into another civil war. He was eventually yanked from the basement bunker where he had been holed up, but the economy will take years to recover.

As we showed in chapter 8, the whole debate over political versus economic reform violates Ayittey's Law, which states that intellectual reform must come before economic reform. Premature economic liberalization results in imperfect capitalism, such as crony or vampire capitalism. Marcos, Suharto, Mobutu, Ben Ali, Gbagbo, and their ilk got wealthy but kept the loot in foreign banks. (The industrialists of the eighteenth century and the robber barons of the nineteenth did not stash their wealth in Swiss bank accounts.) In the developing countries, though the economy got richer, the wealth was not spread among the population. Crises erupted when the masses were hit with falling commodity prices and hikes in the costs of basic food items. People vented their frustrations in the streets and demanded regime change—Tunisia, Egypt, Algeria, Libya, Jordan, Morocco, and so on. This was when the "political ceiling" was reached. If the political space is opened up, the prosperity will continue, as was the case in Chile. In most cases, however, dictators kept the lid on, and the economic gains unraveled when the country imploded: Ivory Coast, Indonesia, Madagascar, and Yugoslavia.

As we noted in the previous chapter, China currently faces the dilemma of economic liberalization *without* political reform. Stubborn resistance to political reform will only lead to disaster. Speaking to Chinese-American business people in New York, Prime Minister Wen said political reform would lead to "a relaxed political environment, so people can better express their independent spirit and creativity."[19] That his speech was censored and blocked from publication in the state-owned media by the powerful Propaganda Department spoke volumes about the importance of intellectual freedom.

HOW THE WEST CAN GET IT RIGHT

The West should decide whether to fight dictators or to do business with them. If it chooses to fight dictators, it can do so in two general ways. The first is to cause no more harm—akin to the Hippocratic oath medical doctors are required to take to uphold ethical standards. If a doctor chooses to treat a patient, he or she must ensure that the treatment does not make the patient's condition worse. If it does, the treatment must be stopped. Similarly, there are several "treatments" the West must stop dispensing to the developing countries. The second way the West can help is by pursuing a few proactive policies or programs that are therapeutic.

The Don'ts

The "bad" medicines the West should stop dispensing to developing countries include the following:

The Unitary State System

This system, which concentrates power and centralizes decision-making, trends toward dictatorship. In developing countries with diverse ethnic minorities, the system always leads to despotism and the persecution of minority groups. Developing countries should be encouraged to move toward more *decentralized* political structures.

The Western-Style Multiparty, Majority Vote, "Winner-Takes-All-and-Eats-All" Model

This model perpetuates dictatorships and leads to ethnic domination, as we have argued in chapter 8. Western-style democracy will *never* work in Iraq, Afghanistan, the Middle East, or Africa no matter how many resources are thrown at it. It will continue to produce coconut republics, failed states, and illiberal democracies. Dictators will *always* win multiparty elections, which explains the frequency of rioting and revolutions after fraudulent elections. Developing countries should be encouraged to move toward consensus-based democratic models because minority positions are accommodated in that model.

The Leader-Centered Approach

The West always looks for a "strong, transformative leader" who can take unpopular steps to transform his society and with whom it can form a nice, cozy relationship called a "partnership"—a leader in the mold of Singapore's Lee Kuan Yeuw, who is visionary, decisive, and forceful. The Clinton administration epitomized this approach in Africa and elsewhere when it sought partnership with an "Abraham Lincoln," who would take charge of his own backyard, and it invested heavily in the rhetoric and personalities of such a "partner." During his March 1998 trip to Africa, President Clinton hailed Presidents Laurent Kabila of the Democratic Republic of the Congo, Yoweri Museveni of Uganda, Paul Kagame of Rwanda, Meles Zenawi of Ethiopia, and Isaiah Afwerki of Eritrea as the "new leaders of Africa" who were taking charge of Africa's own backyard, and he spoke fondly of the "new African renaissance sweeping the continent." But barely two months after Clinton's return to the United States, the so-called new leaders of Africa were at each other's throats in the Congo conflict. And the rest of them turned out to be reform acrobats and crackpot democrats.

Similarly in North Africa and the Arab world, the West has favored "partnerships" and rapprochement with strong leaders; their people did not count. The upheavals in that region have exposed the folly of that approach. As President Barack Obama rightly said in a speech to Ghana's Parliament on July 11, 2009: "Africa doesn't need strongmen, it needs strong institutions."[20]

Strong institutions are established by civil society, not by leaders, who have a conflict of interest. Leaders can't be expected to set up the very institutions that will check their arbitrary use of power and looting. Clinton seems to have learned from his old mistakes. During an interview with the BBC on January 12, 2011, regarding reconstruction efforts in Haiti, a frustrated Clinton said that what will pull Haiti out of its misery is "strong institutions." Amen.

West-Brokered Peace Accords

Since 1970, there have been more than 40 wars fought on the African continent. Populations have been decimated, infrastructure destroyed, and people's homes razed. The economic toll has been horrendous: devastated agriculture, deepening poverty, declining investment, increasing social misery, and a massive refugee population of mostly women and children. One word explains the causes of all these wars: power—the monopolization of it and the reluctance to relinquish or share it in the unitary state system.

Appalled by the gratuitous mayhem and wanton destruction after years of senseless civil war, the conscience of the West or the international community stirs action. Maximum pressure is applied to combatants to reach a cease-fire or a peace accord. This is a Band-Aid solution that treats the symptoms but not the root cause (power in a unitary state system). More than 35 such peace accords have been signed in postcolonial Africa since the 1970s with an abysmal success record.

The reason for the failures lies in the approach often foisted on Africa by well-intentioned Western donors: direct face-to-face negotiation between warring factions. The approach is flawed because it excludes civil society. Africa's own indigenous conflict-resolution mechanism provides a better approach. It requires four parties: an arbiter, the two combatants, and civil society or those directly and indirectly affected by the conflict (the victims). When two disputants cannot resolve their differences by themselves, the case is taken to a chief's court for adjudication. The court is open to all, and anyone affected by the dispute can participate. The complainant makes his case, then the defendant. Next, anybody else who has something to say may speak. After all the arguments have been heard, the chief renders a decision. The guilty party may be fined, say, three goats: one for the chief, for his services; another for the injured party; and the remaining one slaughtered for a village feast. The latter social event is derived from the African belief that it takes a village, not only to raise a child, but also to heal frayed social relations. Thus, traditional jurisprudence lays more emphasis on healing and restoring social harmony and peace than on punishing the guilty.

Further, the interests of the community supersede those of the disputants. If they adopt intransigent positions, they can be sidelined by the will of the community and fined, say, two goats each for disturbing the social peace. In extreme cases, they can be expelled from the village.

Most of the peace accords in Africa failed because they excluded the third critical component—civil society. Only rebels and government officials were represented at the conferences. Fortunately, the lesson is being learned. Said Henry Anyidoho, the deputy political head of the joint UN–African Union peacekeeping mission to Sudan: "We've been promoting the use of traditional methods to solve conflicts . . . You see all over Africa, where that system is broken, you have problems. Where that system is in place, you have no problems."[21] Rwanda is following this path. After the 1994 genocide that saw the slaughter of more than 1 million Tutsis, the UN set up the International Criminal Tribunal for Rwanda, based in Arusha, to prosecute the orchestrators of the violence—over 100,000 suspects. The Rwandan government then discovered that it would take 250 years for the formal court system to try them. So, to restore peace and bring about reconciliation and justice, the government turned to the traditional courts, called *gacaca*. According to *The Economist*, "They got off to a flying start: in October 2001, Rwandans elected 258,208 *gacaca* judges, including 19 for each of the country's 9,170 cells (tiny administrative units sometimes as small as 200 people)."[22]

Government of National Unity (GNU)

This is also sponsored by Western donors in an effort to end political stalemates, often caused by the combination of the unitary state system and Western-style multiparty democracy. It is another Band-Aid solution and may emerge out of a peace accord to end a conflict. It generally seeks to bring the combatants—government and rebel/

opposition forces—together to form a "government of national unity" (GNU) in a power-sharing arrangement. The notion of former bitter enemies sitting down together to govern a country sounds infinitely appealing but defies logic. It is fraught with grave dangers, which explains why the experience with power sharing in Africa in recent times has been anything but salutary.

The first major hurdle that a GNU has to clear is how former mortal enemies, who in the past plotted to kill each other, can bury their intense hatred and work amicably together. Second, a GNU is essentially a formula for joint plunder of the state. Ministerial or government positions will have to be divvied up, and bitter squabbles erupt over the distribution of government posts as nobody is satisfied with the eventual distribution. Squabbling over posts may lead to the resumption of hostilities and renewed conflict—as in Angola in 1992, the Democratic Republic of the Congo in 1999, Sierra Leone in 2000, and Ivory Coast in 2004.

A GNU seldom lasts. Here are some examples:

- Angola's GNU did not last for more than six months in 1992.
- Former president F. W. de Klerk of South Africa pulled out of the GNU after barely one year when apartheid was dismantled in 1994.
- The Democratic Republic of the Congo's GNU in 2003 created four vice presidents but did not bring peace to eastern Congo, especially the Bunia region.
- Burundi's civil war flared up in August 2003 despite the establishment of a GNU brokered by former South African president Nelson Mandela.
- Ivory Coast's GNU, established in January 2003, collapsed in less than a year.
- Sudan's GNU, brokered in Kenya in 2005, barely lasted a year. The rebel movement—now called Sudan People's Liberation Movement (SPLM)—abruptly pulled out of the national unity government on October 12, 2007. In January 2011, South Sudan voted overwhelmingly to break away from the North.
- Kenya's GNU, established in February 2008 after the violent December 2007 elections in which 1,200 people perished, has been floundering.
- Zimbabwe's GNU, signed in 2008, has been ditched.

Once again, the attempt by the international community or the West to resolve a political crisis in Africa is laudable, but the solutions being offered are wrong and ineffective. Like peace accords, most GNUs collapse because of their Western approach—from the direct face-to-face negotiations between former combatants to governing together. An African approach would convene a sovereign national conference, or stakeholders' conference, such as Afghanistan's *loya jirga* or South Africa's CODESA, which we discussed in chapter 8. A stakeholders' conference would include civil society groups as well.

It is important to remember that when a political stalemate occurs, the next step is to open up or widen the forum for mediation by including civil society groups. Rather than threaten the use of legitimate military force to end the stalemate in Ivory Coast, ECOWAS should have convened a national conference with delegates from all sections of society, as Benin did in 1991.

The Dos: Therapeutic Medicine

The West can help defeat dictators and advance the cause of liberty by taking any of the following measures or strategies.

Create a New United Nations

The United Nations could be the perfect body to serve in the vanguard of freedom for the peoples of the world. But it is indisputably dysfunctional. It can neither stand up to dictators nor prevent despotism and seeks only to clean up the trail of devastation and human debris they leave behind. It even succumbs to despots. On March 18, 2011, however, the United Nations did redeem itself by imposing a no-fly zone over Libya to prevent its dictator from slaughtering his people. But the institution still needs to be reformed. At a minimum, this should include the following:

- Enforce the United Nations' own 1948 Universal Declaration of Human Rights. Countries that do not adhere to that declaration should be thrown out of the United Nations. In particular, Article 19, which guarantees freedom of expression, should be rigorously enforced.
- Aggressively apply the principle of reciprocity to member nations. Every September, the United Nations holds a General

Assembly Meeting, in which dictators of various stripes step up to the podium and spit vitriol at whoever peeves them. A corresponding mini-assembly should be organized in each member nation on the same day that its leader is speaking at the General Assembly—or the day after—to enable his citizens to vent their spleen as well.

- End religious persecution. Countries that allow churches or mosques to be desecrated or burnt with impunity should be kicked out of the United Nations.
- End the abuse of veto power. It should be possible to override a Security Council veto with a two-thirds majority vote in the Security Council or the General Assembly, or the Secretary-General should have the power to override.
- Disperse specialized UN agencies strategically around the developing world. For example, locate the Commission on Human Rights in Zimbabwe and the Commission on Economic Development in North Korea.

Make a More Vigorous Push for Intellectual Freedom

A recurrent theme throughout this book has been the advocacy for and defense of freedom of expression. As we argued in chapter 2, this freedom is not a Western invention but has existed in all traditional societies. Former president of South Africa Nelson Mandela once said: "In the 21st Century, the capacity to communicate will almost certainly be a key human right."[23] An opinion or viewpoint can be expressed, written, sung, performed, or aired in a whole variety of media: novels, books, newspapers (print media), in theaters (films, plays), on the air (radio, television), and on the Internet. The combination of all these constitutes intellectual freedom.

Dismantling a dictatorship requires reform and more reform. We have made clear that the establishment of intellectual freedom is the critical first step. A free media is the most effective weapon against all dictatorships. Why are the Communists in China more terrified of a free media than they are of the Japanese? If Wikileaks has a "sanitizing effect" on the conduct of US foreign policy, imagine what a free media in a developing country would do. A free media could:

- Put the brakes on Iran's nuclear programs,
- End North Korea's nuclear threats,

- Cut China's chopstick mercantilism down to size, and
- Put Hugo Chávez back in the military barracks where he belongs.

Had there been a free media in Iraq under Saddam Hussein, the war that has cost so much blood and treasure might not have been necessary. Had there been a free media in Somalia, Rwanda, Burundi, and Liberia, these countries would not have imploded. A free media in a developing country does not threaten the "national interests" of any Western country!

Establish a Radio Free Africa

Of the various types of media, radio is the most powerful force of change in the developing countries. Poor people can't afford to buy and read newspapers or watch television; they listen to the radio because it is free. The average person in the West takes for granted the practical usefulness of radio, without realizing its powerful potential for civic empowerment in the Third World. In Africa, the radio is a political tool for the empowerment of the African masses. Dictators realize this potential, which is why they seek to control it. An African president once told Elizabeth Ohene, the deputy editor of BBC's Africa Service: "You are more powerful than an African president."[24] On a continent where most people lack access to electricity and hence television and the Internet, radio is immensely powerful. Consequently, despots seize control of radio and use it for propaganda purposes, blocking out dissenting or opposition views. For opposition politicians in many African countries to get their views to the masses, BBC and the Voice of America often serve as alternate outlets. The establishment of a Radio Free Africa, similar to Radio Free Asia, will do for Africa what Radio Free Europe did to the Soviet Union. In September 1996, the US Congress created Radio Free Asia (RFA) to express its disgust at the massacre of pro-democracy demonstrators at Tiananmen Square in 1989. The beaming of uncensored news into China so upset Beijing that Washington kept the location of its transmitters a state secret. Recall my statement that Communist China is more terrified of a free media than it is of the Japanese.

North Korea is perhaps the most closed and viciously repressive country in the world. In a bid to open up that secretive Communist country, human rights activists launched a campaign to fly more than

20 balloons, each 6 yards tall and carrying about 30 small radios, into North Korea, which strictly bans its people from listening to or watching outside broadcasts. The Reverend Douglas Shin, a Korean-American human rights activist, estimated that the cost of the "Give Ear to a North Korean" campaign was $7,000.[25]

Ethiopia, laboring under the Zenawi dictatorship, has only one radio station, which is state controlled; the same is true of Eritrea. Establish free FM radio stations in those countries. We told in chapter 6 of the establishment of Radio Eye in Ghana in 1994. Our victory forced the government to issue licenses to many other stations, which led to media pluralism in Ghana that eventually brought about peaceful democratic change in 2000.

Since then, this author has made numerous exhortations in testimonies before Congressional Committees, presentations at the World Bank, and US AID about the need for Radio Free Africa. On July 28, 2009, I made the same suggestion to Secretary of State Hillary Clinton at a State Department dinner. She said she liked the idea, but whether it will be implemented or not is a different matter. The proposal would have to go through the bureaucracy grinder, be stripped by this or that agency, and would be thoroughly discombobulated by the end of the process. So this author went ahead and gathered some young American and African students to establish Radio Free Africa: http://www.radiofreeafrica.org. (The author has also made other suggestions, most of them stated above, to the State Department.)

Focus Smart Aid on Building Institutions

Past efforts to promote democracy in developing countries failed partly because the West resorted to lecturing and using vague language. Donors preached "democracy," "accountability," "rule of law," "good governance," and "market economy," among others, and withheld aid unless "multiparty democracy" was established. They paid little attention to the institutions needed to establish these desirable goals or orders. For example, enforcing the rule of law is not possible without an independent judiciary; nor are free and fair elections possible without an independent electoral commissioner. The focus, then, ought to be on the institutions required to attain those goals.

Vagueness gives despots too much wiggle room for chicanery and tomfoolery. Ask the buffoonish Musugu Babazonga of Tonga to establish rule of law and he will say he is the law. He wrote the constitution and all the laws himself. And since he rules, there is rule of law in his country. Ask him to cut government spending and he will establish a "Ministry of Less Government Spending."

Bad governance, the whole list of gross human rights violations, and many of the problems in developing countries can be traced to the absence of the six key institutions we listed in the previous chapter: a free media; an independent judiciary, electoral commission, central bank; neutral security forces; and a professional civil service. Most of these institutions are also needed to establish a closely related concept that is extremely important for economic development: an enabling environment. It would therefore seem more logical for pro-democracy and human rights advocacy groups, as well as development experts and practitioners, to seek the establishment of these six critical institutions. In a July 11, 2009, speech to Ghana's Parliament, President Obama said:

> In the 21st century, capable, reliable, and transparent institutions are the key to success—strong parliaments; honest police forces; independent judges—(applause); an independent press; a vibrant private sector; a civil society. (Applause.) Those are the things that give life to democracy, because that is what matters in people's everyday lives.[26]

There will be unity of purpose if multilateral financial institutions (such as the World Bank and the IMF), Western donors, and human rights groups focus on fostering the above six institutions. That is where smart aid will put its money. Again, these institutions are reformed or established by civil society, not by leaders.

A free media and an independent judiciary are indispensable to fight corruption, which costs Africa US$148 billion a year according to the World Bank. Back in 1999, the World Bank president, James Wolfensohn, wrote a revealing piece in which he said,

> A free press is not a luxury. A free press is at the absolute core of equitable development, because if you cannot enfranchise poor people, if they do not have a right to expression, if there is no searchlight on corruption and inequitable practices, you cannot build the public consensus needed to bring about change.[27]

Why, then, didn't the World Bank make the establishment of a free press a condition for its loans? According to Wolfensohn, the reason was political and diplomatic. The bank could not use the "C-word" (corruption) because donors felt uncomfortable about it. And if you could not use the C-word, you could not talk about a free press either. "What could be more intrusive on politicians than a free press? What is it that could enfranchise people more than a free press?" It was political correctness run amok.

Wolfensohn went on to argue that corruption and freedom of the press are really economic and social issues and that ending the former and encouraging the latter are essential to development. [28] By defining corruption not as a political issue but as an economic and social one, the World Bank sought to make donors more comfortable with, and more favorable to, fighting corruption. The World Bank finally realized that corruption was the largest single obstacle to equitable economic development.

The World Bank was seeing a correlation not only between press freedom and the control of corruption, but also between "voice and accountability and measures such as per capita income, infant mortality and adult literacy"[29]

So it undertook its own study of 60,000 poor people in 60 of the countries, known as "Voices of the Poor," to prove what should have been obvious: It was not money that separated the poor from the rich, but a "lack of voice." The poor cannot elect their own people to power, and they cannot gain access to power. If they cannot even reach the "authorities" to express themselves, they cannot expose their own inequality. No one speaks for them; they have no representation. And if they cannot make themselves heard—which is a benefit conveyed by the freedom of the press—what hope do they have for the right of equitable development?

Wolfensohn concluded that "each country needs to ensure this right from within. It needs to listen to its own voices to get the ideas moving that can change society."[30]

It is somewhat strange that it took the World Bank, which claims to champion the cause of the poor, over 40 years to realize that the poor have a voice that needs to be heard. What happened next is even more revealing.

After succeeding Wolfensohn in 2005, Paul Wolfowitz made poverty alleviation in Africa his topmost priority, and he was tough on corruption. He suspended loans to Chad over diversion of oil money to purchase weapons and took a hard line against the tyrannical re-

gime of Robert Mugabe of Zimbabwe. But his anti-corruption campaign rankled a World Bank staff that was more interested in advancing
their cushy careers by shoveling money out the door. On May 18, 2007,
they forced his resignation over an alleged "sweetheart deal" for his girl-
friend, Shaha Riza, and the fight against corruption and the promotion
of a free press evaporated.

All donors should come together to set up a Free Media Center in
China, Ethiopia, Eritrea, Iran, Zimbabwe, and other countries, where
anyone can walk in, browse the Internet, read newspapers, and so on.
Add an auditorium for public lectures.[31] If Zenawi tears it down, cut
off the US$1 billion Ethiopia receives in aid. A roadmap is urgently
needed, and it starts with intellectual freedom and a free media. By free
media is not meant the ability of the BBC or the Voice of America to
broadcast freely in, say, Iran. Rather, it means the establishment of an
indigenous free media in Iran itself. The case for democracy has to be
made by the locals themselves. Note the role Al Jazeera played in the
upheavals in North Africa and the Middle East. When first established,
it was embraced by Arab autocrats for its rabid anti-West venom. It
broadcast the audio tapes of Osama bin Laden and gruesome pictures
of beheadings by Islamic extremists. Now, Al Jazeera is spreading revolutionary flames across the Arab world. Hosni Mubarak shut it down
in February 2011, and one of its journalists was killed in Libya. A case
of Arab autocrats being hoisted by their own petard?

The next institution to wrestle out of the control of the despot
is the judiciary. Recall the role of Pakistani judges in ousting military
dictator Musharraf in 2008. Like the civil service and the military, each
institution has a professional code of conduct. As we suggested in chapter 8, these codes should be rewritten and enforced.

Engage the New Democracies

Spreading democracy should not be the function of the West alone.
Newly democratized countries that have successfully discarded the yoke
of tyranny can be extremely helpful. Poland should be commended for
establishing and funding Belsat—a TV station in Warsaw for dissident
Belarusian journalists. It is an effort by the Polish government to foster
democratic change across the border in neighboring Belarus. Poland
also offers scholarships to Belarusian students expelled from university at home because of their political activities. The Polish government
also supports groups that give money to families of political prisoners

and dissidents.[32] Countries such as Botswana, Ghana, and South Africa should emulate Poland's example.

Regional organizations too can be helpful. The Organization of American States (OAS) often takes a hard line on coups and election fraud in Latin America. Its counterpart, the African Union, is a disgrace. At its summit in Addis Ababa, Ethiopia, in February 2011, it chose President Teodoro Obiang of Equatorial Guinea as its new chairman, just as the defunct Organization of African Unity (OAU) chose Field Marshall Idi Amin as its chairman in 1975. The regional organization, the Economic Organization of West African States (ECOWAS), however, has been more sane. And the Arab League? The less said, the better.

Engage the Younger Generation—The Cheetah Generation

The pace of democratization can be accelerated by working with reform-minded people—especially the younger generation. Recent street protests were started by them—Mohamed Bouazizi, for example. In the past, large amounts of effort, time, and resources have been wasted on trying to persuade, cajole, or even bribe aging autocrats and the ruling elites to implement reform. Such obstinate and recalcitrant public officials have been described by this author as Africa's "Hippo Generation." They are of the old 1960s era and mentality—stodgy, pudgy, intellectually astigmatized, and stuck in their muddy colonialist pedagogical patch. Wedded to the old "colonialism-imperialism" paradigm with an abiding faith in the potency of the state, they won't move one foot without complaining and demanding more foreign aid. They lack vision—hippos are nearsighted—and they sit tight in their air-conditioned government offices, comfortable in their belief that the state can solve all of Africa's problems. All the state needs is more power and more foreign aid. They defend their territory ferociously since that is what provides them with their wealth. (Hippos are territorial animals and kill more people in Africa than does any other animal.) The Hippos in government couldn't care less if the whole country collapses around them; they are content as long as their pond is secure. Reform is anathema to the Hippos as it will threaten their lucrative business empires and their grip on political power.

By contrast, the "Cheetah Generation" refers to the new and angry generation of young African university graduates and professionals who look at African issues and problems from a totally different and unique perspective. They are young, dynamic, intellectually agile, pragmatic, and tech-savvy. They may be the "restless generation," but they are Africa's new hope. They brook no nonsense about corruption, inefficiency, ineptitude, incompetence, or buffoonery. They understand and stress transparency, accountability, human rights, and good governance. They also know that many of their current leaders are hopelessly corrupt and that their governments are stubbornly dysfunctional and commit flagrant human rights violations.

The Cheetahs do not look for excuses for government failure by wailing over the legacies of the slave trade, Western colonialism, imperialism, or an unjust international economic system. Unencumbered by the old shibboleths, Cheetahs can analyze issues with remarkable clarity and objectivity.

The outlook and perspectives of the Cheetahs are refreshingly different from those of many African leaders, intellectuals, or elites, whose mental faculties are so foggy and whose reasoning is so befuddled that they cannot distinguish between right and wrong. They blame everyone except themselves for Africa's problems. The Cheetahs are not so intellectually astigmatized. Whereas the Hippos constantly see problems, the Cheetahs see business opportunities. The Cheetah generation has no qualms about getting its hands "dirty." Africa's salvation rests on the back of the Cheetah generation.[33] Mohamed Bouazizi was a Cheetah; he tried to sell fruits and vegetables to support himself rather than relying on the government. Since his death in January 2011, other Cheetahs have been vigorously shaking coconut trees in North Africa and the Middle East. On February 11, 2011, came a loud *"THUD!"* Another coconut down in Egypt, with more to follow.

CHAPTER 10

EPILOGUE

"Those who make peaceful revolution impossible will make violent revolution inevitable."

—President John F. Kennedy in 1962 to Latin American diplomats

THIS BOOK BEGAN BY ASSERTING that the cost of despotism is unacceptable: monumental humanitarian crises, horrendous human suffering, the slaughter of millions of civilians, the brutal repression of millions more, massive numbers of refugees, the economic devastation wrought by the catastrophic collapse of states, the plunder of resources, and naked corruption are all hallmarks of dictatorships—a cost the world must bear. Sadly, this cost has been rising. Dictators have proliferated in recent times, but not because they are "acceptable" to the people in developing countries. In fact, despotism does not inhere in the political cultures of their traditional societies, of which there were two types. At one end were the stateless societies, which elected to dispense with centralized authority altogether. A despot cannot exist in societies or political systems that have no leaders or rulers. At the other end were those states that chose to have leaders—chiefs, sachems, sheikhs, monarchs, and so on—but surrounded them with councils upon councils to prevent them from abusing their powers.

Decision-making in traditional societies was by consensus. When important matters arose, the ruler convened a "village meeting" and put the issue before the people. The issue was then debated until a consensus was reached. Anyone who wished to air an opinion was free to do so. Once a consensus had been reached, everyone, including the ruler, was required to abide by it. This type of governance—for want of a better term—may be described as participatory democracy by consensus. Furthermore, most of these traditional societies had no standing armies. In the event of conflict, the ruler would summon young men of certain ages and lead them into battle. After the cessation of hostilities, the people's army was disbanded and never became a drain on the tribal treasury. Dictatorship can't exist in a political system that is geared toward consensus building and that has no military or means of coercion.

Above the village level, there were larger polities: kingdoms and empires that were, for the most part, confederacies—associations of independent states that drew up a common policy on defense. As such, they were characterized by the decentralization of power and devolution of authority.

This structure was dictated by situational circumstances: Means of communication and transportation were poor or underdeveloped. A few empires had standing armies, but weapons were primitive and could be made by the people themselves. Strong centralized rule was the exception. And rebellious subjects always had an advantage: they could vote with their feet and settle elsewhere. Confederation permitted states to voluntarily join forces for a common purpose while retaining their own local autonomy.

Colonial rule was extractive, oppressive, and exploitative and disrupted the serenity of traditional governance by introducing new forms of governance. Rebellious natives had to be pacified, subjugated, and enslaved. There has been little atonement for this colonial sin and travesty. Since the purpose of colonial rule was extraction and exploitation, the suitable form of government was the authoritarian type, headed by a strong colonial officer or governor—often of the military bent—with sufficient firepower to crush any rebellion among the natives. The unitary system of government, backed by a standing army, was the most expedient. The natives had no say in the administration of the colonies nor was their welfare a priority for the colonialists. After some 80 years, the colonial yoke in Africa was cast off in the 1960s.

The struggle for independence was long and debilitating in many countries. In the Americas, the struggle was led by settlers who sought a break with their European motherlands. Elsewhere, it was led by the elites among the natives. "Free at last" was the resounding cry at independence. When the Americans rebelled against British colonial rule in 1776, they wisely jettisoned the British or European unitary system of government and incorporated several features of the Iroquois confederacy. Unlike the Americans, however, the vast majority of newly independent developing nations have retained nearly all the features of the authoritarian colonial state: a strong leader, centralized decision-making, and the military, to name a few. Thus began the age of despotism.

Today's despot has at his disposal not only the colonial instruments of repression but also improved means of controlling population movements, geographical reach—thanks largely to advances in modern communication and transportation—and lethal firepower, none of which was available to a potential despot in traditional societies. In the case of Africa, true freedom never came to much of the continent after the colonialists left. As we saw, one set of masters (white colonialists) was replaced by another set (black neo-colonialists), and the oppression and exploitation of the African people continued unabated. We examined the proliferation of despotic regimes in the developing countries in chapter 3 and discussed their modus operandi in chapter 4.

Despots seize control of the key state institutions and pack them with their supporters, allies, and cronies, subverting the institutions to serve their interests, not those of the people. Despots rule by instilling fear and intimidation and suspending freedom of expression and other civil liberties. A variety of tactics may be used to deal with the opposition—bribe and co-opt, divide and conquer, and infiltrate and destroy—or simply crush it. However, just as colonial rule did not endure, neither will despotism. Eventually the despotic regime will self-destruct from within, largely owing to internal contradictions and divisions. If that does not happen, the subjugated people will rise up and revolt, as we saw in chapter 5.

The process is predictable. The economy is the despot's Achilles heel. Incendiary rhetoric and policy zigzags take their toll on investment, and nationalization of commercial properties sends investors scurrying away. The economy falters—production falls, goods become scarce, and prices start to rise. Public resentment begins to mount. The despot may take desperate measures to manage the situation—stringent price controls and currency changes—but these measures only exacerbate the crisis. Cash-strapped and unable to afford huge subsidies, he may allow prices to rise. But the people, fed up with deteriorating economic conditions and rampant corruption, take to the streets to vent their frustration and anger. If the despot adamantly refuses to yield, the street riots may provoke a coup, a palace coup, or a rebel insurgency. Such insurgencies often degenerate into civil wars with devastating consequences.

Alternatively, the despot may relent and grudgingly attempt to save his tottering regime by implementing some economic reforms, often at the behest of the World Bank and Western donors. Such reforms may spark economic growth and prosperity but will really only enrich the ruling vampire elites, leaving the mass of the people in abject poverty (crony or vampire capitalism). Growing social inequality, lack of jobs, and deteriorating economic conditions may provoke social unrest and lead to demands for political reform or regime change—as occurred in Tunisia and its subsequent domino effect on Algeria, Egypt, Jordan, Libya, Morocco, and Yemen. A despot who yields and opens up the political space allows the economic prosperity to continue, but that causes him to lose power. Most prefer to keep the lid on, thus sentencing their countries to a ruinous implosion, as in Burundi, Indonesia, Ivory Coast, Rwanda, Somalia, Yugoslavia, and Zaire. Eventually, a despotic regime meets its own demise, which may be peaceful or violent, depending upon its willingness to accept change.

Mass street protests by themselves are not sufficient to dislodge a despot from power and effect political change. Where a despotic regime is willing to accept change, such protests can produce change peacefully—as was the case with the color and flower revolutions. Africa's sovereign national conferences were able to bring peaceful change for the same reason. But when a despotic regime is unwilling to accept change, the aid of an auxiliary institution—such as the military, the judiciary, the media, the electoral commission, and the civil service— is necessary to effect change. Revolutions failed in Burma, Ethiopia, Iran, Kenya, and Zimbabwe for lack of this auxiliary support. The Rose, Black, Yellow, and Bouazizi (or Jasmine) revolutions succeeded because they had such auxiliary support—the security forces, the judiciary, a split in the army, and army neutrality, respectively.

A despot's best ally, however, comes from the most unlikely source—the opposition itself. For every force in nature there is a counterforce. A force dominates if the counterforce is weak or non-existent. Despots have proliferated and dominated the political scene in far too many countries because the opposition—both domestic and international resistance—is weak, fragmented, and constantly bickering. In chapter 7, we discussed how the opposition forces can be strengthened.

No one single individual or political party can by himself or itself remove an entrenched despot from power. It takes an alliance of opposition forces and careful planning. A military junta requires a different set of strategies than a civilian despot. It takes another institution—the civil service or the judiciary—to fight the institution of the military. However, the most effective weapon against *all* dictators is the free media.

Since action is required on many fronts, it is imperative to have a body, which I called an elders' council, to coordinate opposition activities. The members of the council must be eminent and respectable personalities who have no political ambition of their own and who are capable of reaching out to all sections of the political spectrum, including the despotic regime itself, with whom it must be willing to negotiate a deal. If the despot chooses the ballot box, the opposition must be adequately prepared. It must ensure that the playing field is level, that the voters' register is clean, that the electoral commission is independent, and that the electoral process is transparent. Too often, the opposition fails to do its homework, rushes to participate in an election without adequate preparations, and then cries "Foul!" when it is trounced. Such opposition blunders, repeated in one country after another, simply give despots new leases on life.

Despots can be toppled if and only if the opposition can get its act together. This book set out to demonstrate that this can be done, as attested to by successful revolutions in the Philippines, Eastern Europe, Indonesia, Pakistan, and a few countries in Africa. However, there is a sobering caveat: removing a despot does not necessarily restore liberty. As we saw in chapter 8, there have been disturbing reversals of successful revolutions.

Such reversals occur mainly because the reform process is left unfinished. As Tunisians lamented in January 2011, "We got rid of the dictator but not the dictatorship." A complete overhaul of the dictatorship must occur and necessitates reform in many areas: intellectual, political, constitutional, institutional, and economic.

THE REFORM ROAD MAP

We have stressed that a vanquished dictatorship must be reformed in an orderly manner. We stressed that the ideal sequence begins with intellectual freedom (*glasnost*), followed by political reform, constitutional reform, institutional reform, and, lastly, economic reform. We called this sequence Ayittey's Law.

Intellectual freedom is the most potent reforming force, and we argued that it should be the primary focus of human rights advocacy groups. Iranians, Chinese, Africans, and other people have to make their own case for reform after being misled by the West. Reform that comes from within is far more sustainable and durable than that imposed from without—by Western donors, the World Bank, the IMF, and others. To make their own case for reform and freedom, people need to have freedom of expression, which exists in traditional societies but is among the first rights to be snatched away by a despot.

The corollary of freedom of expression is the free media. The West often underestimates its potency, but it is the most effective weapon against *all* dictatorships. Thus, the first order of business is to get the media out of the hands of corrupt and incompetent dictators. Let the people expose, debate, and find their own solutions to their problems. They themselves know that their political system—dominated by one coconut-head and tribe—stinks, and they will demand change or political reform.

Political reform or democratization must be combined with constitutional reform. This requires jettisoning the unitary state system and the Western-style multiparty majority vote system. The concentration of power at the center leads to competition among various groups—ethnic, religious, political, and professional—to capture it. Once captured, this power is used to settle old scores, loot the treasury, and advance the economic interests of one ethnic, religious, political, or professional group. Everybody else is excluded—the politics of exclusion. And those who seize such power are loath to relinquish it. If the Western-style multiparty majority vote system is added, it is a recipe for disaster, for the despot will never lose an election. This combination has caused much grief, turmoil, and strife in developing countries—a slew of coconut republics, failed and collapsed states, and illiberal democracies. Ethnic groups chafing from grievances have picked up guns to launch rebel insurgencies or secede to form their own nations: in Bangladesh, the Balkan states, Eritrea, Slovakia, and southern Sudan.

An alternate model to the unitary state system and Western-style multiparty democracy may lie in a decentralized political structure (federal or confederal) and a democratic system that is based upon consensus, rather than majority vote. Such a system was tried successfully with Africa's sovereign national conferences—in particular, South Africa's Convention for a Democratic South Africa (CODESA), which was used to dismantle apartheid.

A new constitution needs to be written as part of the reform process. It must have an articulating principle—liberty, freedom, justice, equality, or whatever a group decides—and it must have a Bill of Rights. A people should choose which conception best fits their tradition and culture: rights may be assumed to be inalienable and god-given, never to be infringed on by the state; or they may be regarded as given by the state and therefore to be protected by the state. For a developing country, there must be a clear separation between the constitution and not just religion but also ideology and ethnicity. Just as the state can't promote one particular type of religion, neither should it be able to advance the interests of one tribe over others or promote one form of ideology over others.

We have seen that institutional reform requires focus on six critical institutions:

1. A free and independent media
2. An independent judiciary
3. An independent electoral commission
4. An independent central bank
5. A neutral and professional armed and security force
6. An efficient and professional civil service.

As we saw in chapter 9, all six institutions are necessary to ensure good governance, which is, in turn, essential for economic development. These institutions cannot be established by the leaders or the ruling elites; they must be established by civil society. Each professional body has a code of ethics, which should be rewritten by the members themselves to eschew politics and uphold professionalism; for example, the bar code, the military code. These reforms will, in turn, help to establish good governance and an environment that is conducive to investment and economic development.

Good governance cannot exist in despotic and authoritarian systems. To be sure, exceptions such as Lee Kuan Yew of Singapore can be found, but exceptions don't make the rule. Searching for a "Lee Kuan Yew" in Africa, Latin America, or the Middle East is not only futile but also dangerous. It encourages all sorts of coconut-heads to emerge and project themselves as such or as "the Messiah." Such was the fad in the early 1960s when African nationalist leaders attached some vainglorious epithets to their names; similarly in Latin America with the caudillos. Africa and Latin America don't need strongmen or messiahs; they need strong institutions.

Economic reform requires dismantling the state-interventionist behemoth, removing stifling state controls, and returning to a market-based economy. As we showed in chapter 3, free markets, free enterprise, and free trade were not Western inventions but have existed in traditional societies for centuries. This author has consistently argued that Africa's salvation lies in returning to and building upon her own indigenous institutions of participatory democracy based upon consensus, free village markets, free enterprise, and free trade.

Economic liberalization *works!* China's rise is the result of the 1978 economic reforms undertaken by Deng Xiaoping. Economic liberalization also lifted the economies of the Asian Tigers, Japan, Indonesia, Ivory Coast, and many other developing countries. But, as we have made clear, it is the type of reform that should be the last to be undertaken. The reason should be obvious. Economic liberalization under a dictatorship will lead to crony capitalism, which deepens social inequality and fuels the scourge of corruption. Remember that if the necessary institutions have not been created or reformed, the economic playing field will not be level. The ruling elites scoff at the rule of law because there is no independent judiciary. And since there is no free media, the flow of information is controlled. In that environment, only those with special access to information or with political connections can take advantage of new opportunities unleashed by economic liberalization. Since this is not available to all, it is *imperfect capitalism.* The problem is compounded when the ruling elites siphon their wealth into Swiss banks and live ostentatiously. The growing social disparities and deteriorating living conditions for the masses will provoke social unrest and demands for political reform or regime change.

The above is the whole gamut of reforms that are needed. Donors and countries that try to cut corners or violate this process do so at their own peril.

Violations

Revolutions in eastern Europe and elsewhere have suffered reversals for two reasons. First, the overhaul of the dictatorship was not completed. Further, some types of reform were attempted out of sequence. The dictator had been ousted and political change had occurred, but constitutional and institutional reforms were not tackled. In many cases, the key state institutions were purged of allies, tribesmen, and supporters of the ousted dictator and replaced by the allies and supporters of the incoming administrations. Such politically motivated changes hardly restore efficiency, professionalism, and independence to these institutions. "Maggots" who had burrowed deep into the state pork continue to chew away at its foundations. New judges soon become corrupt, the police start taking bribes, and the soldiers start protecting the new bandits. We suggested that, after a dictator has been ousted, an interim period of five years be set aside to clean up all state institutions.

Many foreign aid programs failed because they did not follow Ayittey's Law. First, they were "leader-centered," not institution-based. Western donors have invested much capital in the rhetoric and charisma of too many strongmen.

Second, as we argued in chapter 9, Western donors and multilateral financial institutions such as the World Bank and the IMF pushed economic liberalization ahead of everything else. Premature economic liberalization leads to crony capitalism and eventually meets its political day of reckoning when it provokes social unrest. When that political boiling point is reached, the prosperity will continue only if the despot lifts the lid; if he doesn't, the country could implode and all the economic gains evaporate. China is currently approaching this point and faces a dilemma. If it clamps shut the political space, it risks a violent revolution. In such an eventuality, not only would the economic gains evaporate but the country might break up. If it opens up the political space, the prosperity will continue, but the Communist Party will become extinct. Tibet and the northwest region will still walk away, but they will do so peacefully through the ballot box—as was the case with the Soviet republics. Thus, the real choice China faces is not so much whether to open up the political space or not but whether it would prefer to break up peacefully or violently. As President John F. Kennedy warned Latin American diplomats in 1962, "Those who make peaceful revolution impossible will make violent revolution inevitable."

Third, the West has never really promoted intellectual freedom, which we have identified as the key initial starting point. It was subsumed under "human rights," but freedom of expression, and its corollary, free media, is the sine qua non of all human rights. To be sure, the West can help but with *smart aid*. For example, smart aid to Africa is that which empowers its people to make their own case for reform and instigate change from within. The kind of reform that is internally generated is far more enduring and sustainable than that imposed from without. As we showed in chapter 9, most of the Western measures and solutions prescribed for the developing world have not worked well. These are:

1. The unitary state system
2. Western-style democracy
3. Peace accords
4. Governments of national unity (GNU).

The West can also help by reforming the United Nations and en-gaging the young democracies, as well as the restless educated youth—the Cheetah Generation—supporting their efforts to take back Africa one village at a time. It is the restless youth who have been taking to the streets, and they need to be engaged. Africa's future and hope rest with the Cheetah Generation—not with the Hippos, nor with the professors and intellectuals who are preoccupied with Confucius.

> African academics hailed the establishment of Confucius institutes on the continent at a seminar opened on August 12 in Yaounde, the capital of Cameroon, saying the institutions are serving as a bridge of culture and partnership between Africa and China.
>
> A total of 25 Confucius institutes have been opened in 18 African countries.[1]

One would have expected them to establish Ubuntu or Majimbo Institutes on the continent. Meanwhile, the following African countries are edging toward implosion: Algeria, Burkina Faso, Burundi, Cameroon, Chad, Ethiopia, Eritrea, Libya, Uganda, and Zimbabwe. Will there be more revolutions, more turmoil, and more collapsed states in the coming years? It seems inevitable.

The purpose in writing this book is to help avert these impending disasters. Take a look at Ghana. Its western neighbors—Sierra Leone (1998), Liberia (1999), and Ivory Coast (2002)—and its eastern neighbor, Togo, all imploded. If we saved Ghana from implosion, then other countries can be saved too.

I will end this book with some personal advice to pro-democracy activists. The struggle for democracy in Ghana took 19 years—from 1981 to 2000. It was full of twists and turns. We made many mistakes that should not be repeated. Though we triumphed in the end, it was a struggle that was not for the faint of heart; it required dedication, diligence, sacrifice, and fortitude. The struggle was a test of will, endurance, and the occasional piece of luck.

THE LONG JOURNEY TO VINDICATION

In the 1980s, I found myself having to fight three battles at the same time: political, intellectual/academic, and political correctness. As a result, I carry many bruises.

The Political Battle

For more than 30 years, I—as well as many other Africans—battled African dictators, both in and out of Africa. I detest them, especially the military type, with every fiber in my body. I hold them responsible for the postcolonial destruction and economic ruination of Africa. The military has been the worst—the scourge of the African continent and the bane of its development. All the collapsed and failed states in Africa were ruined by military coconut-heads. I used to hold many of Africa's leaders in high esteem for the struggle they waged to win independence for their respective countries. But there has been a catastrophic failure of leadership on the continent. Of the 211 heads of state Africa has had since 1960, fewer than 20—or less than 10 percent—can be said to have been good leaders. This reflects a huge deficit of leadership. For two years in a row (2009 and 2010), the Mo Ibrahim Foundation could not find a leader it thought worthy of receiving its $5 million prize.

For me, the turning point came in 1974 when I was hauled into the military barracks and questioned about comments I had made on a radio program. Subsequently, my house was raided and copies of my commentaries were seized by security agents of the military junta of Colonel I. K. Acheampong. Ghana has had six military coups since independence in 1957—one too many.

The Intellectual Battle

I left Ghana in 1975 to pursue postgraduate studies in economics at the University of Manitoba in Winnipeg, Canada. I am an economist by training, and it may surprise many readers that I turned out to be a warrior for freedom. It had long occurred to me that the prevailing theories of economic development were not particularly useful or relevant. They could not explain Africa's dire economic situation or paradox—rich in mineral resources yet impoverished. Most theories focused on strictly technical phenomena such as capital formation (investment), savings, growth, and so forth, without social content. Furthermore, I felt that the operational orthodoxy of development economics was vacuous. Economists make the assumption that "all other things are equal . . ." For example, other things being equal, an increase in investment in an African country would raise its Gross National Product (GNP). I rebelled against that orthodoxy. An increase in investment won't raise GNP in a country wracked by civil war, rampant corruption, or crumbled infrastructure.

The title of my PhD dissertation was "Effective Savings: A New Monetary Theory of Development." In a nutshell, standard economic theory states that savings are the resources required for investment. Since investment is the key to economic growth, an increase in the rate of savings would be required to raise the rate of economic growth—and therefore economic development—*all other things being equal.* If savings are inadequate, then foreign investment or aid can fill in the gap.

I argued in my dissertation that these assumptions are not necessarily valid for a developing country because the *environment* in which development takes place cannot be assumed to be conducive or "constant." Corruption, senseless civil wars, and crumbled infrastructure, among others, all have a deleterious impact on this environment. At a minimum, this environment must have some basic functioning infrastructure, some security of persons and property, the rule of law, stability, and some basic freedoms (political, economic, and intellectual). These prerequisites are ensured by the functioning of the key institutions listed above: an independent judiciary, central bank, media, and electoral commission, an efficient civil service, and neutral and professional security forces. It was clear even to the most casual observer that such an enabling environment did not exist in most African countries.

The "development environment" that had prevailed for much of the postcolonial period was one characterized by insecurity, occasioned by senseless wars and ethnic strife; crumbled infrastructure; rule of tyranny and banditry; military vandalism; and debauchery of state institutions. The police are highway robbers. Judges are crooks. We cannot make the assumption that *all other things are equal.* They are *not* equal, and therefore an increase in investment cannot be expected to raise the GNP.

I wrote about the deteriorating environment in Africa and the catastrophic development crisis it would cause. I warned of an impending debt crisis (the inability of African countries to service their foreign debts because not enough foreign income was being generated), incipient rebel insurgencies, impending state collapse, and massive refugee problems. This deterioration, I argued, had little to do with Western colonialism or imperialism but much to do with such internal factors as bad leadership, despotism, corruption, tribalism, senseless civil wars, poor governance, and so on. My thesis committee hit the roof. It objected strenuously and ordered me to expunge all references to "internal factors" from the thesis. I refused, and they withheld approval of my dissertation. For nine months I battled them. In the end, bitterly disappointed, I gave in.

The Externalist Orthodoxy

Even today Africa is often portrayed as the hapless victim of hostile external forces. She is still suffering from the aftereffects of the slave trade, the legacy of colonialism, Western imperialism, an unjust international economic system, and even earthquakes on Jupiter! African leaders are saints; criticizing them is like "blaming the victim." For much of the postcolonial period, this "externalist orthodoxy" held sway and was used to excuse nearly everything that went wrong in Africa, which, the leadership claimed, was the fault of somebody else, seldom themselves. Who was I to claim that an impending crisis in Africa would be due to "internal factors"?

Fte./Lte. John Jerry Rawlings had been my friend in the early 1970s when I was teaching at the University of Ghana. We used to meet on Saturdays and talk for hours about the problems plaguing Ghana: corruption, economic mismanagement, and so on. In 1979 he staged a successful coup, cleaned house, and, after three months, returned to the barracks. Hilla Limann was elected president of Ghana in 1979, but barely two years into his administration, Rawlings staged another military coup in December 1981, which I felt was uncalled for. I had made plans to return to Ghana after receiving my PhD; instead, I diverted to the United States and vowed to fight and remove the canker of military rule from Ghana's political scene. I had condemned military vandalism in my thesis; at that time, it had become a scourge in Benin, Burkina Faso, Chad, Liberia, Mali, Mauritania, Niger, Nigeria, Sierra Leone, and Togo. At one point, 12 of the 15 West African states were ruled by military dictators.

Political Correctness

I came to the United States in 1982, starry-eyed and extremely naïve. I felt mine was a "just cause"—freedom for Africans. They are not free under their own leaders, as I said in my dissertation. I had failed to persuade my dissertation committee that tyranny has adverse economic consequences. In Africa, the risks and dangers of fighting dictators are well known. Courageous editors, journalists, writers, professors, and politicians who fought them were punished severely with beatings and prison terms. Many paid the ultimate price. For speaking out and writing about despotism, corruption, senseless wars, and other problems in Africa, my house was searched by security goons in Ghana (1974); my hotel room was raided by security forces in Nairobi (1991); I was tossed into jail in Dakar (1994); and I was trailed by security forces in Ghana and Zimbabwe (1995).

When I came to the United States in 1982, I felt I had finally come to the land of freedom. I could now publish all those pieces about bad leadership, poor governance, senseless wars, and corruption that I had been ordered to expunge from my dissertation. Further, I could wage a struggle against the military dictatorship in Ghana from a "safe" haven. But a rude shock awaited. My simple message of freedom for Africans found no takers. For three years, nobody would publish those pieces I excised from my dissertation. The basic reason was that the same externalist orthodoxy I had encountered in Canada also held sway in American academia: the tendency to blame Africa's woes on external factors. This was further compounded by political correctness. Whites were reluctant to criticize black African leaders for fear of being labeled "racist." Black Americans felt they had to show "racial solidarity" with African leaders; there is a sizable community of influential black Americans in the media, politics, and academia. I remember that whenever I submitted a critical piece on African leaders to a white editor, he would pass it on for "clearance" to a black American who then spiked it. The white editor did not want to publish anything about Africa that was "negative" or that attacked black African leaders—hence the need for "clearance." And the black American, who often knew little about the situation in Africa, felt he must defend African leaders, who were the victims of colonial oppression.

To be sure, colonialism was invidious. No one disputes the inhumanity of slavery nor the rape of Africa during the colonial period. But the externalist doctrine had unintended consequences. It provided African despots with a convenient alibi, absolving them of any wrongdoing and of responsibility for the mess they created. They could blame their arrant failures on someone else—on external factors. Naturally, they overplayed this externalist card or blame game to cover up their failures. The most fervent adherents of the externalist orthodoxy were such African leaders as Kwame Nkrumah of Ghana, Julius Nyerere of Tanzania, Jerry Rawlings of Ghana, Muammar Qaddafi of Libya, and Robert Mugabe of Zimbabwe.

Up until the new millennium, the internalist camp was pitifully sparse, populated by such luminaries as the writer Chinua Achebe and Nobel Laureate Wole Soyinka, both of Nigeria. Those of us in that camp were pilloried, reviled, and called all sorts of names. I was denounced as a "traitor," "imperialist lackey," "colonial stooge," "Uncle Tom," and a "house nigger" and accused of "bashing Africa" and "washing Africa's dirty linen in public"—as if Africa's dirty linen was invisible to the world.

In 1988, when I applied for promotion at Bloomsburg University in Bloomsburg, Pennsylvania, the committee in the Economics Department flatly rejected my application. A professor of East Indian extraction dismissed my work as "utterly useless." In 1993, when American University refused to renew my visiting scholarship for the third time, about 600 students sent a petition to the university president, demanding that I be rehired. In the end, they kept me on, but to ensure that I could continue my work, I decided to set up the Free Africa Foundation to be a catalyst for reform: www.freeafrica.org. The foundation does not take any money from government agencies, either in the West or in Africa; it relies on private donors.

In 1999, my office at American University was firebombed, causing extensive damage and the destruction of more than 80 percent of its contents. Book manuscripts that I had in files were incinerated. It could have been the work of some agents working for despotic African governments. (Such was the case with the Chilean dissident, Orlando Letelier, who was killed in a car bomb attack in Washington, DC, in 1976.) On January 25, 2011, the website of the Free Africa Foundation was hacked into. Pro-democracy activists should expect such attacks and be prepared for them; I was not. They should also expect to be enticed by lobbyists who work for the dictators. Lobbyists for the regimes of Sani Abacha of Nigeria, Gnassingbé Eyadéma of Togo, Mobutu Sese Seko of Zaire, Omar Bongo of The Gabon, Teodoro Obiang Nguema Mbasogo of Equatorial Guinea, and Paul Biya of Cameroon all approached me, asking me to "work for them." Money was not an issue, they assured me, but I politely declined. I wouldn't sell out my principles.

I received many life-threatening phone calls; they might have come from the lobbyists I refused to work for. Nasty messages were left on my answering machine. But I was not deterred. I found that I was now waging three battles: intellectual, political, and political correctness. I fought white liberal professors, white conservatives, black Americans, and African academics. I also fought the World Bank, the IMF, US AID (the US Agency for International Development), and other donor agencies, whose foreign aid programs were abject failures. They were lonely uphill battles in the wilderness, but I stuck to my guns. Too many warriors give up too easily in the face of daunting hurdles and obligations such as family life and work schedules. I was a university professor with work-time flexibility. The attacks and ostracization continued. Some of my colleagues in academia didn't even want to hear my name mentioned, and African dictators would have been all too eager to feed me to the crocodiles.

I was like an intellectual gadfly or heretic. Numerous organizations, agencies, and personalities dismissed my strictures on Africa, from congressional and parliamentary committees (in the United States and Canada), to the World Bank and the United Nations, to such personalities as the Reverend Jesse Jackson and Randall Robinson, who spearheaded the campaign against apartheid in South Africa. My clash with African American civil rights leaders in the late 1980s was particularly notable.

Apartheid was an abomination, but South Africa was not an exception. Elsewhere on the African continent were equally heinous de facto apartheid regimes: Arab apartheid in Mauritania and Sudan; tribal apartheid in Burundi, Rwanda, and elsewhere; and political apartheid in many African countries that had declared themselves "one-party states."

I advised Reverend Jackson and Mr. Robinson that, to be credible, the campaign against apartheid should be coupled with an equally vigorous campaign to free blacks elsewhere in Africa. They responded by saying that we should free the blacks in South Africa *first*. I countered, nearly screaming: "By then, it will be too late!" As it turned out, we freed the blacks in South Africa in 1994, but we lost Somalia (1991), Burundi (1993), Rwanda (1994), Zaire (1996), Liberia (1997), Sierra Leone (1999), Ivory Coast (2000), and Togo (2005). Winning one and losing eight—with more losses to come—is indeed a pyrrhic victory.

Back in 1993, I predicted the impending implosion of Rwanda. Upon returning from Rwanda in December 1993, a World Bank mission was full of praise for the Hutu-dominated government of the late president Juvénal Habyarimana. "Nonsense. You must be blind!" I told them. They didn't listen. In March 1994, the country descended into an orgy of violence and carnage that resulted in the slaughter of more than one million Tutsis.

A more direct and poignant prediction came at a conference organized by the Mário Soares Foundation in Porto, Portugal, in March 1999. (Mário Soares was a former president of Portugal.) The conference was about resolving conflicts in the Great Lakes Region in Central Africa. I cautioned the audience about too much focus on conflict *resolution* to the detriment of conflict *prevention*. To drive home this point, I stunned the audience by pointing out to them that, while we were gathered trying to resolve conflicts in the Great Lakes Region, other hot spots were brewing that could blow up. That was in March 1999. I warned them that the following African countries were standing ready to implode: Central African Republic, Chad, Guinea, Guinea-Bissau, Ivory Coast, and Zimbabwe. Nine months after that conference, Ivory Coast was the first country on that list to start its descent with a coup in December 1999. Next was Zimbabwe in March 2000. By 2005, all my predictions had come to pass. All those countries were being ruled by dictators.

Five years later, I made another prediction; this time at the IMF Headquarters in Washington, DC. I was invited to a panel discussion on September 16, 2010, to determine how best the IMF could help African and low-income countries achieve the Millennium Development goals (MDGs)—one of which is to halve poverty by 2015. Most African countries are not expected to reach those goals. In a paper delivered, I warned: "Currently, the following countries are teetering on the brink of implosion: *Algeria, Burkina Faso, Cameroon*, Central African Republic, Chad, Congo (Brazzaville), *Egypt*, Equatorial Guinea, Ethiopia, Eritrea, *Libya, Sudan, Uganda*, and Zimbabwe. It is magnanimous of the IMF to speak of helping fragile and collapsed states but prevention is better than cure."[2] That was in September, and by March 2011, those countries in italics were in turmoil, with their leaders either under siege or overthrown.

What kept me going was the support I received from my own people—Ghanaians both at home and in the diaspora. Everywhere I went in both Ghana and the United States, I was accosted by ordinary Ghanaians, expressing admiration for my courageous stance. They had read my articles and books, as well as seen or heard me on television and radio. It gave me a sense of "protection." Once, I took a taxi in Accra. The driver took me to my destination and when I asked him the fare, he said: "Don't worry, I like what you are doing." It has happened to me on many occasions in Washington, DC, as well.

Being an internalist, I aggressively pushed for "internal solutions." I coined the expression "African solutions for Africa's problems" when Somalia collapsed in 1992. The solutions to the myriad of Africa's problems lie in Africa itself—not along the corridors of the World Bank, the inner sanctum of the Soviet presidium, or on the planet of Mars. These solutions lie *within*, and they require returning to Africa's own roots and building upon her own indigenous institutions of participatory democracy based upon consensus, free village markets, free trade, and free enterprise. For far too long, the leadership has looked *outside* Africa, borrowing and blindly copying all sorts of unworkable foreign systems and paraphernalia.

THE VINDICATION

By 1998, the intellectual battle was close to being won. The debt crisis and economic decline that I had predicted in my dissertation had sadly occurred. Rawlings's military coup had thoroughly vindicated the predictions I made in my dissertation. When he seized power in 1981, Ghana's income per capita was US$410. His lunatic Marxist revolutionary policies of blowing up markets, closing down borders, threatening to shoot cocoa smugglers by firing squad, and imposing stringent price controls sent the economy reeling to its nadir in 1983 with an income per capita of US$365. Over one million Ghanaians fled the country. This was not a country into which you pump more investment and expect to raise the GNP. (When Rawlings left office in 2000, income per capita was US$390.)

In 1995, the World Bank admitted that its Structural Adjustment Program (SAP) or economic liberalization programs, on which it had spent US$25 billion, were a failure. Only 6 out of the 29 adjusting countries were deemed to have been "economic success stories." The reasons for failure were all too familiar: poor governance, corruption, political instability, and conflict.

In 1996, the Department of Economics at the University of Manitoba, Winnipeg, invited me to come and give a seminar. They paid me a $5,000 honorarium, which was nice of them. Guess what I talked about—the very pieces that they had asked me to take out of my dissertation back in 1981!

I was also getting speaking invitations from all over. In 1998, for example, I was invited to testify before the Senate Foreign Relations Committee about President Clinton's visit to Africa during which he hailed the leaders of Ethiopia, Eritrea, the Democratic Republic of the Congo, Rwanda, and Uganda as the "new leaders" of Africa. I testified that Africa needed strong institutions, not new leaders.

One Nigerian friend, Emma Etuk, who was concerned about my safety, told me bluntly in 1998: "You are alive today because you have been vindicated. All your predictions have come true. The more countries implode in Africa, the more people wish they had listened to you, instead of attacking you." That was in 1998, and by then, tragically, Somalia, Rwanda, Burundi, Zaire, Liberia, and Sierra Leone were in flames. The Western media could not make any sense out of the implosions, and I became much sought after, appearing on numerous television and radio programs. One American journalist, Jim Fisher-Thompson, told me: "George, I have followed most of your writings over the years and I must say that you've always been *ahead* of the curve."

I was invited to the White House on four occasions (once by George H. W. Bush, once by Bill Clinton, and twice by George W. Bush) and gave lectures at the State Department, the World Bank, the IMF, and the United Nations, among others. I was invited to testify before the Senate of Canada. But I doubt if my ministrations had any impact on Western policies toward Africa. In the end, I gave up and decided to work with people inside the diaspora community, who already understood conditions back home in Africa, so I wouldn't have to convince a skeptical audience. Thus it is best to rely on support for the cause of freedom from your own diaspora community and not from the United States, which has lost much clout in Africa and the Middle East. We brought change to Ghana without any official US government support.

By 2006, corruption was costing Africa US$148 billion a year, according to the African Union. It was then that the World Bank mustered enough courage to start talking about corruption—an issue I had raised in my dissertation way back in 1981. The military had left a trail of devastation across Africa. Africans had started waging a second liberation against crocodile liberators and Swiss Bank socialists. The chaos in Africa was due not so much to external but to internal factors. Tunisians and Egyptians did not blame American imperialists for their woes; they just wanted the regimes of Ben Ali and Mubarak to disappear. The rest of the story is well known.

THE POLITICAL FRONT

Unfortunately, we did not do so well on the political front at home. Remember that for 19 years, Ghana reeled under the brutal military dictatorship of Jerry Rawlings, who seized power in a military coup in December 1981. Intolerant of criticism, his was a regime that dumped human waste in the offices of newspapers that were critical of his inane policies. In the 1990s, the offices of the *Ghanaian Chronicle,* the *Free Press,* and the *Crusading Guide* were "shit-bombed"—as Ghanaians termed that barbaric act. Eventually, I and a small group of Ghanaians numbering about 100—both in and out of Ghana—succeeded in rallying millions of Ghanaian voters to toss Rawlings and his National Democratic Congress (NDC) out of office in the December 2000 elections. There was a core group of about 20, of which I acted as the "glue" or coordinator.

Our campaign was arduous, festooned with uncanny twists and ugly turns. There were moments of exhilaration and then of dashed hopes and despair. It became clear to us early in the 1990s that the West would be of little help to us. It was chastened by racial over-sensitivity and carried too much colonial, diplomatic, and ideological baggage. Further, the West only had stability and democracy on its agenda in the aftermath of the Cold War. We had to wage that battle for freedom by ourselves. Other pro-democracy activists may well have to do the same. In fact, that is what the Iranians are being exhorted to do. Said Akbar Ganji, who spent six years in Tehran's Evin Prison on trumped-up charges of endangering national security:

> Of course, Iran's democratic movement and civil institutions need funding. But this must come from independent Iranian sources. Iranians themselves must support the transition to democracy; it cannot be presented like a gift. Expatriate Iranians can assist the transition.[3]

To wage an effective struggle against the Rawlings regime, however, we did a lot of research and soul-searching. We were determined not to repeat the mistakes others had made. What we found was sobering. To be sure, Rawlings was an evil genius, devilishly crafty and brutally efficient. But his regime endured—not so much because of his ingenuity and craftiness but because of the weakness of the opposition forces arrayed against him. Railing against the atrocities and failings of his regime was pointless. He was not going to change. A far more effective strategy was to focus on strengthening the opposition forces.

In the early 1990s, the opposition parties in Ghana were worse than useless—hopelessly splintered and constantly bickering. Every educated fool wanted to be the one to replace Rawlings, so it was nearly impossible to unite the opposition parties to fight a common enemy. In the end, however, we succeeded in knocking heads together to win the December 2000 elections.

In January 2001, John A. Kufuor, a personal friend, was inaugurated as Ghana's president. I was overcome with joy. When I saw Kufuor take the oath of office, tears welled up in my eyes. Finally, that long struggle had come to a successful end. President Kufuor offered me a position in his cabinet, which I politely declined for two reasons. First, I told him I had not waged that campaign for democracy for my own personal benefit. We had freed Ghana, and it was time to turn our attention to other African countries, such as Ethiopia, Eritrea, and Zimbabwe, that were laboring under repressive regimes. Second, I had to practice what I preached. I had written in my books that the first generation of African leaders should have retired after winning independence for their respective countries. That dictum should also apply to me. For the eight years that President Kufuor was in office, I neither asked for nor received one cent from his government. I never asked for any favors. I did an occasional critique when I felt the regime was going astray, but, by and large, President Kufuor governed well.

This was also the judgment of President Barack Obama when he chose Ghana as the first sub-Saharan African country to visit in July 2009. He selected Ghana because it was a "model of good governance, democracy and strong civil society participation." Kenyans were miffed that he did not visit his fatherland, and the Nigerians smelled a rat, believing that his visit was a conspiracy to destabilize their country. But Nobel Laureate Wole Soyinka had a different take: a visit by Obama would have sanctified the putrid mess called Nigeria. He threatened to have Obama stoned if he set foot in the country. Mercifully, President Obama wasn't stoned in Ghana.

On July 11, 2009, President Obama gave a rousing speech that was hailed across Africa to the discomfort of its aging despots. He ripped into them, denouncing corruption, senseless wars, and the rule of tyranny. Here are some excerpts from that speech to Ghana's parliamentarians:

Development depends upon *good governance*. That is the ingredient which has been missing in far too many places, for far too long. That is the change that can unlock Africa's potential. And that is a responsibility that can only be met by Africans [italics added] . . .

No country is going to create wealth if its leaders exploit the economy to enrich themselves, or police can be bought off by drug traffickers. No business wants to invest in a place where the government skims 20 percent off the top, or the head of the Port Authority is corrupt. No person wants to live in a society where the rule of law gives way to the rule of brutality and bribery. That is not democracy, that is tyranny, and now is the time for it to end . . .

History is on the side of these brave Africans and not with those who use coups or change Constitutions to stay in power. *Africa doesn't need strongmen, it needs strong institutions* [italics added] . . .

As we provide this support, I have directed my Administration to give greater attention to *corruption* in our human rights report [italics added].

I listened to Obama's speech with a bemused sense of vindication. Guess who had been saying these things for the past 30 years or more? Well, "Professor Ayittey is a nobody," said Ghana's ambassador to the United States back in 1996. Now black American and African scholars invite me to write papers on Africa for them.

I did not write this book to seek personal glorification but to help oppressed people elsewhere in the world battling dictators and struggling to bring democratic change to their countries peacefully—*without violence, without firing a shot, and without Western help or intervention.* It is change that is internally generated and, as such, more likely to be sustainable than change that is externally driven. It requires a different way of looking at the problem. Dictators are beyond redemption, and the focus therefore must be on forging a formidable and smart opposition. There will be setbacks; admittedly, it took us from 1981 to 2000. But at least the country did not blow up like its neighbors—Ivory Coast, Liberia, and Sierra Leone. If we did it in Ghana, it can certainly be done in Burma, Iran, North Korea, and Venezuela as well as in many African countries.

That is what this book is all about.

NOTES

INTRODUCTION: ADVANCING THE CAUSE OF LIBERTY

1. USAID, "Ghana Democracy and Governance Strategy Update," August 2009, http://www.usaid.gov/gh/home/DG%20Strategy.pdf

CHAPTER 1: DESPOTIC REGIMES TODAY

1. *Wall Street Journal*, December 22, 2009.
2. Barry Schweid, "Freedom in Decline for 4th Straight Year," http://www.nharnet.com, December 28, 2010.
3. This list by the author was published by in the July/August 2010 issue of *Foreign Policy* magazine.
4. "Lt.-Gen Omar Bashir himself is reputed to have a number of Dinka and Nuer slaves in his own home, from the time he was military commander in Muglad, south-west Sudan" (*New African*, July 1990, 9). "The allegations against me are all lies," he claimed though he "acknowledges that he has four `students' living in his house. One of them, a young black boy from the Nuweir tribe, escaped this year (1995)" (*Washington Times*, April 27, 1995, A18).
5. *New York Times*, October 12, 2010, A6.
6. http://ethiopiaforums.com/ethiopias-meles-zenawi-rejects-poll-criticism.
7. Fiona Hill, "The Changing Face of Eurasia," August 19, 2001, http://www.eurasianet.org/departments/insight/articles/eav082001.shtml.
8. On May 9, 2011, I participated in a Breakfast Forum organized by Civita, a free-market organization in Oslo, Norway. Former president of Peru Alejandro Toledo complained of elected autocrats in Bolivia, Ecuador, Nicaragua, and Venezuela, saying: "They were a façade of democracy but rule from an authoritarian heart." http://www.blip.tv/file/5126016.
9. *The Economist*, September 11, 2010, 17.
10. *The Economist*, December 4, 2010, 57.
11. Ibid.
12. *Washington Post*, January 9, 1998.
13. Inequitable distribution of land is a legitimate issue in Zimbabwe, where whites, who comprise about 10 percent of the population, own about 90 percent of the best farmland. But the issue is not resolved through barbaric and violent invasion of commercial farmlands. Quote from *Bloomberg News:* January 2, 2007.
14. *The Observer* (London), September 30, 2001.
15. *Bloomberg News*, January 2, 2007.
16. Alejandro Chafuen, "What Latin America Needs," *Washington Times*, November 26, 2005.
17. George J. Andreopoulos, "Ethnic Cleansing," *Encyclopedia Britannica*, http://www.britannica.com/EBchecked/topic/194242/ethnic-cleansing.

18. http://www.foreignpolicy.com, March 30, 2010.
19. *Foreign Policy*, June 2009, http://www.foreignpolicy.com/articles/2010/06/21/2010_failed_states_index_interactive_map_and_rankings.
20. United Nations Development Program (UNDP), 2010, http://hdr.undp.org/en/statistics.
21. United Nations Development Program (UNDP), 2009, http://hdr.undp.org/en/statistics/.
22. *New York Times*, August 27, 2008.
23. *Washington Times*, September 21, 2007.
24. Michael Stott, "Russia Corruption 'May Force Western Firms to Quit,'" Reuters, March 15, 2010, http://www.reuters.com/article/2010/03/15/us-russia-corruption-idUSTRE62E1SU20100315
25. *Washington Times*, September 21, 2007.
26. *New York Times*, November 29, 2002.
27. *Telegraph* (London), June 25, 2005.
28. *New African*, September 2000.
29. *Post Express*, July 10, 2000.
30. *Wall Street Journal*, December 10, 1996.
31. Philip Gourevitch, *We Wish to Inform You That Tomorrow We Will Be Killed with Our Families: Stories from Rwanda* (New York: Farrar, Straus and Giroux, 1998), 218.
32. Wole Soyinka. *The Open Sore of a Continent: A Personal Narrative of the Nigerian Crisis* (New York: Oxford University Press, 1996), 139.
33. "George Ayittey's Critique of 'Coconut Republics': Too Good to Keep to Ourselves," June 4, 2007, http://blog.ted.com/2007/06/04/george_ayitteys/
34. Ibid.
35. Ellen Barry, "Uzbekistan, Amid Criticism, Holds Parliamentary Election," *New York Times*, December 28, 2009.
36. *New Vision*, Kampala, December 15, 2004.
37. *New York Times*, January 16, 2003.
38. *New York Times*, September 13, 2003.
39. *Global Voices*, February 8, 2008, http://globalvoicesonline.org/2008/02/09/tanzanias-cabinet-dissolved-after-corruption-scandal/
40. *Washington Post*, April 20, 2001.
41. *Index on Censorship*, March 2000, 99.
42. *The Economist*, October 11, 2007, 48.
43. *The Daily Monitor*, February 25, 2011.
44. "Nigeria Voter Registration Kit Stolen At Airport," BBC News, December 9, 2010, http://www.bbc.co.uk/news/world-africa-11958945.
45. *Washington Post*, October 27, 2010.
46. *Washington Times*, August 28, 2003.
47. *The Economist*, August 30, 2003, 32.
48. Associated Press, December 20, 2010, and *Der Spiegel*, http://www.spiegel.de/international/europe/0,1518,735633,00.html.
49. Benjamin Bidder, "Europe's Last Dictatorship Shows Violent Side," *Der Spiegel*, http://www.spiegel.de/international/europe/0,1518,735633,00.html.
50. *Washington Times*, June 9, 2002.
51. *The Economist*, March 16, 2002, 18.
52. *BBC News* website, May 10, 2002.
53. Richard Borsuk, "The Suharto Regime Blew Many Chances to Amass Wealth," *Wall Street Journal*, December 30, 1998, http://www.wright.edu/~tdung/suharto-wealth.htm.
54. *Washington Post*, November 12, 2001.
55. Ibid.

CHAPTER 2: TRADITIONAL SOCIETIES

1. John Stuart Mill, *On Liberty and Other Essays*, edited by John Gray (Oxford and New York: Oxford University Press, 1998), Chapter 1: Introduction.

2. Ibid.
3. *Washington Post,* October 13, 1994
4. *Wall Street Journal,* February 24, 2011.
5. Ibid.
6. According to J. B. Webster and A. A. Boahen, "Slaves had many privileges in African kingdoms. In Asante, Oyo and Bornu, they held important offices in the bureaucracy, serving as the *Alafin's* Ilari in the subject towns of Oyo, as controller of the treasury in Asante, and as Waziri and army commanders in Bornu. Al-Hajj Umar made a slave emir of Nioro, one of the most important of the emirates of the Tokolor empire, and in the Niger Delta states slaves rose to become heads of Houses, positions next in rank to the king. Jaja, who had once been the lowest kind of slave, became the most respected king in the delta, and was no exception; one of the Alaketus of Ketu, and Rabeh of Bornu, rose from slave to king." *History of West Africa: The Revolutionary Years—1815 to Independence* (New York: Praeger, 1970), 69.
7. Anthropologists define a state as a bureaucracy organized specifically to carry out political activities. See, for example, Paul Bohannan, *Africa and Africans* (New York: Natural History Press, 1964). In a state, there is an interlocking system of offices or positions that must be filled by officials. Authority is then made inherent in these positions. A few anthropologists, however, lump empires and autonomously ruled ethnic groups with centralized authority together as "states."
8. He was interviewed on the American television program *"Sixty Minutes"* (CBS) on May 2, 1993. Asked if his race was a problem, he replied: "Color or race is not important to the Ghanaians, which is their greatest trait. They are color-blind. I am accepted as one of the community." He also listed some of the rules he could not break as a chief: "A chief cannot fall from his palanquin and remain chief," "A chief cannot touch the ground with his bare feet," and "When the chief is taking his bath, he must place his feet on elephant tusks."
9. Lewis H. Morgan, *Ancient Society, or Researches in the Lines of Human Progress from Savagery through Barbarism to Civilization* (London: Macmillan, 1877).
10. UAE Interacti, http://www.uaeinteract.com/government/political_system.asp.
11. In Iran, the Pahlavis came to power with the overthrow of Ahmad Shah Qajar, the last ruler of the Qajar dynasty. The National Assembly of Iran, known as the Majlis, convening as a constituent assembly on December 12, 1925, deposed the young Ahmad Shah Qajar and declared Reza Shah the new monarch of the Imperial State of Persia. In 1935, Reza Shah informed foreign embassies that he had changed to Iran the name of the country that for centuries had been known to the world as Persia. The Pahlavi dynasty ended in 1979 when Reza Shah's son, Mohammad Reza Pahlavi, was overthrown in the Islamic or Iranian Revolution.
12. Michael S. James "What Is a Loya Jirga?" ABC News, May 28, 2002, http://abcnews. go.com/International/story?id=79066.
13. Thomas Jefferson, "Amendment I (Speech and Press)," Thomas Jefferson to Edward Carrington, January 16, 1787, http://press-pubs.uchicago.edu/founders/documents/ amendI_speechs8.html.
14. Jean-François Bayart, *L'État en Afrique: la politique du ventre* (Paris: Fayard, 1989), 58.
15. Bohannan, *Africa and Africans,* 195.
16. Pao Saykao, "Hmong Leadership: The Traditional Model," 1997, http://www.hmong net.org/hmong-au/leader.htm.
17. Michael van Notten, *The Law of the Somalis: A Stable Foundation for Economic Development in the Horn of Africa,* ed. Spencer Heath MacCallum (Trenton, NJ: Red Sea Press, 2005), 82.
18. Near-kritarchies such as Somali society have one fundamental weakness, however. They are defenseless against a powerful external aggressor. As a result, the Somali found themselves cut up in five ways under colonial rule. Some found themselves in Ethiopia (Ogaden), Djibouti, Kenya, Italian Somaliland, and British Somaliland. The same can be said about the Hmong and the Kurds because, traditionally, they have no political leaders.

For more on the Somali, see van Notten, *The Law of the Somalis* and I. M. Lewis, "Lineage Continuity and Modern Commerce in Northern Somaliland," in *Markets In Africa,* edited by Paul Bohannan and George Dalton (Evanston, IL: Northwestern University Press,1962).

19. Igor Kopytoff, ed., *The African Frontier: The Reproduction of Traditional African Societies* (Bloomington: Indiana University Press, 1989), 66.
20. James H. Vaughan, "Population and Social Organization," in *Africa,* edited by Phyllis M. Martin and Patrick O'Meara, 2nd ed. (Bloomington: Indiana University Press, 1986), 177.
21. Basil Davidson, *The African Genius: An Introduction to African Cultural and Social History* (Boston: Atlantic Monthly Press, 1970), 193.
22. "Chinese Gods," *Kidipede,* http://www.historyforkids.org/learn/china/religion/gods .htm.
23. History of China, www.history-of-china.com.
24. Jan Vansina, *Kingdoms of the Savanna* (Madison: University of Wisconsin Press, 1975), 29.
25. James L. Gibbs Jr., *Peoples of Africa* (New York: Holt, Rinehart and Winston, 1965), 460.
26. Randall M. Packard, *Chiefship and Cosmology: An Historical Study of Political Competition* (Bloomington: Indiana University Press, 1981), 6.
27. Bruce E. Johansen, "Native Ideas of Governance and U.S. Constitution," 2009, http:// www.america.gov/st/peopleplace-english/2009/June/20090617110824wrybak cuh0.5986096.html.
28. Frank Douglas Heath, "Tribal Society and Democracy," *The Laissez Faire City Times* 5 (22): May 28, 2001, http://www.afrifund.com/wiki/index.pcgi?page=CtrySomaliland[0].
29. "Pre-Columbian Americas," All Empires, http://www.allempires.com/article/index. php?q=americas_history.
30. Johansen, "Native Ideas of Governance and U.S. Constitution."
31. Heath, "Tribal Society and Democracy."
32. Ibid.
33. "Imperialism," *Encyclopedia of World Geography,* http://world-geography.org/321-imperialism.html.
34. K. Kris Hirst, "Top 8 Top Unknown Ancient Empires," About.com, http://archaeology. about.com/od/ancientcivilizations/tp/unknown_civ.htm.
35. "Forgotten Empire: The World of Ancient Persia," The British Museum, http://www .thebritishmuseum.ac.uk/forgottenempire/persia/people.html.
36. Ancient Persia, http://www.ancientpersia.com/res_f.htm.
37. Ibid.

CHAPTER 3: INDIGENOUS CURBS AGAINST DESPOTISM

1. P. T. Bauer, *Reality and Rhetoric: Studies in the Economics of Development* (Cambridge, MA: Harvard University Press, 1984), 104.
2. "French Revolution," *Wikipedia,* http://en.wikipedia.org/wiki/French_Revolution. See also, "Louis XVI," World Civilization, Washington State University, http://wsu .edu/~dee/REV/LOUISXVI.HTM.
3. Liu Junning, "The Ancient Roots of Chinese Liberalism," *Wall Street Journal,* July 6, 2011, p.A13.
4. Jomo Kenyatta, *Facing Mount Kenya, The Tribal Life of the Gikuyu* (London: Secker and Warburg, 1938), 180.
5. Kenneth S. Carlston, *Social Theory and African Tribal Organization* (Urbana: University of Illinois Press, 1968), 182.
6. "Abu Bakr," *Wikipedia,* http://en.wikipedia.org/wiki/Abu_Bakr. A longer version of his speech can be found at "Anecdotes of Abu Bakr," http://www.witness-pioneer.org/vil /Articles/companion/17_abu_bakr.htm#Sayings of Abu Bakr. The main difference between Sunni and Shi'a Muslims originated in the seventh century BC over how the head of the Muslim community should be selected. Sunnis believe that the head of state, the

caliph, should be selected by *Shura*—that is, elected by Muslims or their representatives—whereas the Shi'a believe he should be an imam descended in a line from the Prophet's son-in-law, Ali. "Sunni Islam," Patheos, http://www.patheos.com/Library/Sunni-Islam.html.

7. G. Y. Amoah, *Groundwork of Government for West Africa* (Illorin, Nigeria: Gbenle Press, 1988), 178.

8. In Ghana, Nana Owongo Nkum III, the chief of Breman Asantem, was destooled by the council at the celebration of Akwasidae Festival at Breman Asikuma. He was found guilty of failing to avert arson and destruction of properties belonging to both members of the royal family and the palace (*Ghana News Agency*, October 4, 2002).

9. "The Laws of Ancient Persians," Pars Times, http://www.parstimes.com/law/ancient_persia_laws.html#5.

10. Paul Bohannan, *Africa and Africans* (New York: Natural History Press, 1964), 191.

11. James H. Vaughan, "Population and Social Organization," in *Africa*, edited by Phyllis M. Martin and Patrick O'Meara, 2nd ed. (Bloomington: Indiana University Press, 1986), 178.

12. *The Guardian*, July 24, 2003.

13. James L. Gibbs Jr., ed., *Peoples of Africa* (New York: Holt, Rinehart and Winston, 1965), 91.

14. Bauer, *Reality and Rhetoric*, 104.

15. Chancellor Williams, *The Destruction of Black Civilization* (Chicago: Third World Press, 1987), 286.

16. Peter Wickins, *An Economic History of Africa from the Earliest Times to Partition* (New York: Praeger, 1981), 228.

17. *BBC News Africa*, December 18, 2010.

18. *The Atlantic*, May 20, 2010.

19. "Profile: Alexander Lukashenko," *BBC News*, January 9, 2007, http://news.bbc.co.uk/2/hi/europe/3882843.stm.

20. Gerald F. Gaus and Chandran Kukathas, eds. *Handbook of Political Theory* (London and Thousand Oaks, CA: Sage Publications, 2004), 141.

21. Christopher Locke, *The Cluetrain Manifesto: The End of Business as Usual* (Cambridge, MA: Perseus Publishing, 2001), Chapter 1.

22. John D. Nebel, Ancient Money, www.ancient-money.org/.

23. Seth Mydans, "A Lone Blacksmith, Where Hammers Ring," *New York Times*, November 25, 2010.

24. Edward Wong, "Silk Craft Fades in Village That Clothed Emperors," *New York Times*, October 11, 2010.

25. Ibid.

26. Ibid.

27. Colin W. Newbury, "Prices and Profitability in Early Nineteenth-Century West African Trade," in *Development of Indigenous Trade and Markets in West Africa: Studies Presented and Discussed at the Tenth International African Seminar at Fourth Bay College, Freetown, December 1969*, edited by Claude Meillassoux (London: Oxford University Press for the International African Institute, 1971).

28. J. B. Webster and A. A. Boahen, *History of West Africa: The Revolutionary Years—1815 to Independence* (New York: Praeger, 1970), 187.

29. Marvin P. Miracle, "Capitalism, Capital Markets, and Competition in West African Trade," in *The Development of Indigenous Trade and Markets in West Africa*, edited by Claude Meillassoux (Oxford: Oxford University Press, 1971).

30. Profit-sharing schemes, it may be noted, underlie the success and stability of Japanese corporations today. These schemes are currently in use in many parts of Africa. For example, the native fishing enterprises in Accra, Ghana, use an abusa-type of scheme. Consider a fishing canoe with a crew of seven, a roll of fishing net, and an outboard motor. Since there may be different owners of the canoe, the net, and the outboard motor, each is considered as a "person" and added to the crew of seven to give a total of ten "persons."

Profits of the operation are then divided ten ways, with each "person" receiving a tenth. If the owners of the canoe, the net, and the motor happen to be the same individual, his share of the profits would amount to 30 percent.

31. There is a story about Nigerian women traders, who can be found in every West African market, that attests to their industriousness and ingenuity. Ask one for an aircraft engine and she will tell you to come the next day. The following day, she will have not just one but two engines—just in case you don't like the first one. Never mind how she got the engine. It is an exaggeration but seeks to speak of the length to which these women traders will go to satisfy a customer's request.

32. The informal sector is defined as an area of economic activity that is unregulated and outside the formal sector, which is characterized by organized management practices, payment of wages, taxes paid, retirement benefits computed, and books or receipts are kept. It is also known as the "parallel economy" but different from the "underground economy" in which banned commodities and services such as narcotics, gambling, prostitution, and so on are traded. A "black market," in which a commodity is traded *above* its legal price, is created when a government imposes a price control on a commodity.

33. Friedrich Schneider and Dominik Enste, "Informal Economies: Size, Causes, and Consequences," *Journal of Economic Literature* 38 (1) (2000): 5-7.

34. Hernando de Soto, *The Mystery of Capital* (New York: Basic Books, 2000), 28.

35. Hernando de Soto, "Egypt's Economic Apartheid," *Wall Street Journal*, February 3, 2011.

36. Ibid.

37. His concept was built on poor peasants' own revolving credit scheme. A borrower must belong to a peer group, which vets all loan applications and is held severally liable in case of default. Peer pressure ensures a repayment rate of as high as 85 percent, which normal banks find difficult to match.

38. Anna Kajumulo Tibaijuka, "Report of the Fact-Finding Mission to Zimbabwe to Assess the Scope and Impact of Operation Murambatsvina by the UN Special Envoy on Human Settlements Issues in Zimbabwe," July 18, 2005, http://www.unhabitat.org/downloads/docs/297_96735_ZimbabweReport.pdf.

39. Ibid.

40. *Washington Post*, December 2, 2009, and January 7, 2010.

CHAPTER 4: THE MODUS OPERANDI OF DESPOTIC REGIMES

1. *New York Times*, October 31, 2010.
2. *Washington Post*, November 15, 2010
3. *The Economist*, February 12, 2011, 47.
4. "Constitution of the People's Republic of China," http://english.peopledaily.com.cn/constitution/constitution.html.
5. "Constitution of Zimbabwe," February 1, 2007, http://www.kubatana.net/html/archive/legisl/070201consti.asp?sector=LEGISL&year=0&range_start=1#download.
6. Sanford J. Ungar, *Africa: The People and Politics of an Emerging Continent* (New York: Simon and Shuster, 1985), 197.
7. *Wall Street Journal*, March 2, 2011.
8. Richard Sandbrook, with Judith Barker, *The Politics of Africa's Stagnation* (New York: Cambridge University Press, 1993), 92.
9. Ibid., 94.
10. *Washington Post*, July 20, 2003.
11. Sandbrook, *Politics of Africa's Stagnation*, 99.
12. Philip Gourevitch, *We Wish to Inform You That Tomorrow We Will Be Killed with Our Families: Stories from Rwanda* (New York: Farrar, Straus and Giroux, 1998), 218.
13. "Stalin & Mind Control: II," YouTube video, http://www.youtube.com/watch?v=GhPCG3nsc38.
14. *Washington Post*, January 25, 2010.
15. *New York Times*, March 9, 2010.

16. *New York Times*, October 10, 2010.
17. Joel Simon, "Attacks on the Press 2009: Introduction," Committee to Protect Journalists, http://cpj.org/2010/02/attacks-on-the-press-2009-introduction.php.
18. "Venezuela Begins Shutdown of 34 Radio Stations," Reuters, August 1, 2009, http://www.reuters.com/article/bondsNews/idUSN0146551720090801.
19. "Attacks on the Press in 2010," Committee to Protect Journalists, http://www.cpj.org/attacks/.
20. *New York Times*, December 22, 2009.
21. K. Anthony Appiah, "Russia's War on Words," *Washington Post*, October 6, 2009, http://www.washingtonpost.com/wp-dyn/content/article/2009/10/06/AR2009100602834.html; *The Economist*, February 5, 2009.
22. "Ali Abdulemam," Oslo Freedom Forum, http://www.oslofreedomforum.com/speakers/ali_abdulemam.html. I also spoke at the human rights event on "How to Defeat a Dictator," and I dedicated my speech to Ali, among others.
23. "Civil Defamation: Undermining Free Expression," Article 19, December 2009, http://www.article19.org/pdfs/publications/civil-defamation.pdf
24. "Tajik Opposition Party Refuses to Print Independent Publications," Radio Free Europe/Radio Liberty, November 3, 2010, http://www.rferl.org/content/Tajik_Opposition_Party_Refuses_To_Print_Independent_Publications/2209265.html.
25. "Civil Defamation."
26. Kenneth R. Timmerman, "Iranian Student Demonstrations Confound Regime," *Newsmax*, December 7, 2009.
27. Loretta Chao and Jason Dean, "China's Censors Thrive in Obscurity," *Wall Street Journal*, April 4, 2010, http://online.wsj.com.
28. *The Economist*, October 23, 2010, 60.
29. Interview on BBC, World Service, September 11, 2004.
30. The most depraved acts of intimidation occurred in Ghana in 1994 when the Rawlings regime dumped human waste in the offices of newspapers critical of his policies. Ghanaians termed this "shit-bombing."
31. *The Zimbabwe Situation*, February 29, 2004, http://www.zimbabwesituation.com/.
32. "Kyrgyzstan: Judges Sacked for Various Misdeeds," November 12, 2008, Euarasianet.org, http://www.eurasianet.org/departments/insightb/articles/eav111308b.shtml.
33. *New York Times*, April 3, 2010.
34. "Government to Restore Judges Sacked by Musharraf: Minister," *Sindh Today*, August 19, 2008, http://www.sindhtoday.net.
35. *The Economist*, August 7, 2010, 43.
36. Josef Stalin Quotes, Brainy Quote, http://www.brainyquote.com/quotes/authors/j/joseph_stalin.html.
37. "Saddam 'Wins 100% of Vote,'" BBC News, October 16, 2002, http://news.bbc.co.uk/2/hi/2331951.stm.
38. Tim Johnston, "Burma's Rulers Keep Tight Grip on Power," *Financial Times*, November 3, 2010.
39. *Daily Mail* (UK), November 5, 2010.
40. *Washington Post*, October 29, 2010.
41. P. L. Hipsher, "Democratization and the Decline of Urban Social Movements in Chile and Spain," *Comparative Politics* 28 (3) (1996): 273-297. See also S. Eckstein and M. A. Garretón Merino, *Power and Popular Protest: Latin American Social Movements* (Berkeley: University of California Press, 2001).
42. *The Sun* (UK), January 31, 2011.
43. Jeevan Vasagar and Rajeev Syal, "LSE Head Quits Over Gaddafi Scandal," *The Guardian* (UK), March 4, 2011.

CHAPTER 5: THE DEMISE OF DESPOTIC REGIMES

1. *New York Times*, September 29, 2010.

2. Michael van Notten, *The Law of the Somalis: A Stable Foundation for Economic Development in the Horn of Africa,* edited by Spencer Heath MacCallum (Trenton, NJ: Red Sea Press, 2006), 14.
3. In the Philippines, it requires 31 procedures involving a whole array of government agencies.
4. Ramin Mostaghim, "Corruption Eats Into Roots of Society," Inter Press Service, July 15, 2004, http://www.ipsnews.org/interna.asp?idnews=24640.
5. Gustavo Coronel, "Corruption, Mismanagement, and Abuse of Power in Hugo Chávez's Venezuela," CATO Development Policy Analysis Number 2. Washington, DC, November 2006, 3.
6. Mark Gregory, "Expanding Business Empire of Iran's Revolutionary Guards," BBC News, July 26, 2010, http://www.bbc.co.uk/news/world-middle-east-10743580.
7. *Bloomberg News,* January 2, 2007.
8. "Fuel Shortages in Northern Iran Sparks Riot," National Council of Resistance in Iran, January 11, 2008, http://www.ncr-iran.org/content/view/4620/152/.
9. *Bloomberg News,* January 2, 2007.
10. *Latin American Herald,* August 10, 2010.
11. Richard Sandbrook, with Judith Barker, *The Politics of Africa's Stagnation* (New York: Cambridge University Press, 1993), 113.
12. "Farmers First, Then Business, Who Next?" Africa News Service, May 8, 2000.
13. *Bloomberg News,* January 2, 2007.
14. *Washington Post,* October 5, 2010.
15. "Venezuela's Economy," *The Economist,* May 10, 2010.
16. Cheikh Anta Diop, *Pre-colonial Black Africa: A Comparative Study of the Political and Social Systems of Europe and Black Africa, from Antiquity to the Formation of the Modern States.* Translated by Harold J. Salemson (Westport, CT: Lawrence Hill, 1987), 65.
17. "'Investing in the Fatherland': Corruption in North Korea," RFA Unplugged, January 30, 2008, http://rfaunplugged.wordpress.com/2008/01/30/investing-in-the-fatherland-corruption.
18. Ibid.
19. Opposition leaders should demand the publication of these annual reports or make them the focus of their demands for reform.
20. "Saddam Hussein's Iraq," Prepared by the US Department of State, September 13, 1999, http://www.fas.org/news/iraq/2000/02/iraq99.htm.
21. *Telegraph* (UK), June 25, 2005. There is a website dedicated to holding corrupt Nigerian government officials accountable and exposing their horrid corruption scandals: http://www.saharareporters.com
22. Gustavo Coronel, "Corruption, Mismanagement, and Abuse of Power in Hugo Chávez's Venezuela," The Cato Institute, November 27, 2006, 3.
23. BBC World News Africa, December 18, 2010
24. *Wall Street Journal,* September 27, 2010.
25. Global Financial Integrity, http://www.gfip.org.
26. Ronald Robinson, ed., *Developing the Third World: The Experience of the 1960s* (Cambridge, UK: Cambridge University Press, 1971), 43.
27. Claude Ake, "As Africa Democratises," *Africa Forum* 1 (2) (1991): 14.
28. *Washington Post,* December 2, 2009.
29. *New York Times,* August 22, 2010.
30. *Washington Post,* September 23, 2010.
31. Mostaghim, 2004.
32. *Wall Street Journal,* September 24, 2010.
33. *The Economist,* World in 2011, 78.
34. *Wall Street Journal,* November 13, 2010.
35. *New York Times,* October 12, 2010.
36. Pro-democracy activists should extract such information but be extremely careful not to embrace such breakaways too closely. They could return to the despot's camp.
37. *Financial Times,* November 24, 2010.

38. Samuel Decalo, *Coups and Army Rule in Africa. Studies in Military Style* (New Haven, CT: Yale University Press, 1976), 36.

39. Sandbrook, *The Politics of Africa's Stagnation*, 99.

40. *New York Times*, December 4, 2009; p.A8.

41. "Ousted Mauritania Leader in Shock," BBC News, August 6, 2005, http://news.bbc.co.uk/2/hi/africa/4126296.stm.

42. "Chinese Officials Stole $120 Billion, Fled Mainly to US," BBC World Service, June 17, 2011, http://www.bbc.co.uk/news/world-asia-pacific-13813688.

CHAPTER 6: STIRRINGS FOR FREEDOM

1. *Wall Street Journal*, October 9, 2010.

2. *Washington Post*, October 22, 2010.

3. *Morning Edition*, National Public Radio, September 27, 2010.

4. *Wall Street Journal*, October 10, 2010.

5. Ibid.

6. Ibid.

7. In total, there were about 100 Ghanaians who brought about democratic change. Of that group, there was a 20-member core group, of which I was one. The group was made of political leaders, lawyers, media practitioners, doctors, and students.

8. "Ghana: Broadening Frontiers of Media Freedom," AllAfrica.com, May 4, 2011, http://allafrica.com/stories/201105050412.html.

9. *The Economist*, December 16, 2000, 54.

10. *New York Times*, May 1, 2001.

11. I would rather call this the Bouazizi Revolution than the Jasmine Revolution to honor the one who triggered it. It has also been called the Twitter Revolution, and even Wikileaks claimed some responsibility for it. Credit should be given where it is due.

12. "Tunisia's Durable President: One-Man Show," *The Economist*, October 29, 2009.

13. The chronicle of events in Tunisia may be found here: Ryan Rifai, "Timeline: Tunisia's Uprising," Al Jazeera, January 23, 2011, http://english.aljazeera.net/indepth/spotlight/tunisia/2011/01/201114142223827361.html.

14. Ibid.

15. Ibid.

16. Mona Eltahawy, "Tunisia's Jasmine Revolution," *Washington Post*, January 15, 2011, http://www.washingtonpost.com/wp-dyn/content/article/2011/01/14/AR2011011405084.html.

17. *Reuters*, January 15, 2011.

18. Rifai, "Timeline."

19. *Wall Street Journal*, February 11, 2011.

20. Ibid.

21. The bellicose trigger-happy Egyptian riot police, who shot, clubbed, and tear-gassed the street demonstrators demanding the ouster of Mubarak, themselves went on street demonstrations on February 13, 2011, to demand ouster of their boss and higher pay!

22. A possible exception may be that of the 1979 Iranian Revolution, when the shah fled the country, leaving a power vacuum. In that case, the ruler had already seen the signs on the wall, and it was only a matter of time before the monarchy collapsed completely.

23. Duncan McCargo, *Media and Politics in Pacific Asia* (London: Routledge, 2002), 20.

24. "EDSA People Power Revolution," Philippine History, http://www.philippine-history.org/edsa-people-power-revolution.htm.

25. The Sensible Archive, October 3, 2007, http://captainsensible.multiply.com/journal/?&page_start=60.

26. "Monks Lead Largest Burma Protest," BBC News, September 24, 2007, http://news.bbc.co.uk/2/hi/asia-pacific/7009825.stm.

27. Ibid.

28. Charles Evans, "1979: Iranian Revolution," http://novaonline.nvcc.edu/eli/evans/his135/Events/Iran79.htm. "Iranian Revolution," *Wikipedia*, http://en.wikipedia.org/wiki/Iranian_Revolution.

29. "Divisions Emerge Among Iran's Conservatives," *PBS NewsHour*, September 16, 2010, http://www.pbs.org.

CHAPTER 7: THE STRATEGY

1. *The Economist*, November 6, 2010.
2. This is akin to the famous quote by Grace Speare: "For every force, there is a counter force. For every negative there is a positive. For every action there is a reaction. For every cause there is an effect."
3. *The Economist*, September 3, 2011.
4. "30 January," Still Sudan, http://stillsudan.blogspot.com/2011/01/30-january.html.
5. *Der Spiegel*, http://www.spiegel.de/international/europe/0,1518,735633,00.html.
6. *Washington Times*, October 15, 1996.
7. This author first made this proposal during an appearance on the Rev. Jesse Jackson's CNN TV program, *Both Sides*, on August 4, 1994. The purpose of the program was to explore what to do in Nigeria. I suggested that, if General Abacha would not implement reform, "we should place $1 million dollars in a Swiss bank" to entice him out of the country ("safe passage" out). The Nigerian ambassador, who also appeared on the program, was livid. Later one commentator who watched the program joked that what drew the ire of the ambassador was not the suggestion but rather the amount offered. In an article published in *African News Weekly* (March 31, 1995), I subsequently raised this figure to $1 billion.
8. *The Guardian* (UK), December 18, 2010.
9. Emphasis added, *Daily Graphic*, January 29, 2011.
10. "Constitution of the People's Republic of China," http://english.peopledaily.com.cn/constitution/constitution.html.
11. "Iran—Constitution," http://www.servat.unibe.ch/icl/ir00000_.html.
12. "Constitution of Zimbabwe," February 1, 2007, http://www.kubatana.net/html/archive/legisl/070201consti.asp?sector=LEGISL&year=0&range_start=1#download.
13. "African [Banjul] Charter on Human and Peoples' Rights," University of Minnesota Human Rights Library, http://www1.umn.edu/humanrts/instree/z1afchar.htm.
14. *New York Times*, October 23, 2010, A19.
15. "ECOWAS Court Orders Gambia to Compensate Tortured Journalist," *Africa News Service*, December 20, 2010.
16. His story is culled from an interview with Steve Inskeep, "Mohammad Reza Shajarian: Protest Through Poetry," *All Things Considered*, National Public Radio, aired on September 27, 2010.
17. *New York Times*, September 19, 2010.
18. "A Violinist's Tribute to a Nobel Laureate," *All Things Considered*, November 23, 2010, http://www.npr.org/templates/story/story.php?storyId=131548541.
19. "Kim Il-sung's 'Awful' Advice Blamed for N. Korea's Economic Malaise," The Chosunilbo, April 1, 2010, http://www.english.chosun.com.
20. "Newspaper Editor Arrested in Harare," SW Radio Africa, December 1, 2010, http://www.swradioafrica.com.
21. William Easterly, "Accountability in Development: The Double Standard." Paper presented at a conference at the New School for Social Research, "From Impunity to Accountability: Africa's Development in the 21st Century," November 19, 2010.
22. *Financial Post* (Canada), May 10, 1999.
23. Marcus Brauchli, "Speak No Evil," *Wall Street Journal*, July 14, 1998.
24. Author's testimony before the House Foreign Affairs Sub-Committee on Africa, US House of Representatives, November 12, 1991, in *Congressional Record*.
25. *Washington Post*, November 27, 1993.
26. Patricia Adams, *Odious Debts* (Toronto: Earthscan, 1991).
27. *New Internationalist*, May 1999, 23; *Financial Post*, May 10, 1999.

28. *Financial Post,* May 10, 1999.

29. *The Atlantic,* November 2003, 39–46.

30. It is important to note that the US Congress resorted to this tactic. Over the years, it refused to pay the United Nations a debt of over $1.3 billion in past dues and overdue assessments. It claimed that it would not pay for an inefficient and bloated UN bureaucracy. Eventually legislation was passed in June 1997 that would pay the United Nations $819 million (about two-thirds of the debt) provided the world body met congressional demands to cut budget and staff members and restrict its activities. "'This Bill will prohibit the payment by the American taxpayers of any so-called U.N. arrears until these congressionally mandated benchmarks have been met by the U.N.,' said the Chairman of the Senate Foreign Relations Committee, Sen. Jesse Helms. 'The measure to the U.N. is simple but clear: No reform, no American taxpayer money for arrears,' Helms added." *Washington Post,* June 14, 1997.

31. Ghanaians in the diaspora did this in 1997 to the electoral commissioner, Dr. Kwadwo Afari-Gyan, who was accused of rigging the 1996 elections. When cornered about statistical inconsistencies, he admitted that he did not know what the population of Ghana was. Imagine. We hammered him in the media, demanding that he should be sacked. Anyone who did not know how many people were in Ghana obviously would not know how many were eligible to vote and, therefore, was not qualified to be the electoral commissioner.

CHAPTER 8: REVERSALS IN REVOLUTIONS—*AND HOW TO AVOID THEM*

1. *New York Times,* October 23, 2010.

2. "EDSA Revolution of 2001," Reference.com, http://mwh.reference.com/browse/EDSA+Revolution.

3. "Georgia's Mental Revolution," *The Economist,* August 19, 2010.

4. *New York Times,* October 26, 2010.

5. Gregory L. White, "Gorbachev Warns of Egypt-Style Russian Revolt," *Wall Street Journal,* February 17, 2011.

6. Mikhail Gorbachev, "Perestroika Lost," *New York Times,* March 13, 2010.

7. *Washington Times,* December 11, 2001.

8. *The Economist,* January 22, 2011, 33.

9. "Constitution," OurConvention.com, http://www.ourconvention.com/Constitution/encyclopedia.htm#Key_features.

10. The Constitution of India is the longest written constitution in the world, containing 444 articles, 12 schedules, and 94 amendments, with 117,369 words in its English-language version, while the US Constitution is the shortest written constitution. The constitution of the Bolivarian Republic of Venezuela is thought to be the second longest written constitution in the world.

11. Steve Hanke, "Lessons from America's Founding Fathers and US Experience," in *Reaganomics Goes Global: What Can the EU, Russia, and Other Transition Countries Learn from the USA?,* edited by Wojciech Bienkowski, Josef C. Brada, and Mariusz-Jan Radło (New York: Palgrave Macmillan, 2004), 7.

12. Fareed Zakaria, *The Future of Freedom: Illiberal Democracy at Home and Abroad* (New York: W.W. Norton, 2003).

13. "Pakistan's President Zardari Closer to Losing Powers," *Christian Science Monitor,* April 1, 2010.

14. "The Loya Jirga," Afghanland.com, http://www.afghanland.com/history/loyajirga.html.

15. Ibid.

16. "What Is Good Governance," United Nations Economic and Social Commission for Asia and the Pacific, http://www.unescap.org/pdd/prs/ProjectActivities/Ongoing/gg/governance.asp.

17. *Wall Street Journal,* February 12, 2011.

18. They are Roman Abramovich, Vagit Alekperov, Boris Berezovsky, Olag Deripaska, Mikhail Fridman, Vladimir Gusinsky, Mikhail Khodorkovsky, and Vladimir Potanin.
19. David Gauthter, "How 'The Family' Controlled Tunisia," *Wall Street Journal*, June 20, 2011, A1.
20. A market is said to be perfectly competitive if it meets five conditions: many buyers and sellers; homogenous product (no brands), no price discrimination, perfect information (all market participants have access to the same information), freedom of entry and exit. Under imperfect capitalism, at least two requirements are violated: perfect information and freedom of entry and exit.
21. *Wall Street Journal*, March 31, 2011, A10.
22. *Washington Post*, October 19, 2010.
23. *Wall Street Journal*, January 10, 2001.
24. *New York Times*, September 30, 2010.
25. *Christian Science Monitor*, October 31, 2008.
26. *New York Times*, September 29, 2010.
27. *The Economist*, August 28, 2010, 35.
28. *Wall Street Journal*, October 14, 2010.
29. Václav Havel and Desmond Tutu, "If China Frees Nobel Winner, It Will Show Its Strength," *Washington Post*, October 22, 2010.
30. *New York Times*, October 27, 2010.
31. Liu Junning, "Ancient Roots," A13.

CHAPTER 9: INTERNATIONAL IMPOTENCE AND HINDRANCE

1. Editorial, *Wall Street Journal*, January 12, 2010.
2. *Washington Post*, October 4, 2010.
3. "The West" is used interchangeably with "the international community" since it is generally the West or the rich countries that have the wherewithal to back international action.
4. *Wall Street Journal*, March 22, 2011.
5. Francis Fukuyama, *The End of History* (New York: Avon Books, 1992), 7.
6. Fareed Zakaria, *The Future of Freedom: Illiberal Democracy at Home and Abroad* (New York: W.W. Norton, 2003), 27.
7. Fareed Zakaria, "The Rise of Illiberal Democracy," *Foreign Affairs*, November/December 1997.
8. *Boston Herald*, January 24, 2011.
9. Ibid.
10. BBC World Service, January 31, 2011.
11. *Wall Street Journal*, February 8, 2011.
12. Ibid.
13. *The Economist*, January 22, 2011.
14. *Weekly Standard*, April 30, 2001, 23.
15. *Washington Times*, May 17, 2001.
16. Yi Feng, "Democracy and Growth: The Sub-Saharan Africa Case," *Review of Black Political Economy* 25 (1) (1996): 95.
17. Ibid., 98.
18. *Washington Post*, January 9, 1998.
19. *New York Times*, September 29, 2010.
20. "Obama's Speech in Ghana," July 11, 2009, http://www.america.gov/st/texttrans-english/2009/July/20090711110050abretnuh0.1079783.html.
21. *Washington Post*, July 5, 2008.
22. *The Economist*, May 17, 2003, 42.
23. "The Right to Communicate,"Article 19, London, February 19, 1999.
24. *The Economist*, January 16, 1999.
25. *Washington Times*, August 12, 2003.

26. "Obama's Speech in Ghana," July 11, 2009, http://www.america.gov/st/texttrans-english/2009/July/20090711110050abretnuh0.1079783.html.
27. *Washington Post*, November 9, 1999.
28. Ibid.
29. Ibid.
30. Ibid.
31. The British Council in Ghana provides such a facility. In 1996, I gave a public lecture at the Council and the place was packed, causing a massive traffic jam four blocks around the British Council. The despotic regime of Rawlings even sent his aides to attend the lecture.
32. *Wall Street Journal*, January 29, 2011.
33. This author seeks to mobilize the Cheetahs, set up a Cheetah Fund, and provide them with "meso capital"—loans in the range of $50,000–$500,000 to set up businesses. The loans will be paid back. Micro-credit finance can't be used to develop Africa. See the website: www.cheetahgeneration.org.

CHAPTER 10: EPILOGUE

1. *Xinhua*, August 14, 2010.
2. The title of my paper was, "Reaching the Millennium Development Goals: Macroeconomic Prospects and Challenges for Low-Income Countries." A synopsis was posted at their website: http://www.imf.org/external/np/exr/cs/news/2010/cso143.htm.
3. *Washington Post*, October 26, 2007.

BIBLIOGRAPHY

US GOVERNMENT PUBLICATIONS

US Senate Committee on Foreign Relations Report. 1996. *Economic Development and U.S. Development Aid Programs.* Washington, DC: U.S. Senate Committee on Foreign Relations, September 19.

BOOKS AND ARTICLES

Adams, Patricia. 1991. *Odious Debts.* Toronto: Earthscan.

Ake, Claude. 1991. "As Africa Democratises." *Africa Forum* 1 (2): 13–18.

Amoah, G. Y. 1988. *Groundwork of Government for West Africa.* Illorin, Nigeria: Gbenle Press.

Ayittey, George B. N. 2006. *Indigenous African Institutions.* Dobbs Ferry, NY: Transnational.

———. 2005. *Africa Unchained: The Blueprint for Africa's Future.* New York: Palgrave Macmillan.

———. 1998. *Africa in Chaos.* New York: St. Martin's Press.

———. 1992. *Africa Betrayed.* New York: St. Martin's Press.

Bauer, P. T. 1984. *Reality and Rhetoric: Studies in the Economics of Development.* Cambridge, MA: Harvard University Press.

Bayart, Jean-François. 1989. *L'État en Afrique: la politique du ventre.* Paris: Fayard.

Bohannan, Paul. 1964. *Africa and Africans.* New York: Natural History Press.

Bohannan, Paul, and George Dalton, eds. 1962. *Markets in Africa.* Evanston, IL: Northwestern University Press.

Carlston, Kenneth S. 1968. *Social Theory and African Tribal Organization.* Urbana: University of Illinois Press.

Chafuen, Alejandro. 2005. "What Latin America Needs." *Washington Times,* November 26.

Coronel, Gustavo. 2006. "Corruption, Mismanagement, and Abuse of Power in Hugo Chávez's Venezuela." CATO Development Policy Analysis Number 2. Washington, DC, November.

Davidson, Basil. 1970. *The African Genius: An Introduction to African Cultural and Social History.* Boston: Atlantic Monthly Press.

Decalo, Samuel. 1976. *Coups and Army Rule in Africa. Studies in Military Style.* New Haven, CT: Yale University Press.

De Soto, Hernando. 2000. *The Mystery of Capital.* New York: Basic Books.

Diamond, Larry. 2002. "Thinking about Hybrid Regimes." *Journal of Democracy* 13 (2): 21–35.

Diop, Cheikh Anta. 1987. *Pre-Colonial Black Africa: A Comparative Study of the Political and Social Systems of Europe and Black Africa, from Antiquity to the Formation of the Modern States.* Translated by Harold J. Salemson. Westport, CT: Lawrence Hill.

Easterly, W. 2010. "Accountability in Development: The Double Standard." Paper presented at a conference at the New School for Social Research: "From Impunity to Accountability: Africa's Development in the 21st Century," November 19.

Eckstein, S., and M. A. Garretón Merino. 2001. *Power and Popular Protest: Latin American Social Movements.* Berkeley: University of California Press.

Feng, Yi. 1996. "Democracy and Growth: The Sub-Saharan Africa Case." *Review of Black Political Economy* 25 (1): 95–126.

Fukuyama, Francis. 1992. *The End of History.* New York: Avon Books.

Gaus, Gerald F., and Chandran Kukathas, eds. 2004. *Handbook of Political Theory.* London and Thousand Oaks, CA: Sage Publications.

Gibbs, James L., Jr., ed. 1965. *Peoples of Africa.* New York: Holt, Rinehart and Winston.

Gorbachev, Mikhail. 2010. "Perestroika Lost." *New York Times,* March 13.

Gourevitch, Philip. 1998. *We Wish to Inform You That Tomorrow We Will Be Killed with Our Families: Stories from Rwanda.* New York: Farrar, Straus and Giroux.

Hanke, Steve. 2006. "Lessons from America's Founding Fathers and US Experience." In *Reaganomics Goes Global: What Can the EU, Russia, and Other Transition Countries Learn from the USA?,* edited by Wojciech Bienkowski, Josef C. Brada, and Mariusz-Jan Radło, 3–7. New York: Palgrave Macmillan.

Heath, Frank Douglas. 2001. "Tribal Society and Democracy." *The Laissez Faire City Times,* 5 (22): May 28.

Hipsher, P. L. 1996. "Democratization and the Decline of Urban Social Movements in Chile and Spain." *Comparative Politics* 28 (3): 273–297.

Johansen, Bruce E. 2009. "Native American Ideas of Governance and U.S. Constitution." http://www.america.gov/st/peopleplace-english/2009/June/20090617110824wrybakcuh0.5986096.html.

Junning, Liu (2011). "The Ancient Roots of Chinese Liberalism," *The Wall Street Journal,* July 6, 2011, A13.

Kenyatta, Jomo. 1938. *Facing Mount Kenya: The Tribal Life of the Gikuyu.* London: Secker and Warburg.

Kopytoff, Igor, ed. 1987. *The African Frontier: The Reproduction of Traditional Africa Societies.* Bloomington: Indiana University Press.

Lewis, I. M. 1962. "Lineage Continuity and Modern Commerce in Northern Somaliland." In *Markets In Africa,* edited by Paul Bohannan and George Dalton, 365–85. Evanston, IL: Northwestern University Press.

Locke, Christopher. 2001. *The Cluetrain Manifesto: The End of Business as Usual.* Cambridge, MA: Perseus Publishing.

McCargo, Duncan. 2002. *Media and Politics in Pacific Asia.* London: Routledge.

Meillassoux, Claude, ed. 1971. *The Development of Indigenous Trade and Markets in West Africa.* Oxford: Oxford University Press.

Mill, John Stuart. 1991. *On Liberty and Other Essays.* Edited by John Gray. Oxford and New York: Oxford University Press.

Miracle, Marvin P. 1971. "Capitalism, Capital Markets, and Competition in West African Trade," in Meillassoux (1971).

Miracle, Marvin P. 1962. "African Markets and Trade in the Copperbelt." In *Markets in Africa,* edited by Paul Bohannan and George Dalton, 698–738. Evanston, IL: Northwestern University Press.

Morgan, Lewis H. 1877. *Ancient Society, or Researches in the Lines of Human Progress from Savagery through Barbarism to Civilization.* London: Macmillan.

Newbury, Colin W. 1971. "Prices and Profitability in Early Nineteenth-Century West African Trade." In *Development of Indigenous Trade and Markets in West Africa: Studies Presented and Discussed at the Tenth International African Seminar at Fourth Bay College, Freetown, December 1969,* edited by Claude Meillassoux, 91–106. London: Oxford University Press for the International African Institute.

Notten, Michael van. 2005. *The Law of the Somalis: A Stable Foundation for Economic Development in the Horn of Africa.* Edited by Spencer Heath MacCallum. Trenton, NJ: Red Sea Press.

Packard, Randall M. 1981. *Chiefship and Cosmology: An Historical Study of Political Competition.* Bloomington: Indiana University Press.

Robinson, Ronald, ed. 1971. *Developing the Third World: The Experience of the 1960s.* Cambridge, UK: Cambridge University Press.

Sandbrook, Richard, with Judith Barker. 1993. *The Politics of Africa's Stagnation.* New York: Cambridge University Press.

Saykao, Pao. 1997. "Hmong Leadership: The Traditional Model." Retrieved September 19, 2006, from http://www.hmongnet.org/hmong-au/leader.htm.

Schneider, Friedrich, and Dominik Enste. 2000. "Informal Economies: Size, Causes, and Consequences." *Journal of Economic Literature* 38 (1): 77–114.

Sharp, Gene, 2010. *From Dictatorship to Democracy: A Conceptual Framework for Liberation.* 3rd ed. Boston: Albert Einstein Institution.

Soyinka, Wole. 1996. *The Open Sore of a Continent: A Personal Narrative of the Nigerian Crisis.* New York: Oxford University Press.

Ungar, Sanford J. 1985. *Africa: The People and Politics of an Emerging Continent.* New York: Simon and Shuster.

Vansina, Jan. 1966. *Kingdoms of the Savanna.* Madison: University of Wisconsin Press.

Vaughan, James H. 1986. "Population and Social Organization." In *Africa,* edited by Phyllis M. Martin and Patrick O'Meara, 169–176. 2nd ed. Bloomington: Indiana University Press.

Webster, J. B., and A. A. Boahen. 1970. *History of West Africa: The Revolutionary Years–1815 to Independence.* New York: Praeger.

Wickins, Peter. 1981. *An Economic History of Africa from the Earliest Times to Partition.* Oxford: Oxford University Press.

Williams, Chancellor. (1987). *The Destruction of Black Civilization.* Chicago: Third World Press.

Wong, Edward. 2010. "Silk Craft Fades in Village that Clothed Emperors." *New York Times,* October 11.

Zakaria, Fareed. 2003. *The Future of Freedom: Illiberal Democracy at Home and Abroad.* New York: W.W. Norton.

PERIODICALS

Africa Forum, private quarterly magazine published in New York by Olusegun Abasanjo (ex-head of state of Nigeria).

Africa Recovery, quarterly publication of the United Nations Development Program (UNDP) on prospects of Africa's economic recovery.

Africa Report, monthly magazine published by the African American Institute in New York.

African News Weekly, weekly newspaper published by Africans in Charlotte, North Carolina.

The African Observer, private newspaper published bi-weekly by Africans in New York.

The Atlantic, private monthly magazine published in Washington.

Business Week, private magazine published weekly in the United States.

Christian Messenger, private Presbyterian Church monthly, published in Accra, Ghana.

Daily Graphic (name changed to *People's Graphic*), daily newspaper published in Accra, Ghana, owned by the government of Ghana.

Daily Nation, independent daily published in Nairobi, Kenya, and owned by the Nation Media Group, listed on the Nairobi Stock Exchange.

The Economist, private weekly published in London.

Financial Times, private weekly published in London.

The Ghanaian Times, government-owned daily newspaper, published in Accra, Ghana.

Global Times, a daily tabloid produced under the auspices of the Communist Party but often displays an independent streak.

The Independent, private daily published in London.

Index on Censorship, private monthly magazine published in London and dedicated to the defense of freedom of expression.

Insight, private monthly magazine published in Washington, DC.

New African, private monthly published in London.

New Internationalist, a private monthly magazine published in London.

Newsweek, private weekly magazine published in the United States.

New York Times, private daily published in New York.

Post Express Wired, private weekly published in Lagos, Nigeria.

Wall Street Journal, private daily published in New York.

Washington Post, private daily published in Washington, D.C.

Washington Times, private daily published in Washington, D.C.

Time, private weekly magazine published in United States.

West Africa, private weekly published in London.

Xinhua, a daily paper published by the Chinese Communist Government.

INDEX